AMERICAN
SHIP MODELS

AMERICAN SHIP MODELS
and How to Build Them

V. R. GRIMWOOD

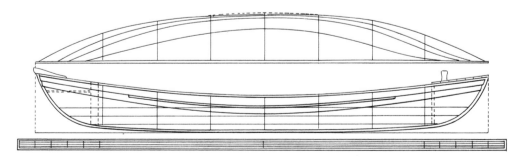

DOVER PUBLICATIONS, INC.
Mineola, New York

Bibliographical Note

This Dover edition, first published in 2003, is an unabridged republication of
the work published by W. W. Norton, New York, in 1942. For this edition the
original fold-out plates have been converted to double-page spreads.

Library of Congress Cataloging-in-Publication Data

Grimwood, V. R. (Victor Redmond), b. 1882.
    American ship models and how to build them / V. R. Grimwood.
        p. cm.
    Originally published: 1st ed. New York : W.W. Norton, c1943.
    ISBN 0-486-42612-2 (pbk.)
    1. Sailing ships—Models—United States. 2. Ship models—United States.
I. Title.

VM298.G723 2003
623.8'2012—dc21
                                                              2003043995

Manufactured in the United States of America
Dover Publications, Inc., 31 East 2nd Street, Mineola, N.Y. 11501

FOREWORD

THOUGH many books have been written for ship modelers, few are suitable for a beginner in the art. The aim of this book is to supply that need, not only in text but in plans made as authentic as possible and selected to permit the building of accurate and correct models in a sequence related to the growing skill of a beginner. The technic described is popular and easy to learn.

The plans selected for the beginner are redrawn, in most cases, from builders' plans, or from measurements of existing craft. Mr. Grimwood has made a great effort to make them accurate. In the case of old vessels, naturally, some reconstruction has been necessary, but this is done with due regard to accuracy as great as present knowledge permits. In the larger and more complicated vessels some simplification of details was required and minor omissions were necessary in order to permit small-scale construction without requiring exceptional skill on the part of the model builder. In the small and more simple craft, however, such simplification has not been necessary and these plans are intended to show all details needed for building very accurate scale models. In general, the plates are arranged in the order of difficulty for the builder, both as to whole and as to detail; the simple rigging and head structure of the skipjack will give the modeler valuable experience toward the complex corresponding work on the merchant ship *Republican*.

I am very much pleased to find attention given to that class of vessels best described as "local types." Most books on models limit discussion to square-rigged ships, merchantmen, and men-of-war, and totally neglect the highly distinctive and decorative American small craft of the period of sail. Some of these latter require less time to model than the square-rigged ships; some of them require equal skill to build and rig. The wide

5

variations in shape and appearance of local types of sailing craft offer a great relief from the dreary *Constitution* and *Flying Cloud* models so commonly attempted by beginners whose skill is not great enough for the undertaking. With the few examples of local types illustrated in this book as an inspiration, the model builder may be led to look about him for subjects of great value and interest—the odd and unusual but hard-working small craft. Canal boats, lighters, schooners, sloops, and other types are disappearing rapidly from waters where once they were very common, and so some preservation of their form and appearance, in models, is highly desirable.

Mr. Grimwood has confined his discussion to the description of one method of building models. He has described each essential step in construction, fitting and rigging, according to the limitations of technic. Being aware that the selected method of construction is not suitable for all models, he has not attempted to describe methods applicable to models best built by other methods.

The beginner will do well to consider carefully Mr. Grimwood's suggestions as to sequence of models. Even though the particular ship or type that the beginner would like to construct is not included in the book, it would be well to begin with the models suggested for a very good and sufficient reason. Unless the beginner has exceptional knowledge and skill he must learn by experience, and by instruction, beginning with easy steps. To try to build a complicated ship model with little knowledge of the use of tools, of methods of construction, and of the type and rig of the vessel will lead only to disappointment. Too often the beginner's "first" model is a crude, ill-proportioned and inaccurate representation of one of the most beautiful works of man, the sailing ship. This mischance can be avoided by attempting only such models as do not lie beyond one's skill and knowledge.

The very sound plan of this book—working from relatively simple models to complicated square-riggers—is emphasized by the fact that the author had no need to make any sacrifice in accuracy of detail in the simple models to obtain ease in building, yet achieved his aim by a suitable selection of model types. That this aim can be achieved is now made evident, and this book consequently opens a new field to ship-model builders which will lead to better and more interesting models than we have seen in the past. Best of all, these new models can be made without great skill and without undue expenditure of time. It seems to me that Mr. Grimwood's demonstration of this possibility makes his book the best in the field of ship modeling.

HOWARD I. CHAPELLE

Cambridge, Maryland

CONTENTS

FOREWORD By Howard I. Chapelle   5

INTRODUCTION   13

Chapter One CONSTRUCTION OF A HALF-HULL SHIP
MODEL. Plate I.   17

Chapter Two THE BUILDING OF A WHOLE-HULL
MODEL. Plate I.   44

Chapter Three TWELVE AMERICAN SAILING VESSELS 56

Chapter Four RIGGING   126

Chapter Five GEAR AND FURNITURE   143

Chapter Six TOOLS AND MATERIALS   149

9

APPENDICES 157

RECOMMENDED READINGS FOR SHIP-MODEL
BUILDERS 165

GLOSSARY 167

INDEX 181

PLATES

FOLLOWING PAGE

I CHESAPEAKE BAY SKIPJACK   "CARRIE PRICE"   16

II PISCATAQUA GONDALOW   "FANNIE M."   16

III AN ANCHOR HOY   Lines found in Grice papers   32

IV COLONIAL FISHING SCHOONER   H. I. Chapelle   32

V WHALING SCHOONER   "AGATE"   48

VI SCOW SCHOONER   "REGENIA S."   64

VII CHESAPEAKE BAY BUGEYE   "EDITH F. TODD"   80

VIII BRIG OF WAR   "BOXER"   96

IX THE SHIP SLOOP   "WASP"   96

X SHIP, MERCHANTMAN   "REPUBLICAN"   112

PLATES

XI Ship, Privateer "OLIVER CROMWELL" 112

XII Sailing Model Yacht 50–800 128

XIII Rigging 144

XIV Gear and Furniture 160

ERRATA

Plate I. The water lines in the body plan are reversed. The lower lift should be Lift 1, and the upper lift should be Lift 2.

Plate VI. In the deck plan of the *Regenia S.* the jibsheet horse is shown abaft the foremast whereas it should be before the foremast.

INTRODUCTION

AT THE outset this book was started with the idea of presenting a collection of ship plans suitable for use by the novice model builder—plans that would produce miniature ships of correct form, proportion, and rig. I hoped that these plans would supply the want that I encountered when I undertook the building of my first ship models. I did not then know where to find suitable plans—and often, when I found them, they were expensive to buy. Another difficulty lay in the fact that the majority of available plans were lacking in essential detail, being in most cases designers' draughts. Complete plans were sadly lacking. Such as I found were drawn, for the most part, for the use of those initiated in the shipbuilding art, and left much to be desired by the novice. The lines as given were mostly drawn to the inside of planking, necessitating redrawing before a correct model could be built. Deck, spar, and rigging plans were also most difficult to find and much time had to be spent in research.

I have endeavored to make the twelve plans presented here as complete as possible and all plans have been redrawn to outside of planking. Some of the waterlines, as shown in the original draught of certain of the plans, have been omitted, as were also some station lines, in order to simplify the building of the model. The builder will no doubt wish to increase the scale from that shown on the plates, but work may proceed directly from the plans by simply increasing the scale proportionately. Redrawing is unnecessary.

At first the plans selected were of ships well known to all Americans, famous ships that played a part in our naval or maritime history—the *Constitution*, the *America*, and others. Before the book was finished all the original plans were supplanted by others of vessels of less popular reputation. In talks with Mr. Robert E. Farlow and Mr. Howard I. Chapelle it was agreed that the book might well be the means of bringing to the modelmaker's attention certain types of American sailing craft that have been neglected by collectors of ship models, examples of which are needed to round out both private and public collections.

Modelmaking can be a most enjoyable pastime and it can also be a source of considerable remuneration. I know one young and skillful modelist who is putting himself through school by the returns from his hobby. During a recent summer he built a model of a Chesapeake Bay bugeye for one of America's marine museums. I believe the plans selected here are capable of producing examples of the modelmaker's art worthy of a place in any marine collection. They have been so arranged that the novice builder will be carried through a progressive course in construction and will find a certain relationship between the simplest model of Plate I and the complicated, full-rigged ship of Plate X.

As this book is intended for the use of the novice, much is written that has been said before; however, the initiate should find in its pages and plates something of interest. I hope also that those who love a ship for itself—and because of that would like to build a model—and those who love the use of tools and wish to try their skill will find in these pages an aid to the accomplishment of their desires.

AMERICAN
SHIP MODELS

PLATE I

Chesapeake Bay Skipjack

CARRIE PRICE

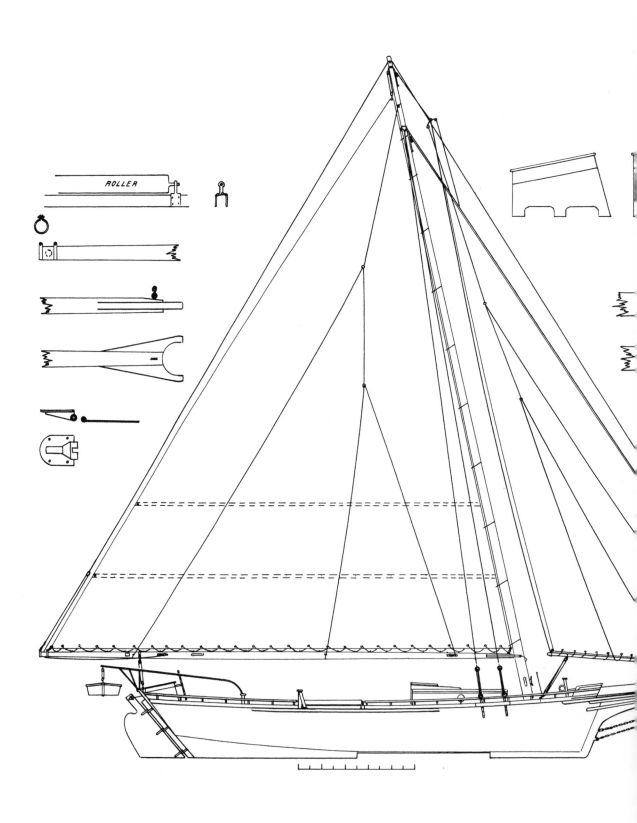

ROLLER

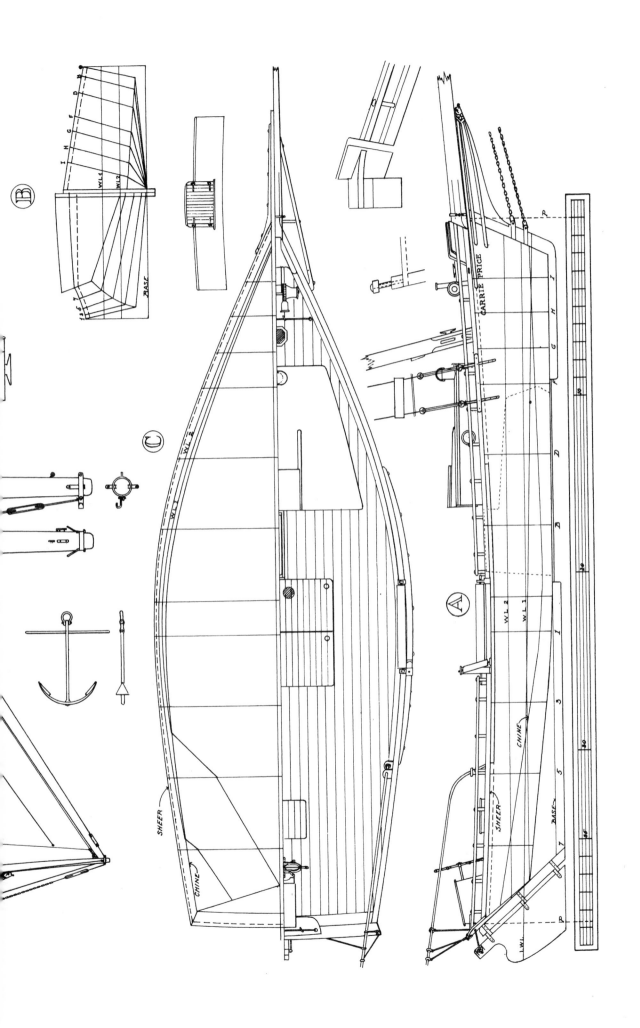

B

C

A

CARRIE PRICE

WL1
WL2
WL2
WL1
WL1

BASE
SHEER
CHINE

PLATE II

Piscataqua Gondalow
FANNY M

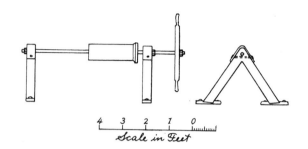

4 3 2 1 0
Scale in Feet

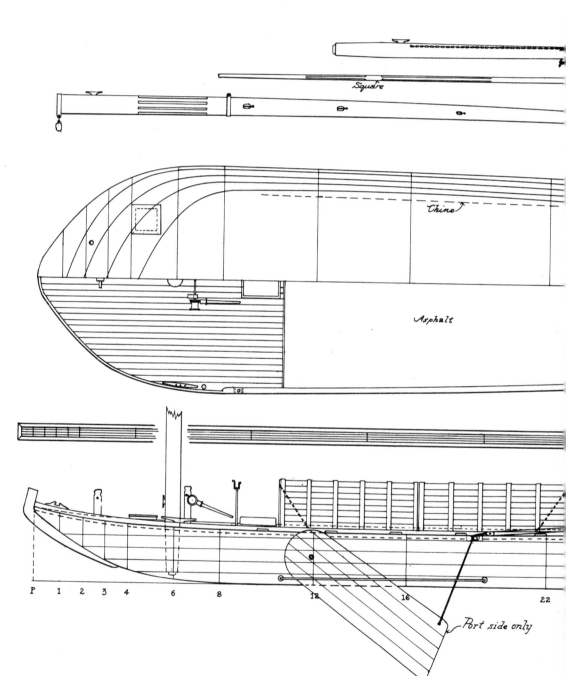

Square

Chine

Asphalt

P   1   2   3   4   6   8   12   16   22

Port side only

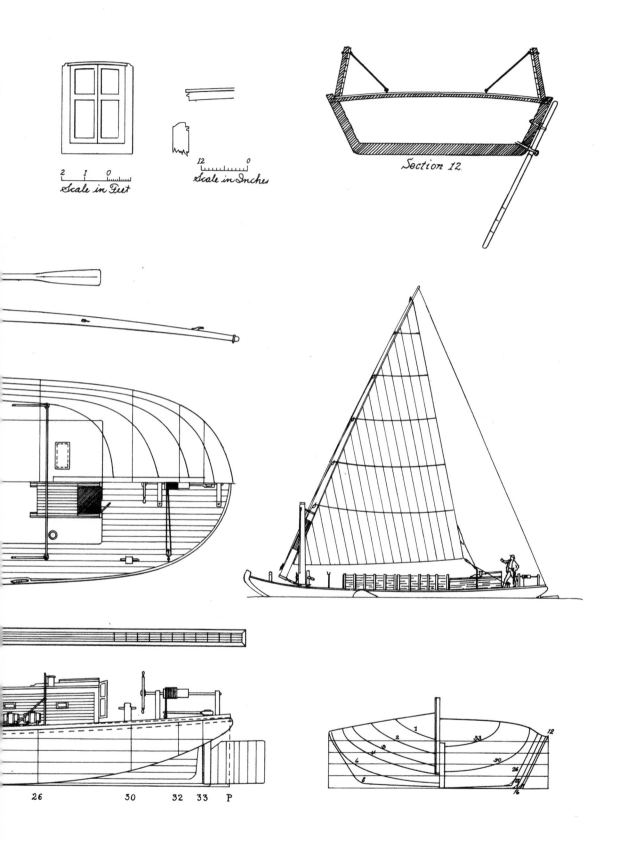

Section 12.

2 1 0
Scale in Feet

12   0
Scale in Inches

26   30   32 33   P

Victor R. Grimwood '41
AFTER D.F. TAYLOR.

CHAPTER ONE

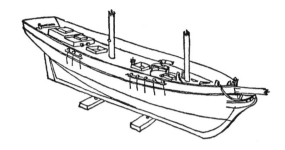

CONSTRUCTION *of a* HALF-HULL SHIP MODEL

THE art of building ship models is as old as its parent art, shipbuild-ing. Archaeologists have found models of great antiquity in all parts of the world. The tombs of ancient Egypt have yielded many beautiful little models. The Egyptian room of the Boston Museum of Fine Arts has on display eight clay models of Nile craft; numerous others are in the collection of the Metropolitan Museum, while some thirty-two other ancient Egyptian examples are distributed among the other museums of this country. Manned by miniature crews, each member performing some sailorman's duty, they give us an exact knowledge of the types of craft and the seafaring methods and manners of the earliest great maritime nation.

Since these models of potter's clay were made, models have been fashioned from a great variety of materials and in many ways. Goldsmiths and silversmiths have turned their hands to modelmaking. A notable example is a gold cup of 1503 now in the Germanic National Museum, Nuremberg, that is a miniature replica of a fifteenth-century carrack. Prisoners of war built fine models of bone during the seventeenth and eighteenth centuries. I have a little model of an eighteenth-century man-of-war made of cardboard, with ivory spars and rigged with spun glass. Some truly wonderful models were made entirely of ivory and examples

17

are to be seen in nearly all good ship-model collections. Elephant and walrus ivory, as well as whales' teeth, were commonly used for hull and spars, and there were models partially rigged with ivory scraped as thin as a hair, the lighter rigging being of white silk and sometimes black or white horsehair. Even human hair has sometimes been used in the rigging of delicate models. Pastry cooks and confectioners have even contrived models out of sugar and flour. Wood, however, is the material generally favored by modelmakers, and the greatest modelists worked in that medium. It is obvious that wood can produce a better replica than other materials of an object built originally of wood.

The finest examples of the modelmaker's art are the so-called Admiralty models. These were built by the naval architects, master-shipwrights, or shipbuilders from the original plans before the ships themselves were built. They were submitted to the Admiralty Board along with the plans for the Board's approval. So complete in detail, so handsomely carved and decorated, so carefully rigged were they, that today the Admiralty models that are preserved to us rank high among the art treasures of the world. Models of construction similar to these are known as "built-up models," or "framed and planked models." In this method of model-making, shipbuilding practice is followed almost exactly: a keel is laid, frames cut to the proper shapes are mounted across it, and the hull is wholly or partly planked and decked—a very difficult method of construction, requiring an intimate knowledge of the art of shipbuilding.

The most prolific producers of miniature ships were the sailors. Their models are mostly jackknife-carved from solid blocks of wood and are known as "sailorman's models." Many very early models of this kind are to be found hanging in churches abroad. They were the only offering poor Jack could make in appreciation of his safe return from a hazardous voyage. Collectors know these as "church ships" or "votive models." As a rule with exceptions, votive models were crude, lacking accuracy of line and proportion; but they are nevertheless representative of ship types and rigs of various periods. They antedate the Admiralty models and are the link, historically, between the Egyptian models and those of later origin. I know of only one church in this country in which hang some of these votive models: St. Ann's on Clinton Street, Brooklyn.

Still another type of model, one with which we are directly concerned, is the "shipbuilder's half-hull model." Several methods of construction were employed: frame and batten, sectional, and lift. It is in the last type that we are most interested. Half-hull models of this character proved to be most useful to the shipbuilder, and were made prolifically. The earliest examples of them date from about 1790. It is often stated that either Enos Briggs of Salem or Orlando Merrill of Newburyport originated them. A half-hull lift model is also called a "waterline model." It represents a longitudinal half of a hull and corresponds to the sheer, or profile, plan as set down on paper by the ship's designer. It is built up in lifts, or layers, each line where the layers join representing a water-line, as shown in the plan of the vessel. This method of construction—the employment of lifts in the building of a complete hull—is the simplest and best way for the modelmaker to obtain correctness of hull shape. It is also a time- and labor-saving method of construction and, if care is given to finishing and rigging, a model built in this way will amply reward the builder for his efforts. This is the method that will later be followed in a step-by-step description of the building of a model of the Chesapeake Bay skipjack (Plate I).

Before we begin actual work on the first little ship I wish to insert here a word of admonition and advice. Ships and their gear and rigging are all dated and influenced by the use to which they were put and the materials available to the builders. Men of the sea did not do things in the way they did just to be different from the landsman, but because experience taught them the way best suited to their needs. "Shipshape" means more than tidiness. There is a reason for the way each piece of rigging is rove and the way it is made fast. For each piece of gear, for the shape and character of each piece of deck furniture, for the placing of hatches and deck houses, there is a logical reason, based on efficiency or safety. For instance, no sharp corners are to be found aboard ship on deckhouses, bitts, or hatchways. In rough weather men are often hurled about the decks, to bring up against something solid, and rounded corners have saved sailors many a cracked pate or broken bone. Don't put some piece of gear that did not come into use until 1850 on your model of an eighteenth-century ship. If you are uncertain about some detail, learn how and why it was used and made. Every item should be a miniature replica of its prototype.

Proper proportions should also be kept strictly in mind and adhered to. To do this is often very difficult on small-scale models, where it is hard to make things small enough and still keep them shipshape. I have never seen a model too lightly rigged, but I have seen a great many with such heavy cordage and big blocks and deadeyes that they were ridiculous. Scale the rigging as well as the furniture and the hull. This is very important.

Two further things contribute to the appearance of a model: the texture and color of materials used for rigging and gear. Linen thread used for rigging should look like rope. Hardware, though made of some substitute material, should wear the look of the iron it simulates. And about the whole little ship there should be an atmosphere of the sea. Just how to obtain this is hard to describe; probably an avoidance of overnicety, of glittering paint, and of polished surfaces will help do it.

Good models are made by taking infinite pains, and the three most essential traits of the modelmaker are care, accuracy and patience.

An important thing to be acquired before starting operations is a working understanding of a set of ship plans, properly known as a "draught." Let us examine Plate I and see if we can decipher this complex-looking maze of lines.

It is customary in a draught to show the lines of a vessel as viewed from one side, from above, and from each end. Only one half of the ship is projected in each view; to project the other side would be unnecessary duplication; and thus they are shown in the plate.

View A. This is the sheer or profile plan, showing the lines of the vessel as viewed from the side.

View B. This is the body plan, divided vertically; one half shows the vessel as looked at from in front, the other half as looked at from astern.

View C. This is the half-breadth plan, divided longitudinally; one half shows the lines of the ship, the other half the plan of the deck in detail—

deck houses, hatchways, pinrails, and other furniture properly located.

The sheer and body plans are crossed by straight lines running horizontally, known as waterlines. They are marked with the symbol *WL* and are numbered 1 and 2 in Plate I. One other horizontal line is shown, and is marked *base*. In this plan it comes at the lower edge of the keel and is the line from which all elevations are taken.

Let us imagine that we have a hull the shape and size of the one in our plan and let us further imagine that we cut this hull along waterlines 1 and 2, making three horizontal layers similar to the layers of a cake. Separating them and looking down upon the upper surface of layer or lift 1, you will see that it corresponds in shape to the curved line in View C that is marked *WL* 1 and that the other slice corresponds in shape with the line marked *WL* 2 in View C. Therefore the curved lines in View C are the shapes of the boat at given heights above the base lines as shown in View A. Such slices would show the complete outline of the vessel; only half of it is shown in the plate. Also shown in the sheer plan (View A) are curved lines indicating the sheer line (the line just under the top rail of the vessel), so marked in the plan, and the location of the deck (the dot and dash line). There are two other curved lines running from the stem to the sternpost in View A. The heavy black line marks the bottom of lift 1, where the keel meets the hull. In a set of designer's plans this is the rabbet line and is always so designated. The other, or lighter line, is the chine, that is, the line where the sides of the boat meet the floor or bottom, forming a sharp angle. The sheer plan also shows stem and stern posts, rudder, channels, rails, and other details. The sheer line and the shape of the deck are also shown in the half-breadth plan (C) and are distinctly marked.

The vertical lines designated by numbers and letters in Views A, B, and C are known as station lines. The station having the greatest capacity (area in cross section) is marked with the symbol $\oplus$ and is known as the "dead-flat." From here forward the stations are designated by letters, aft by numbers. The last vertical line at each end of the plan (generally a dotted line is used) is called a "perpendicular," marked *P* in the plate. These lines are located at the point where the line indicating the main deck meets the line of the stem and sternpost. The length of the vessel is generally measured between these two points, and is referred to as the length between perpendiculars.

Again let us cut up our imaginary hull, this time as though it were a loaf of bread, making a cut at one of the station lines in View A and thus obtaining a cross section of the vessel. Its shape would correspond with the bent line in the body plan (View B) bearing the number or letter of the station at the point where the cut was made. A little study of these views and their lines will acquaint one with their purposes and show how the Views A, B, and C are related to one another.

Place one leg of a pair of dividers on the center line at station F in View C and measure the distance to the point where WL 1 intersects line F—then you have one-half the width of the vessel at this point. Going to the body plan (View B), place one end of the dividers on the center line at WL 1. Mark off horizontally along this WL the distance shown on the dividers—then the curved line F in this view will cross WL 1 at this point. All breadths along the waterlines, deck, and sheer lines will check from the half-breadth plan to the body plan and all elevations will check from the sheer plan to the body plan. Study the plans until the meaning of each line is clear to you. When you are certain you know what each line represents, then proceed to the actual work of construction.

Before attempting to make a complete model, and in order to familiarize yourself with the principles of lift-model construction, let us first build a half-hull model. This need not be a wasted effort, as such a half hull can be made a very attractive and interesting example of model building. As decorations such models have certain advantages in that they may be hung like pictures, whereas a complete model must have something to rest upon and often requires a case. Half-hull models make very attractive overmantels, fit over doorways, and lend themselves to many decorative effects.

In building such a model you must first determine whether it shall be natural wood, varnished, or painted when finished. It was the general practice of shipbuilders to leave these models unpainted in order to show the waterlines. We describe the building of our present model with that object in view.

Secondly, scale or size must be determined. The larger the model is, the easier the work. Experienced modelists consider ¼ inch to 1 foot to be about as small a scale as should be used, to permit the working out of proper proportions of the blocks, cordage, and gear. In the reproduction of larger ships ¼-inch scale produces overly large models suitable only for display in very large rooms. At ¼-inch scale a 160-foot hull becomes 40 inches long. Add to this the length of projecting spars, say another 15 or 20 inches, and the model becomes 5 feet long. It then becomes necessary, if the model is desired for display in the average home, to work on a smaller scale, regardless of the disadvantages. Most of the plans in this book have been drawn so that doubling the scale as shown will produce a model of reasonable size and permit the proper working out of details. In Plate I, Views A, B, and C were originally drawn on a scale of ⅜ inch to 1 foot. They scale in the reproduction one-half that size, or ³⁄₁₆ inch to 1 foot. Double this and we get a model measuring just under 15 inches between perpendiculars, a very suitable size. So we will build our half model on a scale ⅜ inch to 1 foot. To build the hull, three pieces of wood are required for the lifts, each 16 inches long by 3 inches wide. Lifts 1 and 3 should be white pine, while lift 2 (between *WL* 1 and *WL* 2, View A) should be of a contrasting wood—say mahogany. (See Chapter Six on materials and tools.) Buy the wood from a mill that will finish the pieces to required thicknesses on a planer or sander. Lift 1 should be finished to exactly ¹⁹⁄₃₂ inch thick; lift 2, exactly ⅜ inch thick; and lift 3, approximately ⅞ inch thick.

Operation 1

Form the lifts into a block (Figure 1). Drive a thin wire nail at each corner, leaving the head projecting so that the nails can be withdrawn later. Now finish the sides and ends of the block so that each face of it forms a right angle to all adjoining faces. Study the plan, and on the upper surface of lift 3 draw the station line ⊕. Be sure to locate this mark so that the forward and after ends of the hull come approximately the same distance from each end of the block. Mark each lift so that its position in the block will remain unchanged during succeeding operations. Draw on top of the block all station lines, using a square and starting from the side of the block that is away from you when the bow end of the block is to your right hand. Carry these lines around the block. If the block is truly squared up they will finish at their exact starting points. If they do not, check the block with the square for error and correct now; to do this is important, for on it depends the accuracy of shape of the finished model; this statement applies to all other models of lift construction.

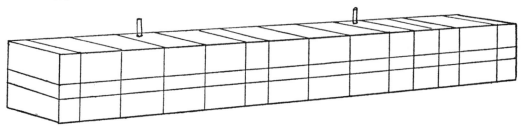

FIGURE 1. *The lifts put together into a block and doweled.*

Between Stations *I* and *K* forward, and 4 and 7 aft, and ⅜ inch from the back edge, drill two ¼-inch holes straight downward through lifts 3 and 2 and into lift 1 to a depth of just ⅛ inch. Be sure not to exceed this, in order to avoid breaking through the bottom of the hull. Get a ¼-inch dowel stick and make two pins 1½ inches long, cutting them from the dowel stick where it is perfectly straight. These pins should fit snugly into the holes and will serve to keep the lifts in place when the corner nails are removed. The block should now appear as in Figure 1.

Operation 2

Pull the nails and separate the lifts. Using the marks on the sides to guide you, draw the station lines on the tops of lifts 1 and 2. Then draw on these lifts the outline of the hull at these elevations, or *WL* 1 and *WL* 2 as shown in View C of Plate I. Note the waterlines are to be drawn with the center line away from you instead of toward you as shown in the plate.

To draw these outlines accurately, start at the ⊕ and measure the distance from the center line along this station line to where *WL* 1 intersects it, as shown in the plan. It is to be remembered that the scale of the plan as reproduced is ³⁄₁₆ inch to 1 foot and that we are building to a scale of ⅜ inch to 1 foot, which is just double the original, and all measurements should be so calculated. Mark this distance off on the ⊕ station on the lift. Repeat this procedure at each station line until you have marked off the proper distances on each one. With these marks to guide you, draw the curved outline of *WL* 1 and *WL* 2 on the corresponding lifts. If you lack the instruments designed for the purpose, use a light, flexible wooden batten to rule in the curved lines. Examine your drawing and see that the sweep of these curves is true and fair (see Figure 2).

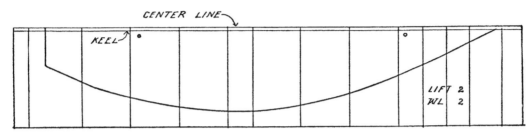

FIGURE 2. *Waterline 2 drawn on lift 2.*

Reassemble the block, putting in the wooden pins, and on the side of the block toward you draw the profile of the hull. Follow the heavy black line in the profile plan, View A, and the dotted line representing the underside of the deck. The block should now appear as in Figure 3. Cut away the shaded part of the block at each end, then the part at the top, and lastly the shaded part at the bottom.

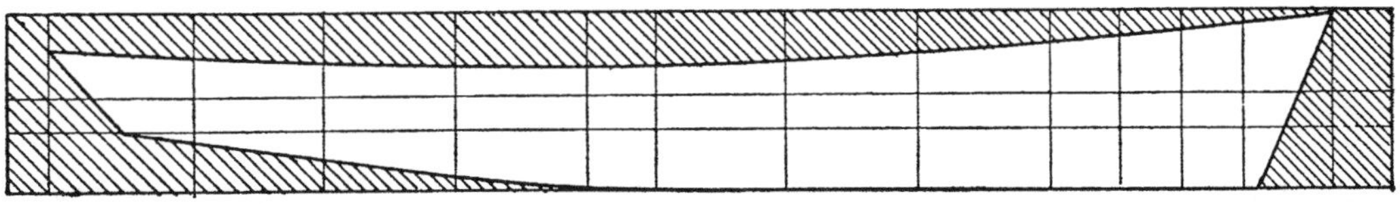

FIGURE 3. *The reassembled block with the profile of the hull drawn on the side.*

Here is a dictum that applies to all further operations of this nature: in making a cut to a mark, never cut exactly on the line but always leave a little excess wood. This excess is an insurance against error, and is removed in the finishing, which we will start with the upper surface of the block. Finishing is best accomplished with a medium-coarse wood rasp followed by coarse and fine sandpaper. Glue the sandpaper, or otherwise fasten it, onto wood blocks wide enough to reach entirely across the hull. Make your cutting strokes with the rasp and the sander length-wise of the block, cutting entirely across it at each stroke as though you were using a plane. Hold the sanding blocks flat and remove all humps and unevenness, testing occasionally with the square, leaving the top a true and fair sweep of surface from stem to stern. Now finish the bottom in the same manner, but leave the ends till later; the block should appear as in Figure 4 when you reassemble the lifts.

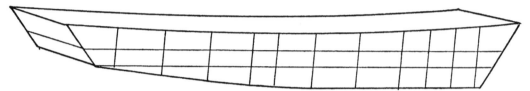

FIGURE 4. *The block after cutting away the shaded portion in Figure 3, leaving the profile.*

You have now cut away the marks made on the top and bottom of the block representing the station lines. They are still on the sides, however, and, using these as guides, redraw the station lines on the top and bottom. Then draw on the top the outline of half the deck as shown by the dotted line in View C.

Operation 3

Again separating the block, cut each lift to the shape of the lines marked upon it. I want to call your attention to the fact that the back line represents the center line, as in the plan View C. The waterlines drawn on the block do not meet this center line but meet the line that represents the width of the keel; from these meeting points to the center line the lift is cut square across the block at right angles to the center line. When the lifts are finished this squared cut makes the seat for the stem and sternpost. Do not cut into it. Also, when you come to shape the bottom later, cut only to the keel line. Look at the body plan and see how the section lines come to the keel at an angle and then run straight across the keel to the center line, thus making a seat for the keel, which must be flat since this joint must be very close.

Don't try to cut exactly on the lines marked on the lifts—leave a margin as directed. Then finish the edges of the lifts carefully down to the marks. Be careful and see that the sweep of the curves is fair and true. A small plane is a good tool to use for this shaping, followed by the inevitable sand-

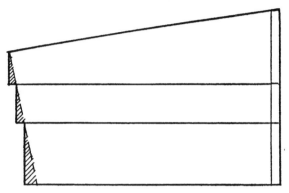

FIGURE 5. *The lifts in position after being cut to waterlines. The shaded portion is to be cut away in the next operation.*

paper on a block. Run your fingers along the finished edges and you will find the spots that are out of true. Fix them now. I find that I can detect irregularities with my fingers more quickly and surely than I can with my eyes. The ends of the lifts should be cut at the lines indicating their extreme lengths and at an exact right angle to the center line. When all are finished to your satisfaction, reform the block. It will look as in Figure 5.

Operation 4

Reassemble the block, this time permanently. Glue the lifts together. Use hot cabinetmaker's glue, applied thinly, and force the lifts together with clamps. See that the joints between lifts are tight and use the wooden pins to assure alignment. Let the glue dry well before proceeding with the work.

You now have the shape of the hull at the underside of the deck and at *WL* 1 and *WL* 2. However, the lower edges of lifts 3 and 2 do not meet the upper edges of the lifts immediately below them, but project beyond them.

Cut away this projecting or excess wood until the shape of the lower edge of lift 3 coincides with the upper edge of lift 2, and lift 2 coincides with lift 1. The hull begins to assume its final shape. In this model the cutting away is a very simple process, as there is no curve to the model's sides above the chine (see body plan, Plate I, View B). In cutting away this projecting wood, again let me caution you not to cut too closely. Also let

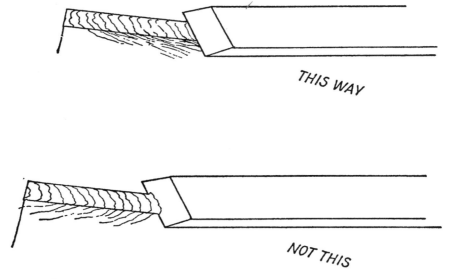

FIGURE 6. *The right way and the wrong way to cut—with the grain of the wood, not against it.*

me advise you to work with the grain and not against it. Cuts made against the grain have a tendency to follow it and you are apt to cut in too deeply and spoil your work, especially if you use a chisel. Against-the-grain cutting tends to cause the wood to split out (see Figure 6). When using a sweep or slightly curved gouge it is often practical, in roughing out the work, to cut diagonally across the grain of the wood, as this will speed up the work.

Good woodworkers proceed on the theory of cutting little and often. Do not be greedy and take large bites.

Operation 5

When you have roughly removed the excess and the angle of the side is fixed, mark on the side the line showing the chine or place where the side meets the rising floor that bends sharply inward to join the keel. As the block is now, its bottom should be perfectly flat from stem to ⊕. From here aft it curves upward to the stern, which it intersects at the point where the top of lift 1 meets the stern (the heavy line in View A marks the bottom of the block). From bow to stern along this line the block should be flat across the bottom, from the side to center line. Mark the width of the keel on this surface, paralleling the center line, and be sure that during the next operation you do not cut into this strip. One way to protect it is to fit on a temporary keel of the proper width. It may be made of softwood and should be the same depth as shown in the plan. The reason for making the keel of the right depth is that it will later aid in using the templates for accurately shaping the hull.

Operation 6

Turn to the body plan, View B, and make a template of the ⊕ section. Since templates should be used in shaping the hulls of all models made by the lift method, familiarize yourself now with their use. According to lexicographer Noah Webster, a template is "a gauge, pattern, or mold, commonly a thin plate or board, . . . used as a guide to the form of the work to be executed."

For our purposes thin wood, sheet fiber, cardboard, or sheet metal all make suitable templates. Whichever material you select should not be too flexible, but must be susceptible of accurate cutting. I prefer a material that I can cut and trim with scissors. A pair of curved manicure scissors will be found very handy in cutting the sharper curves, particularly in cardboard templates.

Draw on the material the outline of the ⊕ section. Mark the waterlines and the base line on it. Cut the top accurately at the under deck line. The depth of the keel should be marked and the template cut to fit correctly against the keel. Look at Figure 7.

At the dead-flat, and this is always the place to start shaping, the hull should fit into the template perfectly, the top of the block meeting the top of the template and the keel (temporary or permanent) fitting into the notch at the bottom. The waterlines marked on the template should coincide with those on the block. This accurate fitting will only be consum-

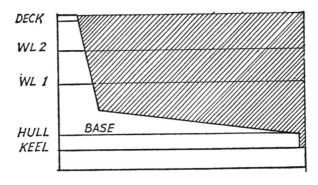

FIGURE 7. *The template for the dead-flat section* ⊕.

mated after the hull is finished. But repeated testing with the template while the work of shaping goes forward is necessary. When the hull roughly fits the template, make templates of other stations and work toward the ends of the block from the ⊕.

To hold the model while working on it, fasten a block of wood across the top surface with screws. Put the screws where there is no danger of their coming through to the outside of the model and spoiling the work. Make the block of a size to fit in the jaws of your vise. This will permit it to be turned three ways in the vise. Don't put the model in a vise as you may destroy it by exerting too much force in attempting to hold it. For shaping the hull a broad chisel followed by a plane will do all the rough work. Later, when making hulls of more complicated form, it will be necessary to have recourse to other tools. Whatever cutting tool you do use should be sharp. In order to do good work tools must cut readily and easily. Look at a man's tools and you can judge his ability. Have respect for your tools and keep them in condition.

As the work of shaping develops, see that the line or bend of the hull at the chine runs in a true sweep from stem to stern, as definite as the line in the plan. It comes to a knife edge. After the plane, use a sharp but not too coarse rasp to remove all unevenness. Then remove all rasp marks with sandpaper.

Operation 7

The half hull is now complete except for the deck. A mahogany deck will give this model a distinctive finishing touch, so obtain a piece of mahogany $15\frac{1}{2}$ inches long by $2\frac{7}{8}$ inches wide and $\frac{3}{16}$ inch thick.

The deck planking of the skipjack is $2\frac{1}{2}$ inches thick or $\frac{5}{64}$ inch by scale. This plank dimension is shown between the dotted line and the sheer line in View A. All ships' decks are built with a crown or camber, to provide for draining surface water off the deck. That is, a line athwartship forms an arc with its high point along the center line of the vessel. The amount of camber varies; custom decrees a camber of 5 inches to 20 feet of beam. Men-of-war, however, have less camber than merchant ships— when heavy guns had to be moved about the decks they would roll easier on flatter surfaces.

The original of our model had a beam of 14 feet, so the amount of deck camber would have been $\frac{14}{20}$ of 5 inches, or $3\frac{1}{2}$ inches. Inasmuch as the deck of our model is to be $\frac{5}{64}$ inch thick on the outboard edge, so at the center line it must have this thickness plus the amount of camber, or $\frac{5}{64}$ inch plus $\frac{7}{64}$ inch, that is, $\frac{3}{16}$ inch exactly. Incidentally, this skipjack has much less deck crown than many of her type.

Decks of a real ship are given their camber by having the deck beams to which the deck planking is fastened arched athwartship. Since this model has no deck beams to shape it, we must obtain the camber in some other way and fashion it from one piece of wood. In order to shape this piece to the proper camber, a guide or gauge is necessary. Therefore we will make a template of the deck camber at the dead-flat. Figure 8 shows a deck template that will serve for this half-hull model and also for the whole-hull model that will be our next undertaking.

The shaping of this piece is the most difficult piece of work so far undertaken. Its shape as seen from above is shown in the deck plan (View C, lower half). Draw this outline on the deck piece. Since this view is projected on a flat surface, the length of the deck as shown does not measure as much as it would if measured along the curved surface of the hull (along the sheer line representing the top of the deck in the sheer plan or View A). This difference is not much, amounting to less than ⅟₁₆ inch, but in cutting the piece allow for it and leave the piece ⅟₃₂ inch longer at each end. Also allow for the stem; cut the bow end straight across to create a flat seat for the stem piece.

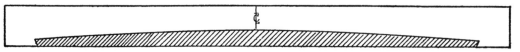

FIGURE 8. *The template for shaping deck camber, at the dead-flat ⊕.*

Cut the deck piece to the outline, leaving plenty of excess wood, not only to allow for finishing but to compensate for any change in shape that may occur when it is bent to the curve of the top of the hull. With a scratch awl or other gauge, measuring up from the bottom of the deck piece, mark on the curved or outboard edge the depth or the thickness of the deck, ⁵⁄₆₄ inch. Carry the mark across the bow end (the seat for the stem) but not across the stern. See that this line is truly marked—no variations or waviness. Take off the vise block, and then, using glue only, no nails or screws, fasten the piece in place on the block.

Bevel off the edge of the deck piece, starting about ⅜ inch from the edge and cutting a sharp bevel down to the mark on the edge representing the thickness of the deck; then roughly finish the edge to the flare of the model's side from the stem to where it turns across the stern. This flare is shown in the small figure of the rail detail in Plate I. The outboard end of the template for the deck camber is cut at an angle that corresponds to the flare of the model's side at the ⊕.

Some further shaping of the deck piece remains to be accomplished, and before you begin look at Figure 9 and get the contours of the deck's surface firmly fixed in your mind.

In this figure the outboard edge of the deck piece is shown by two parallel lines, one a dotted line and the other above it lightly drawn. Above

PLATE III

Anchor Hoy. U.S.N.

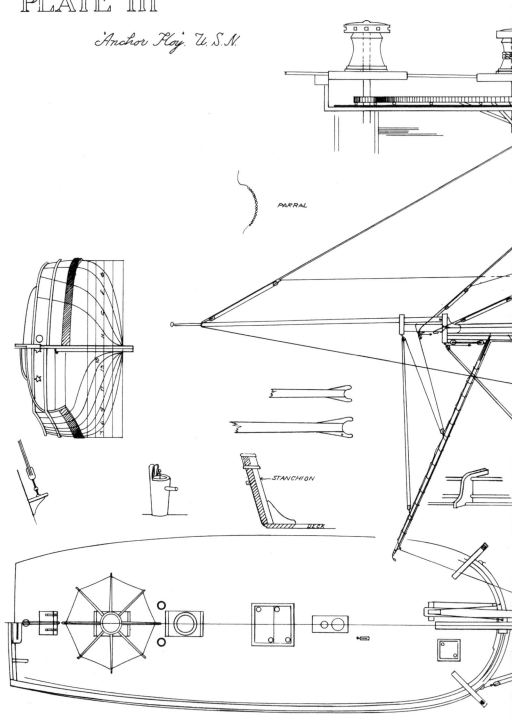

PARRAL

STANCHION

DECK

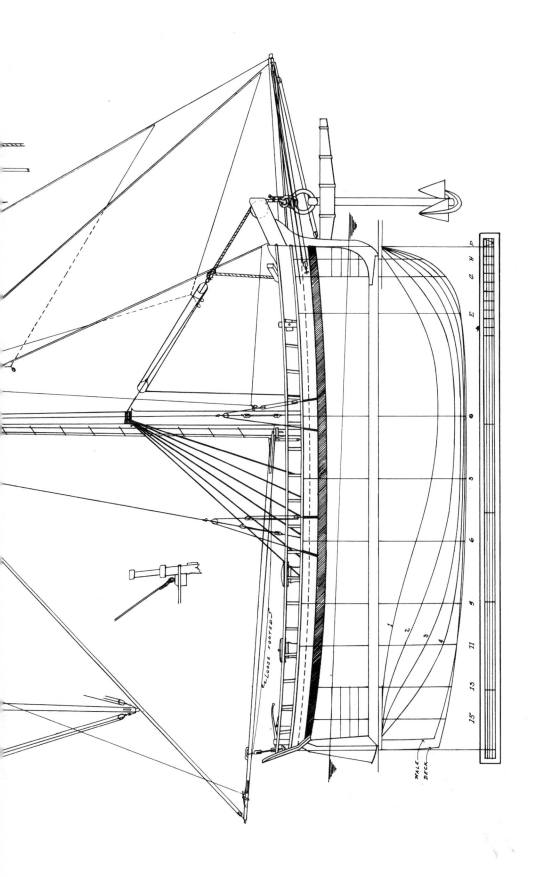

Colonial Fishing Schooner
from a reconstruction by H. I. Chapelle.

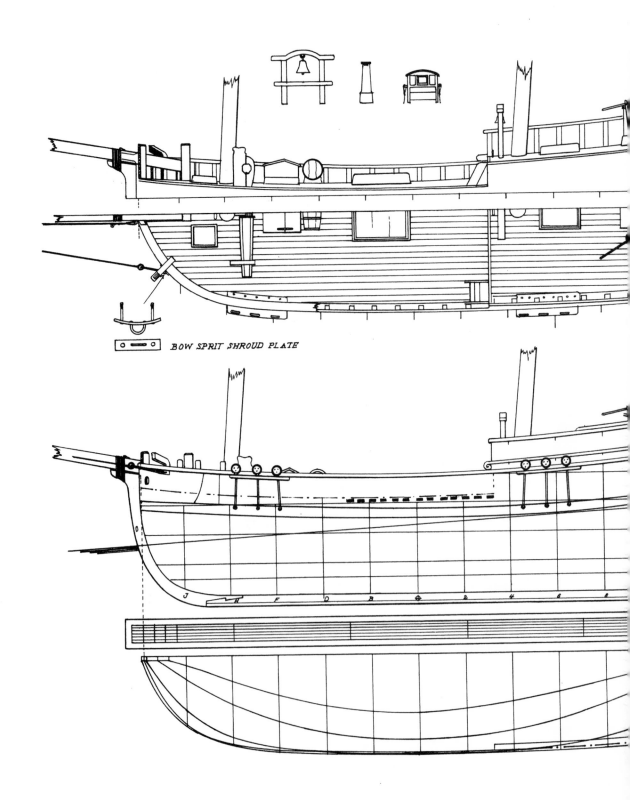

BOW SPRIT SHROUD PLATE

PLATE IV

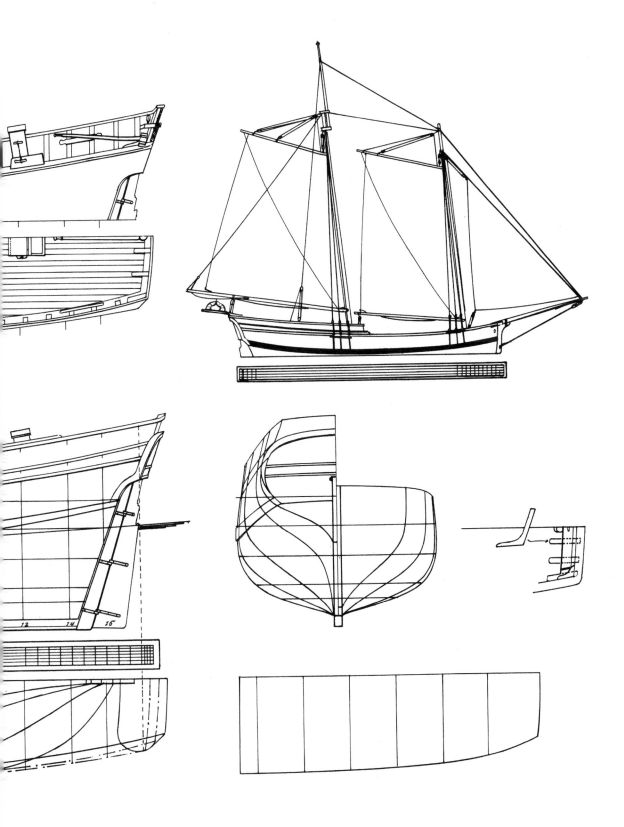

this light line is a darker line (not shown in Plate I) that represents the sheer of the deck piece along the center line of the model. Note that it varies in its height above the line representing the top of the deck at the side. It is exactly 3½ inches by scale (⁷⁄₆₄ inch in our model) above this line at the ⊕; it meets this line at the stem; and at the stern it is 3 inches above it. Its sweep is a true curve from stern to stem. Mark these heights on the inboard (or back) edge of the deck piece, measuring up from the

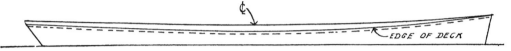

FIGURE 9. *The sheer of the deck camber.*

bottom of the deck piece and adding the thickness of the piece at the outboard edge (2½ inches). These totals will be 5½ inches (¹¹⁄₆₄ inch) at the stern, 6 inches or ³⁄₁₆ inch on our model, at the ⊕, and 2½ inches by scale at the seat of the stem piece. With these marks as a guide, draw on the edge of the deck piece a line representing the sweep of the sheer along the center line, at the back of the model. To make certain that this marking is accurately accomplished and a true sweep obtained, make a template of the sheer and use it to guide you in the work. In shaping, remember you are to cut with the grain of the wood. Cut away the back edge of the piece down to the mark you have made, and roughly finish. You now have the deck piece cut to proper thickness along the inboard and outboard edges but have not shaped it athwartship; that is, it is not as yet shaped to the proper camber or crown.

Making *frequent* use of the template you made for the camber, shape the deck properly at the dead-flat. In using this template, always apply it to the outboard edge and gauge the camber from there. As the hull narrows up fore and aft and the camber remains constant; the factor in maintaining the camber is the change in the thickness of the deck piece at the center line. Therefore, we must start fitting the template at the outboard edge of the piece where the thickness is always the same. A plane will not work on the curved surface of the deck, but a drawknife or small spokeshave is just the tool for this shaping. Follow with a rasp or sandpaper.

Operation 8

It is customary in the construction of half-hull models to attach the keel, stem, sternpost, rudder, and—if the boat has one—the centerboard partly lowered.

Make all these parts of mahogany. Start with the stem piece and make it long enough to extend ¹⁄₁₆ inch below the keel. It must be remembered that in building models one departs from shipbuilding practice in many details of construction. Keels, stemposts, and sternposts of ships are not fastened on the outside of the hulls as they are when building such a model as this. They are integral parts of the ship's frame and the outside planking of the hull is rabbeted into them (see the description of Plate VIII). In order to disguise the fact that in the model these pieces are attached to the outside of the hull, very nice fitting of them is necessary.

Until now you have left the fore end of the hull (the seat for the stem piece) roughly finished. In this model (see Plate I) the forward end of the hull is perfectly straight as it rises from the keel to the top of the deck. Also the forward face must be perfectly flat. Finish this end now until it is perfect in both respects. Use fine sandpaper on a truly flat hardwood block, and true the seat both ways at once by holding the block properly against the hull. Finish the seats for the keel and sternpost as carefully. The stempost tapers slightly from where it comes against the hull to its outer face and this taper is repeated throughout the length of the longhead. The upper part of the outer face of the stem piece is recessed in profile to receive the heel of the long-head (see View A, Plate I). Here, again, be careful to make these parts tight fitting, particularly at the lip at the lower end of the recess. There is no objection to making the stem piece and longhead all in one, if you wish, but some part of a piece so made will be very delicate, since the grain of the wood will run crosswise somewhere. Made in two parts it will be much stronger. Fasten the stem piece to the hull with glue and small brads. Do not drive the brads home flush but let the heads stick out slightly to look like boltheads. If the longhead is a separate piece, do not put it in place yet.

Next make the keel, in two pieces, as shown in the plans, and attach. Use the sandpaper as directed to seat the keel properly. Then make and put in place the sternpost. Make the longhead and notice that it tapers slightly to its outboard end. The eagle head which is characteristic of the skipjack can be made in one piece with the longhead. It should be carved in bas relief, that is, not widening out from the longhead, the eyes and features being more or less suggestions. These eagle heads were in reality very crude examples of the ship carver's art. Actually the eagle head was made separately from the longhead and let into a V-shaped notch in its forward end, the after end of the eagle head being pointed to fit the V. Next make the rudder and then the rail of the head and the cheek knees as shown in the plan, Views A and B of Plate I. The cheek knees have a slight upward curve which you can give them by bending when you put them on. The arrangement of the rail of the head and the cheek knees is a survival from the days when the prows of ships were a maze of involved timbering with extravagantly carved rails and braces surmounted by a beautiful figure or group of figures. These were not pure adornment, but served certain definite purposes, chiefly the support of the head. For a more complicated form of this construction about the bows of a ship, see Plate X. The practice of constructing this simplified form will serve you well when you come to build the *Oliver Cromwell*.

Lay these parts aside for the time being and proceed to the next operation.

Operation 9

Half-hull models are usually mounted on wooden panels. This model fits nicely on a ¾-inch panel 24 by 8 inches. It may be of whatever wood you elect. Bevel the edges to suggest a frame. Go over the hull now with the finest of sandpaper and finish it to a high degree of smoothness. Mount the hull on the panel, attaching with screws from the back.

The load waterline of the hull should be parallel with the bottom of the panel. Sometimes this line is drawn on the hull. If you wish to show it, do so with a carefully drawn, narrow black line (View A, Plate I). More often it is shown by a short black line on the panel only, which would be a continuation of the line on the hull, but the line is omitted on the model. Sometimes it is not shown at all.

With the model in place, next put on the longhead and cutwater, gluing them in place to the stem piece and the panel. Put on the cheek knees and then the rail of the head. This requires great care and careful proportioning. The inside edges of the cheek knees fit against the stem and the longhead and are bolted to both. The lower cheek knee is slightly longer than the upper one in the part that fits against the hull so that the ends of the cheek knees are parallel with the rake of the stem. Details of the head can be visualized by studying Figure 24, the cutwater of the schooner *Agate*. Now the rudder, without "braces," is glued in place entirely independent of the hull. See that its forward edge is parallel to the after edge of the sternpost.

The space between the inboard ends of the keel pieces is where the centerboard comes through the hull. When you come to make a whole-hull model, an opening 3½ inches by scale must be cut through lift 1 for it. The slot extends from the forward keel piece to the after keel piece. A strip of wood or "shoe" ¾ inch wide by 1 inch deep by scale goes along each edge of the opening and butts against the ends of the keel pieces (see View A in the plate). Put on this "shoe" and then make the centerboard. This is not made in full and is supposed to represent the centerboard partially lowered. The board is 3 inches thick by scale in a whole model, so it will be 1½ inches ($^3\!/_{64}$ inch) in our half hull. Fit the board into the recess formed by the shoe up against the hull and glue fast to the panel (see Figure 10).

This finishes the work on the hull. Give a final rubdown with fine sandpaper to panel and all. Run the sandpaper lightly over the edges of the longhead, keel, stem, and sternpost, so that they show slightly rounded edges instead of sharp corners. Polish to a very smooth finish.

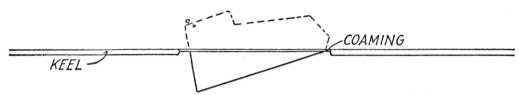

FIGURE 10. *Detail for centerboard, keel pieces, and shoe.*

Operation 10

Apply one coat of varnish. When it is dry, put on three coats of any good varnish. Varnish works better when warm and should be used very thin. When the first and second coats dry, rub them down with fine sandpaper or steel wool and see that the varnish does not form any unsightly lumps.

After you have compared the model with the plan and are sure that everything is in place, your work is finished.

A MORE DECORATIVE FORM OF THE HALF-HULL MODEL

This model, since it will be painted, should be made entirely of pine. Models of this type can, of course, be varnished, and they can be very handsome. If you choose to paint your model, follow all the directions as given for the construction of the model. The following directions for making the deck furniture refer to a painted model. In the case of skipjacks, painting is more in keeping with the original, as there is no bright or varnished work to be found about them. Skipjacks are work boats, not yachts. However, if you do finish in varnish, make the deck furniture of hardwood and carry out the construction in detail. It is not necessary to hollow out the hull or to have the hatchways and companionway open into the hull, but hatch coamings should be built properly with mitered corners, rabbeted to take the covers. The wheelbox, cabin trunk, and hatch covers should show that they are constructed of matched boards. Do not use dummies made of blocks that will look all right if painted but very badly if varnished.

There will be a little more detail to work out on the deck in either a painted or varnished model. See the directions for finishing the deck piece to show planking and waterways as given in the instructions for building a whole-hull model (page 46) and follow them in building this half model.

Make the bowsprit and fit it in place. It is square in section inboard. Outboard its edges are chamfered off, making it nearly octagonal for 2 feet by scale (¾ inch), and then it is rounded to the cap. As you are still working on a half-hull model, you show only one-half the bowsprit; that is, it is 5 inches wide by 10 inches deep inboard. At the heel, put on the oblong piece that is shown there in the plan. The butt of the bowsprit rakes slightly aft and this piece fits against the butt. It is properly called a samson post. In the real boat it is stepped on the keel and extends through the deck. It carries the axle of the winch and the hawser is bent around it when anchoring. It also takes the forward mooring lines when making fast to a dock. Paint this samson post and the bowsprit white.

Either buy or make a winch and mount it in place. If you purchase one from a dealer in model fittings, get it to scale, ⅜ inch to 1 foot. It will probably be made complete and you will have to cut it in two. If you have a small lathe it is simple to turn a winch out of metal; brass is best. The winch can be turned from one piece. You will have to file out the throat piece to hold the winchbar. It can be made of brass. Paint or color it to look like iron. Solder it fast to the winch in its proper place and remove all excess solder lumps.

For making such metal pieces as the horse for the foresheet block, get an assortment of women's black hairpins. They can be purchased in several sizes and thicknesses of wire. Get straight ones. Let the center end of the wire into the panel and bend the other end down and put it into a hole in the deck. A nice refinement is to make a round deck plate to fit over this hole through which the horse goes. It should be 3 inches in diameter by scale (³⁄₃₂ inch) and can be cut out of any thin metal. Put a small ring, or traveler, on the horse for the jib sheet-block and paint it black. Fishing-tackle dealers sell small rings that are very useful to model-makers. They come both split and solid and in all small diameters.

Next make the half sections of the octagonal mast partners as shown in the plate and construct a short half-section mast stump. The mast is also octagonal for 3 feet 9 inches ($1\frac{13}{32}$ inches) above the deck, where the round starts. Make the stump about 7 feet high by scale. Cut the top square across, put on the partner, insert the lower end of the mast, and glue in place. Paint the partner white, leaving the mast unpainted.

Next comes the cabin trunk, with companionway, slide and door. The cabin can be made of a solid block fitted to the camber of the deck and cambered on top. Glue a thin piece on for a roof, rounding the projecting sides. Drill a hole of the proper size for a port and make a ring from a copper washer to fit around the hole. Countersink the ring till it sets in a little from the side of the cabin. Under it fit a piece of clear photo film and fasten in place with three small brass nails. Put on the sill for the companionway door next, then an upright piece for the door frame, and finally the door. Glue these pieces on the after end of the block. Make a cover with cambered top and track for it to slide on, gluing it in place on top of the cabin. The slide cover should not project aft beyond the top of the door.

In gluing small parts, wipe off the excess glue which squeezes out of the seams before it hardens, as it is difficult to chip hardened pieces of glue off afterwards without injuring delicate work. Also, avoid using too much glue and don't spread it around when wiping it off. Remember —glue fills up the wood; varnish will not take properly over it, and if stains are used they will not penetrate the glue. All models shrink a little in time, and excess glue left in seams or in corners will chip off during this shrinking process, taking the paint with it and occasionally cracking fine moldings.

Paint the sides of the cabin trunk white and the top a slate blue. Paint the track for the slide white; also the cover. The door and molding and sill of the companionway should be white too.

Between the cabin trunk and the main hatch comes the centerboard trunk. This is a coaming $2\frac{1}{2}$ inches high ($\frac{5}{64}$ inch), closed at each end and butting against the cabin under the companionway and against the main hatch coaming aft. The top of the centerboard when raised comes about 1½ inches (³⁄₆₄ inch) above the coaming. The centerboard has a hole through its after end ½ inch in diameter by scale (¹⁄₆₄ inch) with the lower edge of the hole even with the top of the coaming. To hold the centerboard in the raised position an iron pin is slipped through the hole to rest on the coaming. There is also an iron eyebolt in the extreme after end of the board to which a rope is made fast with an eye splice. This rope leads aft over the hatches and is belayed to a cleat on the after hatch. All the skipjacks on the Bay show deep scores in the forward hatch coaming cut by this rope. Paint the coaming white and the board blue like the top of the cabin trunk.

Next make the hatch coamings, but without the inside shoulder for the covers to rest on. They are cambered like the deck. Now make two covers out of pine as thick as the hatch coaming is high for the forward hatch and one for the smaller after hatch. Camber them top and bottom, wipe the top edges with sandpaper to round them very slightly, fit them in place inside the coaming, and glue fast on the deck. Countersink the rings at the corners of the hatch covers. The rings are handholds so that the covers can be lifted. Paint the covers slate blue and the coaming white. The rings should be black.

Abaft the small hatch come the wheel and wheelbox. Except for the handles, the wheels in use on skipjacks are all metal. Proper wheels to scale can be bought from dealers in model findings for a few cents and you may find it more expedient to buy one than to attempt to make one. If you elect to do the latter, make it complete and cut it in two afterward. The felly can be turned out on a metal-working lathe, also the hub and axle (in one piece). Drill holes for the spokes, which can be made of hairpin wire. Insert the spokes, soldering them fast in place and letting the ends of the wire project beyond the felly enough to take the handles. Make the handles of boxwood, drill a hole up into them from the bottom—not all the way through—and slip them on the spoke ends. Fishing-rod cement, known as ferrule cement, will fasten them on securely. Paint the felly and hub white and the spokes and axle black, but do not paint the handles. These should be stained a weathered gray.

Make the half portion of the wheelbox. Drill a small hole with a No. 60 twist drill through the axle so you can pin the wheel to the panel and thus hold it securely in place. The rods that move the rudder enter the wheelbox from the back and run parallel to the axle of the wheel, to which they are geared inside the box. The model box can be a solid piece of pine set on feet with a thin piece glued on for a top. These boxes open at the line shown on the side of the box; the opening runs parallel to the axle of the wheel, the whole top part lifting off. Score a line around the box to represent this. The hole through the back of the box is spaced 4½ inches (⁹⁄₆₄ inch) from the center line and is cut through where the cover and box join. The hole for the half axle is also cut through here. Put the box in place and insert the axle in the groove, pinning it fast to the panel. Use a headless pin driven home and touch with black paint. The wheelbox is to be white. It has an unpainted cleat on the portside, which, of course, will not show in the model but must not be omitted when you build a complete model of the skipjack.

Rudders are hung by means of pintles and gudgeons, hingelike parts on which they turn. To make the pintle, bend a strip of sheet brass around a pin that is soldered fast. Form an eye in the center of another strip, touch with solder to keep it in shape to make a gudgeon, the female part of the device. The forward edge of the rudder is notched out and the hinge operates in the notch, allowing the rudder to come flush against the stern-post. The edges of both are beveled 45° to allow the rudder to turn. For this half-hull model, straps alone will suffice, as the rudder is glued fast to the panel. Brads (simulating bolts) to hold the straps on the rudder may be driven through and into the panel, making the rudder doubly secure.

Make the after part of the rail and the stern board before you do the forward part. The stanchions are made of brass tubing with a round-headed pin through them. Get the pins long enough to go through the lower rail to help secure it to the hull (for details see Plate I). The rails hold the stern board at the sides while the shelf for the mainsheet horse will make it fast across the stern. The curve at the stern is so slight that the board can be bent to it. Drill a hole through the stern board in line with the hole in the after end of the wheelbox for the rod that actuates the rudder. Put on the metal part at the rudderhead and connect the rod. The rod has an eye in the outer end and fits into the housing on the rudderhead. It is held fast by a bolt dropped down through the housing. Paint the metal parts black.

Return to the forward end and put on the wooden breasthook that rides over the bowsprit. The sides of this piece are beveled to correspond with the flare of the rail. The two big wooden pieces sticking up above the rail on each side of the bowsprit are the knightheads. They also cant outward at the top like the rail and the forward end of the top rail is bolted to the knighthead. The top rail is of double thickness at the knighthead, the after end of the doubled part curving down to the proper thickness of the top rail at the after end of the knight. The space between the main rail and the top rail at the knight is filled in solid to give added strength here.

Amidships in each rail of the skipjack is a roller of iron with pins in the ends for axles. The wire rope of the dredge runs over it. There is also an upright roller, at the after end of each of the horizontal rollers, that comes into play when the dredge is towing. This wire rope goes to a power-operated winch on deck, which is in place only during the oyster season and is therefore not shown; it is part of the fishing gear.

Below the rollers is a wooden piece that projects out from the side of the hull to make a guard. This is fastened to the hull with bolts; for the model, use small brads with heads that will project just a bit, like bolt-heads.

Put the straps on the stem for the bobstays and an eyebolt for the bowsprit shrouds, the chain plates, and lower deadeyes. The straps, or properly the "chain plates," for the latter are protected where they cross the rails by short wooden battens about an inch thick. They bolt to the log rails. The plan shows these details.

The boat davits at the stern shown in the plan are 1½-inch iron pipe (¾₆₄-inch wire), bent to shape. The outboard end is flattened and a hole is drilled through the flattened part; to it is shackled a treble block for the boat falls. The supports for the davits are iron rods bolted to the stern board. Paint the davits and supports white.

The waterway around the deck should be painted the same color as the cabin top. The deck and the rails should be white. The stanchions should be either white or the color of the waterways and the hulls are invariably white above the waterline and copper red below. The rudder is painted like the hull, white and red. The eagle head may be almost any color you fancy and the name is generally most crudely lettered in black.

Finishing in varnish requires that all work be perfectly done, as any carelessness is readily apparent. Paint covers a multitude of sins.

CHAPTER TWO

THE BUILDING *of a*
WHOLE-HULL MODEL

THE building of a whole-hull model follows closely the manner of building the half hull—of course with the exception that measurements of width are doubled. The pieces for the lifts will be 16 by 6 inches and all of the same wood—pine. See that the pieces when piled up form a perfectly square block, true and smooth on all faces. Accuracy is easiest to obtain with the lifts held securely in place by nails driven at the corners of the block. Mark each lift with an identifying symbol and a designating mark at each end. With the bow end held to your right, put the marks on the sides of the lifts toward you and do all subsequent measuring from this side of each lift. This procedure will assure that the marks on any lift will coincide with the marks on all the other lifts.

In the half model, the back of the block represented the center line, but for the whole-hull model we must determine the position of this line by measurement. Accuracy is best obtained by using a depth gauge. Mark the center line on the top, bottom, and each end of the block. Then mark the station lines all around. On each side of the center line draw parallel lines to mark the width of the keel, stem and sternpost. Drill two holes for the dowel pins, one on each side of the center line (one aft,

44

one forward), ⅜ inch off center and between the same stations as for the half-hull model.

Draw on the sides of the block the profile of the hull, this time cutting away the shaded portion at the ends of the block only. Cut at an exact right angle across the block. This is to fix the accurate seating of the stem and sternpost pieces when you come to put them on later. Pull the pins and separate the lifts, marking on the upper faces of lifts 1 and 2 the outlines of waterlines 1 and 2 (View C, Plate I). On lift 3 draw the outline of the under side of the deck (the dotted line, View C) and cut and finish the lifts to these shapes. Put lift 2 on lift 1 and put in the pins to hold it in place. Drill a hole the size of an applicator (see Chapter Six on Tools and Materials) near each side of the hull at the ⊕ through lift 2 into lift 1 to a depth of ¼ inch. Put on lift 3 and repeat the operation, but do not drill the hole immediately over the hole in the lower lift. The holes should be placed ¼ inch in from the side of the hull, paralleling the angle of the side as shown in the plate (View B).

Again separate the lifts and, leaving a shell of wood, cut out the inside portion of lifts 2 and 3. Leave plenty of wood at the bow and stern, and about ⅜ inch at the sides of the lifts. Glue lift 2 in place on lift 1. Put a little glue on an applicator and drive it through the hole at each side of lift 2 into the holes in lift 1, thus forcing the lifts into place. Repeat with lift 3. Use clamps to force the lifts into a tight joining and let the glue dry thoroughly.

Now cut the top lift to the sheer line and the bottom to the keel line from the ⊕ aft. Finish the top, first with a rasp, cutting across both sides at the same time to assure their being alike, then finish with a sandpaper block in the same manner.

Next cut away the projecting edges of the lifts, as when building the half hull. Smooth up the inside of the hull and give it two coats of paint or orange shellac. This is not absolutely necessary, but painting the inside of the models tends to preserve them and prevent checking. Cut the slot for the centerboard 3½ inches wide (⁷⁄₆₄ inch), reaching from the forward keel piece to the after keel piece. The axle for the skipjack centerboard is a piece of wood or metal put through the board at right angles. About

$\frac{7}{32}$ inch long, it projects $\frac{1}{16}$ inch on each side. Its location is shown in the plate. Cut a groove down from the top of lift 1, just deep enough to allow this model axle to be dropped into it and rest on the bottom of the groove. Make the centerboard to scale, paint it slate blue, and hang it. A piece of wood glued into each groove above the axle will hold it in place.

The deck of this model is to be made of pine or holly. Follow in general the instructions for building the half-hull deck. But remember that in this case the greatest thickness is at the center line.

The waterways of a skipjack around the edge of her deck are made flush with the deck planking. To imitate this construction score a line all around the deck, parallel to the outside edge of the deck and 7 inches inside it, by scale. Before scoring this line see that the outer edge of the deck is perfectly finished and that its sweep is sweet and true from stem to stern.

The deck planks are 6 inches wide. Beginning with the center line, therefore, score marks 6 inches apart lengthwise of the deck to represent the planking. If you elect to make the hatchways in detail, cut openings for them before you put the deck on, and in any case cut a slot $3\frac{1}{2}$ inches wide by scale between the cabin and the main hatch for the centerboard opening. Fasten the deck to the hull with glue and small screws around the outside edge and see that they are placed so that the main rail will cover them when that goes on later. Also see to it that the screws do not come under the stanchions that support the top rail. Cut the hole for the mast, which must be made to correspond with the rake of that spar.

Make and put on the stem, the keel, the coaming about the centerboard slot, the sternpost, and the longhead. In all cases be most particular about the seating of these parts. In the building of real vessels they are bolted to members inside the hull; in the model, small brads can be used to fasten them, leaving the heads projecting slightly in imitation of boltheads. One brad through the foot of the longhead into the stem will serve to hold it in place until the cheek knees are put on, whose purpose is to support this member. They may be put on now or later, but do not put on the rail of the head until there is no danger of breaking it. "Setting the head," which is the assembly of the cutwater and rails, knees, and carving, requires great accuracy. The smallest error will spoil the whole appearance of an other-wise perfect model. In oldtime shipyards, setting the head was done by a skilled workman, often the carver. The model builder should always compare the "head" of the model with that shown in the plans, as each step is completed, to make certain the model head is *exactly* like that shown in the plans in *every* respect.

Fasten the pieces that form the cabin sides to the sides of the hole made for it in the deck, and join them carefully at the corners, which should be mitered. The tops of the athwartship pieces should be cambered. The roof should be very thin, scaled to the drawing, and should have a hole cut in the after end for the companionway. Build the frame for the doors and then put on the slide track and the sliding cover with the cambered top. The camber of all pieces of furniture corresponds to the camber of the deck. Put a waterway around the cabin as shown in the plate.

Note that the bowsprit is not a straight spar, but is hogged. The curve must be cut into the under side of the stick to scale. Make the metal band and fittings and put them on before inserting the bowsprit. Then comes the rest of the deck furniture, as described for the building of the half hull, leaving the rail of the head until last.

The anchor and the flat-bottomed skiff should not be put in place until last of all. The inboard end of each of the stern davits fits into a cup hous-ing with a flat base that is bolted to the deck. For additional support a metal piece with the ends bent over is bolted to the deck and to the inside of the rails. Through the piece that is bent over at the top a hole is made and the metal pipe of the davit goes through the hole. To make it strong, an additional plate is welded on the top and a collar goes around the hole. You can carry out that detail or make the piece simply by cutting a piece of sheet metal to the proper width and length, bending over the top and drill-ing the hole. Three iron rods support the outboard end. Two of these have the ends flattened and are bolted to the stern board; the other has the end split and forked to go over the top edge of the board. They are fas-tened to the pipe of the davit with clevises. Bending their ends around the pipe and touching with solder will suffice to imitate this fastening. The boatfall consists of a treble block on the davit and a double block and hook at the lower end. The fall is rove from the arse of the double block to the treble block twice around and then through the third sheave of the treble block and is belayed around the davit and one of the supports. A plank is lashed athwartship, across the davits over the skiff, and when the skiff is hoisted, gripes lashed around it and the plank keep it steady.

Put on the chain plates and deadeyes (see rigging, Plate XIII) and the straps on the stem for the bobstays to shackle to. These are simply two parallel metal straps put on each side of the stem with holes in the outer ends. A shackle bolt goes through them and the last link of the chain bobstay.

It is better to paint the model before the operation of rigging is undertaken. Start with the deck. A painted deck is characteristic of the skipjack; it is invariably white, with waterways of a contrasting color, generally a slate-gray blue, light in color. Hatch coamings, cabin, wheelbox, and rails are white. The wheel is as previously described. Stanchions of the rail are slate blue, as are also the tops of the cabin, the slide, and the wheelbox. The stern davits are white and all other metal parts black, to look like iron. The bowsprit is white. Cleats are unpainted. The small boat is like the hull. The hatch covers are slate blue like the centerboard.

The hull is painted white down to the waterline. For the underbody use red copper marine paint. Use all paint very thin; thick paint is just as out of proportion on a model as an oversize spar or too heavy cordage. See that the paint does not gather thickly in corners; brush it out well.

The setting up of the spars and rigging is next, and there is a further description in detail of the rigging of this model in Chapter Three. The history of the skipjack type and of the *Carrie Price* in particular is given in Chapter Three.

The first thing to consider in the rigging of any model is the material used. About 1860, wire rope supplanted hemp for the standing rigging on most vessels, and since the skipjack is a modern type her standing rigging (as well as that of the bugeye, the scow schooner, and the model yacht) will all be wire. How to make suitable model wire rope is described in Chapter Four. For the skipjack, two sizes of wire rope are required, and

Whaling Schooner
AGATE

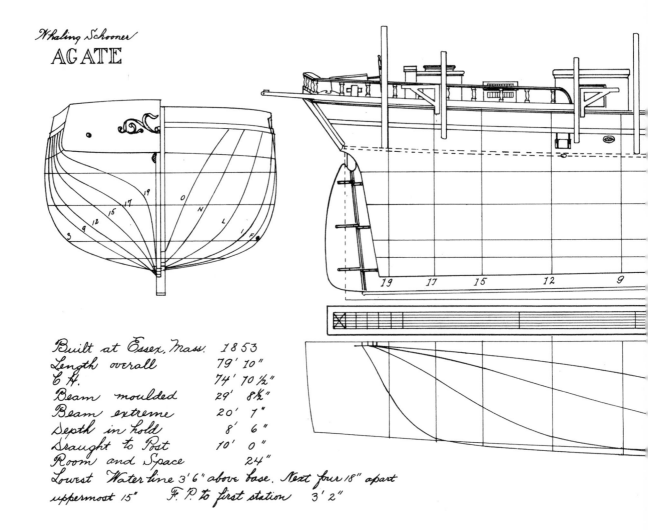

Built at Essex, Mass.   1853
Length overall   79' 10"
C.H.   74' 10½"
Beam moulded   29' 8½"
Beam extreme   20' 7"
Depth in hold   8' 6"
Draught to Post   10' 0"
Room and Space   24"
Lowest Water line 3' 6" above base. Next four 18" apart
uppermost 15"   F. P. to first station   3' 2"

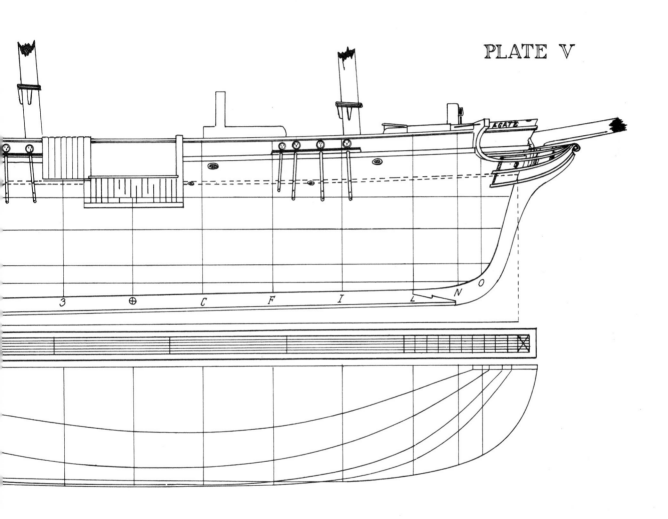

PLATE V

"AGATE"

BAIL FOR STAYS

2 1 0
Scale in Feet

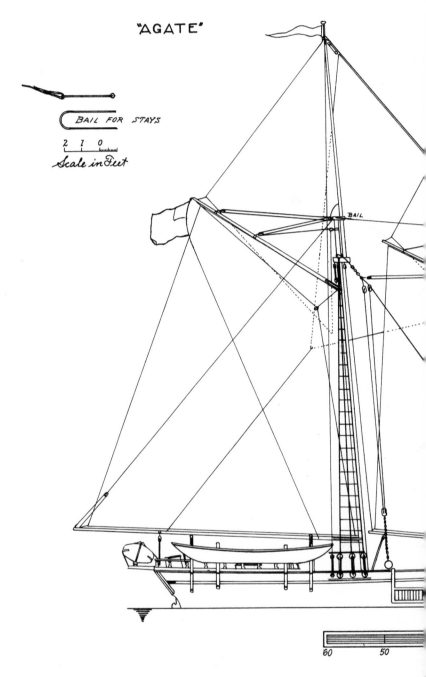

BAIL

60   50

AGA

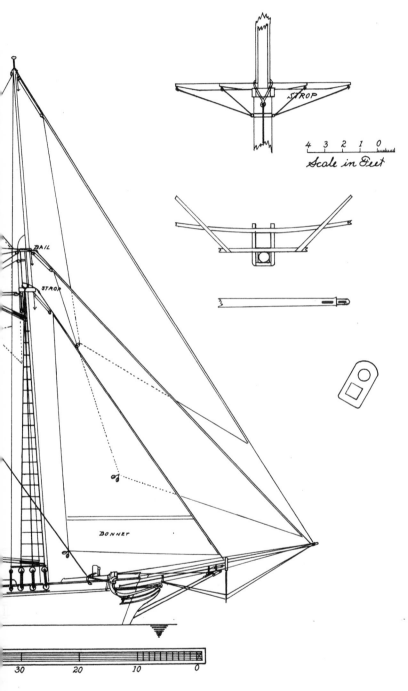

STROP

4 3 2 1 0

Scale in Feet

BAIL

STROP

BONNET

30   20   10   0

plan and rigging details.

2 pieces of 3-inch chain. The wire rope should be ¾ inch in diameter for the main shrouds and jibstay and ½ inch for the balance of the rigging by scale.

It is presumed that the bowsprit is in place on the model and is fitted with the metal cap or band at the outer end. If you have not put this fitting on the outer end of the spar, make it now as it is shown in Plate I, with eyes top and bottom and with nosing pieces for the bowsprit shrouds (see Chapter Four on iron work).

It is best to rig the bowsprit first and then progress to the other spars, since the bowsprit controls the rigging of them to some extent. So first secure the bowsprit in place. It is held down in its bed by the gammoning (the metal band that fastens it to the stem of the hull). Its shape is shown in the plate. The outer end of the bowsprit is held down by a chain bobstay connected to the under eye of the cap iron by a turnbuckle, as shown, and the two bowsprit shrouds that reeve through the nosing pieces of the cap iron, the end being seized to itself. The after ends set up to eyebolts in the hull, just aft of and a little below the after end of the longhead. Sometimes the shrouds are of chain at the after end and wire rope from the end of the chains out to the nosing pieces.

Put this bowsprit rigging in place and then step the mast. It is best that all fittings, cleats, blocks, and hoops be in place on the mast before it is stepped, and to that end Figure 11 shows the mast with these pieces in place but without the rigging.

The first of the standing rigging to go over the masthead is the starboard pair of shrouds; next comes the port pair (see Chapter Four). These shrouds are made like the shrouds of a ship. Reeve the laniards and tighten them up to give the mast the proper rake, but do not finish off the laniards until the jibstay is set up, which allows you to make any adjustments. Next get the wire jibstay over the head and reeve it through the sheave hole in the outer end of the bowsprit to the chain bobstay that fastens to the bobstay plate on the stem. The end of the stay has a thimble turned in at its end and sets up on itself, being held by two seizings. Shrouds and jibstay are ¾-inch (by scale) wire rope. Next comes the forestay of ½-inch (by scale) wire rope that sets up to the eye on the top of the bowsprit cap iron and has a thimble turned in its end. It is seized fast to itself. All the standing rigging of the skipjack is now complete.

The next spar to rig is the boom. Make this complete with all its fittings before you fasten it in place. There are lots of fittings to be made before the boom is ready. Beginning at the outboard end, the plate shows there are two iron straps, or bands; the upper sides of these are left open and

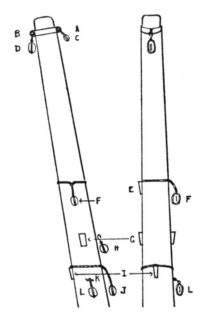

FIGURE 11. *Detail of the masthead, ready for stepping.*

the ends bent up to form lugs or ears, so that a bolt can be passed through them to hold each to the boom. To these straps the outhaul for the main-sail and the topping lift are bent. Their shape and construction are shown in the plate. Between these bands is a sheave in the boom, for the fall of the topping lift. Going inboard, directly under the outermost cringle in the upper reef band, there is a small sheave, in a cleat (or cheekblock) on each side of the boom, for the reef tackle. Just forward of this comes the mainsheet band that the mainsheet block makes fast to (see the *Edith F. Todd* sail plans). Then on the starboard side (only) is a cleat for the fall of the topping lift to belay to, and 3 feet (by scale) further inboard is another cleat (one on each side) for belaying the reef tackle. About a foot from where the jaws of the boom begin there is a small cleat (one on each side) for the lazyjack of the mainsail. On top of the boom, about 4 inches in from the throat, is an eye with a ring, for the lift for the inboard end of the boom; and along the whole length of the spar are eyes for lacing the mainsail to the boom.

The jaws are shown in Plate I. The sides of the boom where the jaws go are generally left square to make a seat for them, and the jaws are held in place by being bolted through the boom. Do not neglect the small eyes for the lazyjack to pass through, there being two of these each side of the boom.

Put the boom in place and fasten it to the mast with a wire parral about the size of heavy bail wire. This parral goes from jaw to jaw, passing around the mast and allowing some play. To hold the boom up in its place on the mast, a long pendant is employed. A hook is seized in at its lower end, which hooks into the ring on the boom. The other end of the pendant reeves through a block up on the mast, and has a single-sheave block turned in this end. This latter block hangs about halfway down the mast. Another rope is hooked in the same way into the ring on the boom and is rove through the block in the pendant and is then brought down and belayed around the starboard shroud at the sheer pole, being the hauling part or fall of the tackle. Originally this may have been a Spanish burton.

The after topping lift is bent to the eye of the cap at the top of the mast. This should come down to within about 5 feet (by scale) of the outboard end of the boom and have a single-sheave block turned in. A laniard is made fast to the pin, or bolt, in the after ring on the boom; it reeves through the block in the topping-lift pendant, back around the sheave at the outer end of the boom between the bands, and belays to the outermost cleat on the boom. All the running rigging of the boom is of manila rope. The lift pendants should be manila rope of ¾-inch diameter (by scale) and the other ropes of ½-inch size, or less, depending on the strain imposed on them.

Few models look well with sails, owing to the fact that most miniature sails are such bad copies of the sails of a vessel, as regards both construction and material. However, the models of the skipjack and the bugeye are improved by being equipped with sails. Real sails are made of strips of canvas, as a rule either 22 or 24 inches wide, sewn together in strips and showing, when finished, a strip about 20 or 21 inches in width. The sails of a skipjack are made with the strips of canvas running parallel to the roach of the sail. They have two sets of reef points, the first row 6 feet above the foot of the sail and the next row 6 feet higher. The reef points are passed through little metal cringles and are of light stuff and hang pendant about 2 feet down on each side of the sail. The reef band is made by reinforcing

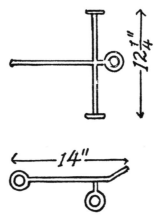

FIGURE 12. *Jack iron.*

the sail with a horizontal strip of the sail canvas through which the cringles go.

The head of a pointed mainsail is generally reinforced by a wooden plate or headboard in a pocket sewn into the canvas, but this is omitted on the headsails. Some skipjacks have no headboard; some have a very short gunter yard to keep the sail properly set at the head. The gunter yard is laced to the luff of the sail and stands vertically against the mast when the sail is set.

Rig the jib first. A single becket block is turned in the end of the rope that is to serve as a halliard. This block hooks into the cringle at the head of the jib. The halliard is then rove through a double-sheave block on the mast back through the single-sheave block at the jib head and then back to the block on the mast from where the halliard leads down and is belayed to the cleat on the port side of the mast. The jib is made fast to the jibstay with metal hanks and its tack cringle is made fast with a length of marline to the eyebolt just aft of the sheave in the outer end of the bowsprit. The jib downhaul is bent to the uppermost cringle, leads down through the hanks, reeves through the sheave on the port side of the bowsprit, and then comes inboard to belay around the cleat on the bowsprit. Attach the club and rig the lazyjack, as in the plate. The lazyjack reeves through

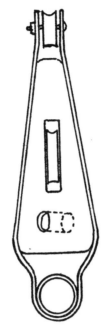

FIGURE 13. *Horse block.*

small eyes on the club and cringles in the foot of the jib. There is a small metal spreader (Figure 12), called a jack iron, running on the forestay, into which the various parts of the lazyjack are bent. A halliard is bent to the upper eye of the jack iron and is rove through a block at the mast-head, whence it leads down and is belayed to the port shroud at the sheer pole. Just afore the mast on deck is an iron horse for the foresheet. A ring or traveler slides on this horse and carries a pear-shaped block of peculiar construction. For the shape of this block see Figure 13. The sheet is seized to the becket of the block, leads around the block on the club, back through the sheave of the horse block again, around the cringle block, and leads back to and through the fairlead or dumb sheave in the horse block. It then goes aloft, through the sheave of a single block on the mast (under the jibstay), and then comes down on deck and is belayed to the cleat on the fore side of the mast.

The mainsail fastens to the mast with wooden hoops and is laced to the boom through cringles in the foot of the sail and small eyes let in the upper side of the boom (see Plate I). The lead of the main halliard is from the becket of a single-sheave block at the head of the sail through a sheave in a double block at the masthead, back through the sheave of the becket block, then back through the sheave of the double block at the masthead, and then down to the starboard cleat on the mast, where it is belayed.

The after lazyjack is belayed on the first cleat abaft the boom jaws, after being rove through the thimbles of its other parts, and it is the same on both sides of the sail. When the sail is hoisted the reef tackle is belayed first on a cleat to port, then reeves through the sheave on that side, passes upward to and through the outermost cringle in the second reef band, comes down to the starboard sheave, through which it reeves, and goes back and belays to the starboard cleat on the boom. The sail is hauled out and made fast with marline to the bolt of the inner ring at the end of the boom.

The sheet is next to rig. A single-sheave block with hook is required at deck. The block hooks into the ring or traveler (and the hook is moused, or lashed) on the mainsheet horse mounted on the shelf just aft the wheel-box. The sheet is spliced to the becket of this block and then leads through a sheave in a double block that is hooked into the horse band, on the boom, leads back through a sheave in the first block, goes again through a sheave in the double block, and then leads back to a hole or fairlead in the shelf. After passing through this hole it is belayed to a cleat on the port side of the wheelbox.

The centerboard is raised and lowered by a rope that is bent to an eye in the top after end of the board. It comes aft over the main hatch, cutting a fairlead for itself, by use, in the hatch cover, and belays to a cleat on the after hatch coaming, within reach of the steersman. The boat falls belay around the boat davits, where they are supported by the brace. The anchors are bent to chain cables and hang at each side of the vessel aft of the head rail, being fastened to the monkey rail with small stuff. The chain cable leads from the anchor ring out to the hook that is secured under the bowsprit cap and held in place by the bolt that goes through the eye at the under side of the cap to hold the bobstay turnbuckle. It then leads back inboard to the winch or is belayed around the samson post at the after end of the bowsprit. Its bitter end is stowed in the forepeak, going through an opening in the main hatch.

With the anchors in place the model is complete and you can proceed to build the next model.

CHAPTER THREE

TWELVE AMERICAN SAILING VESSELS

PLATE I: THE SKIPJACK *CARRIE PRICE*

WHEN the Conservation Department of the state of Maryland formulated and put into effect the laws that regulate the oyster crop and its taking, it was not the intention of the department to keep from extinction certain types of sailing craft. However, such regulations, to the delight of lovers of wind-driven craft, have had just that happy result. The use of power-driven craft for the dredging of the oyster crop is prohibited by law, in the waters of Maryland, though tonging with power boats is permitted.

So today, under these provisions, five types of sailing craft are preserved to us. Every season, beginning on the fifteenth of October, they join the large fleet of Chesapeake Bay oyster dredgers. These five types are the sloop, the schooner, the skipjack, the bugeye, and the three-sail bateau, the last being a hybrid that stems from the skipjack and the bugeye. The sloop and schooner show little out of common with other vessels of their type and cannot claim the Chesapeake and its environs for their place of birth. But the other three types, without doubt, did originate in those shallow waters, and as these types proved their worth they were adapted to the oystering, a matter of equipping them with the gear of that trade.

These pages include plates and discussion of the skipjack and the bug-eye, both of intense interest to the student of marine development. Both types are essentially working craft but in some instances both skipjacks and bugeyes have been converted into pleasure craft with highly satisfactory results.

We have described the skipjack quite thoroughly in the preceding chapter, but have not surveyed its development. Its history is not a matter of printed record. Only local tradition and the evidence gathered by travelers and by those who cruised the waters of the Bay are available to shed some light on the origin of the skipjack. It appears that the type was not in existence before the Civil War; indeed there is no mention of a similar type being used about the Bay much before 1890, when Kunhardt, then yachting editor of *Forest and Stream* magazine, first described the "Hampton flattie." We may consider this type the progenitor of the skipjack. Kunhardt describes the flattie as a gaff-rigged sloop having a mainsail and jib but without a bowsprit, flat-bottomed forward but V-bottomed from about amidships aft to the transom. The same writer, in the second edition of "Small Yachts" (1891), gives working drawings of one of these boats, and reports that they were used for hauling produce on the local creeks and rivers and for oystering.

Hard on the heels of the flattie appears a boat type designated by the strange name of "Black Nancy." This name seems to have been applied on the Western Shore of the Bay more commonly than on the Eastern Shore. Very similar to the flattie in hull, it exhibits a change in the rig: a bowsprit is added and the mainsail is no longer gaff-headed but has become of leg-o'-mutton shape. Somewhere about the year 1895 the modern skipjack appears, with its characteristic longhead (or cutwater). This boat retained some of the simplicity of the hull found in the Hampton flattie, but in rig it was similar to the Black Nancy in that it had a bowsprit and "sharp" mainsail. So it appears that the skipjack's development can be traced from a flat-bottomed sharpie type hull, through the Hampton flattie (with V bottom aft) and the Black Nancy. Small craft of the type called crabbing bateau were also developed, similar to the dredging skipjacks, and of equal beauty. Skipjacks, as a type, ranged in length from 18 or 20 to 72 feet, some of the larger ones being given the rig of bugeyes for convenience in handling (see Plate VII, showing this rig). When so rigged, the vessel was called a three-sail bateau.

There is no better example of the worth of the chine-built boat than that furnished by the skipjack. It is a very fast and able boat, and with the centerboard is perfectly suited to navigate the shallow waters of the Chesapeake Bay region. In fact, skipjacks were so fast that some were used for poaching on the oyster beds that the Commission had closed to "drudging" (dredging for oysters). The modern Star-class racing boat is built on the general hull form of the skipjack but substitutes a fin and keel for the centerboard, thereby somewhat limiting its use. However, these boats clearly demonstrate the value of the chine hull form.

The *Carrie Price*, the subject of Plate I, is a typical skipjack, so much so that her lines and plan were selected for inclusion in the Historic American Merchant Marine Survey made by the Smithsonian Institution, Washington, D.C. (Survey 5–5). A comparison of the *Carrie Price*, which is still afloat, with the plans and lines of that survey shows some differences, but the plans and lines here given correspond with the boat as she is. Actually, she shows somewhat sharper lines and has an easier sweep of chine. Her main hatch is also much larger than the Historic American Merchant Marine Survey shows, and there are radical differences in fittings and rig. These are shown in the accompanying plans, which differ from those of the Survey just mentioned.

The *Carrie Price* was one of the early skipjacks, which makes her inclusion in the government's survey a very happy one. James Henry Price built her at Holland Island, Maryland, in 1897, shortly after the type was first recognizable. He built her for his son, Adam P. Price, and she was named for his son's wife, Carrie. For many years the *Carrie Price* was reckoned one of the fastest of the skipjacks, a crown now worn by a newer boat, the *Joy C. Parks* of Cambridge, Maryland. After a summer spent in refitting and painting the *Carrie Price* will no doubt again put out in search of the Chesapeake Bay oyster.

The *Carrie Price* measures:

Length between *PP*	39′	10″
Extreme beam	14′	4″
Draught aft	2′	6″
Draught at forefoot	1′	5″
Mast, overall	59′	8″
Mast, above deck	55′	6″
Mast, diameter at partners		11″
Mast, diameter at heel (lift 1 of model)		7⅓″
Mast, diameter at truck (top of mast)		5½″
Boom, length overall (throat to end)	39′	10″
Boom, diameter (⅓ from throat)		7⅘″
Boom, diameter at throat		7″
Boom, diameter outboard		5″

As far as I can determine there is no fixed masting rule that covers the making of spars for the skipjacks. Most of these boats were built by rule of thumb and sparmaking was a matter of judgment, left to the builder; but it is safe to say that diameters of the masts were about 1 inch to every 5 feet of length, that the boom was invariably the length of the boat, and that the same rule for finding the diameter of the mast applied to the boom. The length of the mast is roughly 4 times the extreme beam or the sum of length of hull plus beam; the length of the bowsprit outboard is roughly equal to the beam. However, the plate shows these sizes exactly as fitted to the *Carrie Price*, and should be followed. As to the mast taper, a diagram is given in Chapter Four on rigging that applies to mast making for both the skipjack and the bugeye. The greatest diameter of the bowsprit is at the heel and at the knightheads, and it is characteristically hogged. It tapers to the outer end, where the diameter is one-half of the greatest diameter. The gear and fittings of the skipjack and bugeye are very similar, except where the two-masted rig of the bugeye calls for necessary divergence. The hog in a Chesapeake Bay vessel's bowsprit is cut into the stick, not sprung in.

PLATE II: THE PISCATAQUA RIVER GUNDALOW

The Piscataqua River boatbuilders produced one of the strangest-appearing small work boats that plied the waters of the North Atlantic seaboard. The boat was exotic in appearance because it employed the lateen rig, the pet of Mediterranean seafaring people. It is probable that the early builders in this country were influenced by shipbuilding as practiced in foreign yards and it is not strange to find a Mediterranean rig employed on the boats built in parts of our country that were settled by Mediterranean peoples. But very little of this influence was to be found in New England, where this type originated and was employed in the coastal carrying of the region. There is no doubt that the builders along the Piscataqua River were familiar with the rig and adopted it for its usefulness rather than because of hereditary influence, being in need of a rig that would serve best on a low-cost vessel designed to carry deck loads and to pass under low bridges.

The Piscataqua River gundalow, with its strange-looking rig, is a thing of the past and has not carried freight for some time. Although there is no vessel of the type afloat today we are enabled to visualize its appearance and to reproduce an example because of the effort and interest of Mr. D. Foster Taylor of Wollaston, Massachusetts. This reproduction happily can be accomplished in miniature with fine results, and so we give in Plate II the lines and plans of one of these vessels, drawn from very careful drawings made under the supervision of Mr. Taylor. His drawings and report form part of the Historic American Merchant Marine Survey in the archives of the United States National Museum at Washington, D.C. Mr. Taylor measured the wreck of the *Fannie M.* at Dover Point, N.H., and with an original builder's model to help him made measured drawings of the lines and the details of this craft. He also built a very handsome model of the vessel, which he presented to the Peabody Museum at Salem, Massachusetts. He has taken the trouble to preserve for us a visual record of this strange craft and so we owe much to Mr. Taylor.

There were plenty of vessels called gundalows engaged in the freighting of goods on our rivers. The name gundalow was used to designate a vessel with a scow- or bargelike hull, suitable for the transportation of heavy articles in and about quiet waters. In fact the scow schooner, whose lines and plans are depicted in Plate VI, is a vessel of this derivation. Evidently the name gundalow, as used in this country, signified a vessel that was designed with square bilges to work in shallow water without regard to rig. How such a vessel was rigged was a secondary consideration. Gondola is without doubt the correct form of the name, which New England had to twist into gondalow or gundalow. Webster's dictionary says that gondola, as used in the United States, is the name of "a heavy flat bottomed barge, used especially in parts of New England." The very fast racing scows, now in more use on the Great Lakes than elsewhere, are distant relatives of these New England vessels. The Piscataqua River gundalows used a modified lateen rig, which enabled them to lower spars and sails easily and quickly for passing under bridges; this was the sole reason for its use.

The *Fannie M.*, whose lines are reproduced here, was built by Captain Adams of Adams Point, Massachusetts, in 1886. It was from his original builder's model that Mr. Taylor worked, as well as the abandoned wreck of the hull.

The *Fannie M.* measured, as per survey:

Overall on deck	68′	10″
Extreme beam	19′	2″
Draught, with board up	4′	6″
Draught, without board	3′	2″
Mast, above deck	19′	2″
Mast, diameter at partner		15″
Yard, overall length	68′	10″
Yard, diameter at heel		21″
Yard, at cap		6″

To build the lift model, five pieces are needed—four of them ¼ inch by 17½ inches and one (for the top lift) ⅝ inch by 17½ inches, assuming the scale is to be ¼ inch to the foot. The procedure of construction is like that used for the skipjack, as far as possible.

After completing the hull, make the mast and step it first. It has an 8-inch sheave in a sheave hole which is made through the mast 10 inches down from the top. The top is capped with a metal band. There is a cleat on the forward side of the mast and a large single-sheave block is fastened to the mast just above the deck and below this cleat. There are no shrouds or stays to support the mast.

The yard is made next. It has a metal band with eye at the top or outboard end, into which the topping lift is spliced. The topping lift belays to a cleat at the stern of the vessel. Three feet below the band there is a cleat on the forward side of the boom which serves as an outhaul for the lateen sail. Fasten the blocks for the brails on both sides of the yard where they are shown in Plate II, making them fast to the spar with eyebolts. Below the last brail block there is a metal band, with eye forward, fitted around the boom; into this eye is shackled a chain halliard which passes through the sheave hole in the mast and is secured at its lower end by a pin driven into the mast. This halliard secures the yard to the mast and is a permanent fixture. Where the yard comes in contact with the mast it is protected with battens 6 feet 3 inches long and 3 inches wide by ½ inch thick. There is a small cleat on the forward side of the yard to which the brails belay and, at the heel, the yard is capped with a metal band with an eye aft into which a double-sheave block is shackled. The tack tackle lead is from the becket of the double-sheave block at the mast around one sheave of the double-sheave block on the yard, back around a sheave of the block at the mast and again to the yard and back to the mast block, thence belaying to the cleat on the mast.

The sail is fastened to the yard with stops; the last one passes around the yard above the topmost cleat, which serves to hold it up on the yard. The brails are rove through the blocks and spliced to a single fall that is belayed, while the sail is held down by passing a length of marline through a cringle at the foot of the sail and making it fast to the eye at the foot of the yard. The brails pass through cringles formed in the bolt rope of the sail and the lead and fastening of the mainsheet is clearly shown in the plate.

The leeboard is held to the hull by the iron bar, shown in Plate II, when the pressure of the water comes against its windward side and would tend to rip it off were it not so reinforced. The deck of the *Fannie M.* had a camber of about 4 inches and was asphalted over to prevent damage from deck loads (coal for example) that had to be moved with shovels. The portable deck rails provided a retaining space for the deck loads.

PLATE III: AN ANCHOR HOY

Francis Grice, born in New Jersey, served a shipbuilding apprenticeship in and about the shipyards of Philadelphia, and later worked on Chesapeake Bay. During this formative period he conceived the ardent admiration for the Baltimore clippers and the Virginia pilot boats that afterward affected his designs.

In partnership with his brother Joseph, Francis Grice opened a yard in Philadelphia, in which the firm built the frigate *Guerrière* for the United States Navy in the year 1814. This, and other experience, led to his appointment as a naval constructor on May 7, 1817. He was appointed chief naval constructor in 1847 and continued to head the Naval Construction Department until illness forced him to take sick leave in 1859. His death came in 1865. He left behind him an indelible record of achievement as an able designer of vessels that served our country, nearly all of which showed in their lines the elements of design that prevailed in the fast ships of the Chesapeake Bay builders.

In addition to others, Grice designed and built the ship-sloop *Albany* and the brigs *Truxton* and *Perry*. These brigs were among the last wind-driven ships in our Navy. Before his retirement, Grice saw the introduction of steam and designed some of our first Navy vessels so propelled, among them the noted side-wheeler *Powhatan*.

With his skill in the designing of great ships it is not strange that Grice should be one of the few to leave a record of a lowly work boat. Among his papers, preserved by the national government in the Office of Naval Records and Library at Washington, are to be found the lines and plan of an anchor hoy. Not much to get excited about as an example of naval architecture, it incorporates in its design features now unfamiliar. Since the anchor hoy has vanished from the ken of man, this design of Grice's becomes a very valuable contribution to the history of American water craft. It is a great pleasure to reproduce it (Plate III).

No more unconventional craft were to be found than the anchor hoys. They were designed to carry huge anchors, and the gear for raising and transporting these set the vessels apart. They combined this special function and that of water boats with the usual duties of hoys, namely the servicing and provisioning of other and larger ships. The hoy, *per se*, did not have gear for handling anchors. Anchor hoys pursued their duties wherever ships gathered in port and they were almost indispensable in and about the navy yards. However, familiar as was the appearance of these craft to mariners of the times, few notes were kept as to their construction and there are only fragmentary records of their looks. The tracing in the Grice papers gives the best picture of these craft, an example probably designed and built for duty at the Norfolk Navy Yard in handling moorings and as a water boat.

The measurements of the anchor hoy in Plate III are:

Length, between *PP*	56′	9″
Beam, extreme	20′	
Bowsprit	31′	
Bowsprit, outboard	20′	1½″
Mast, above deck	53′	6″
doubling	5′	9″
Mast, shoulder for shrouds	20′	
Topmast	32′	
Gaff	26′	6″
Boom	44′	

The arrangement of an anchor hoy below deck is different from that of an ordinary craft. Forward, there is an open hold or space which might have been used as quarters for the crew or might have contained the galley, but Grice does not show this feature. If we look within this space we do see some features of her construction. We see the lower or after end of the great cat that projects from her bow and that has a large sheave

PLATE VI

Scow Schooner

"REGENIA S."

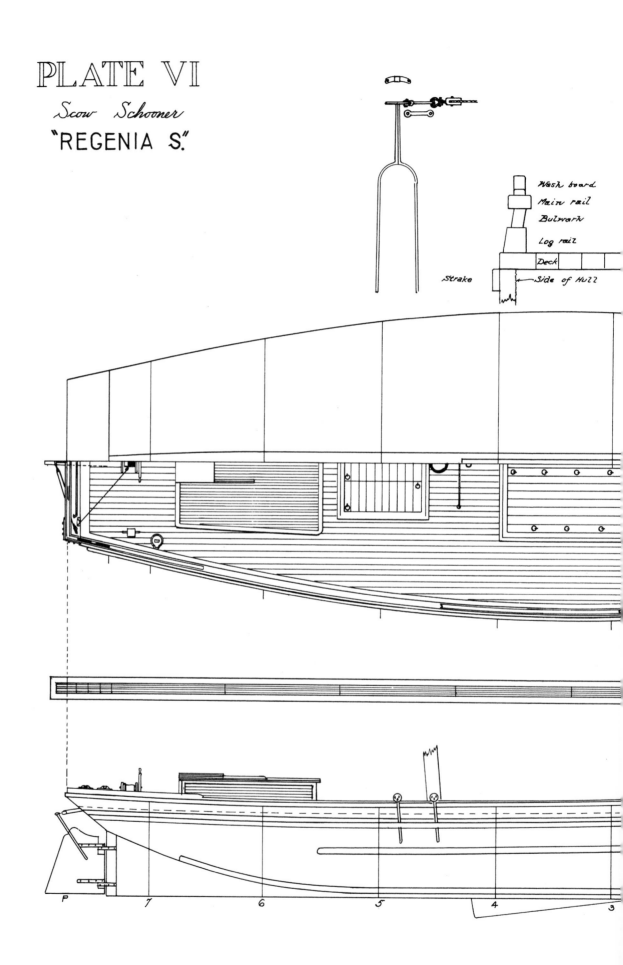

Wash board
Main rail
Bulwark
Log rail
Deck
Strake
Side of Hull

P   7   6   5   4   3

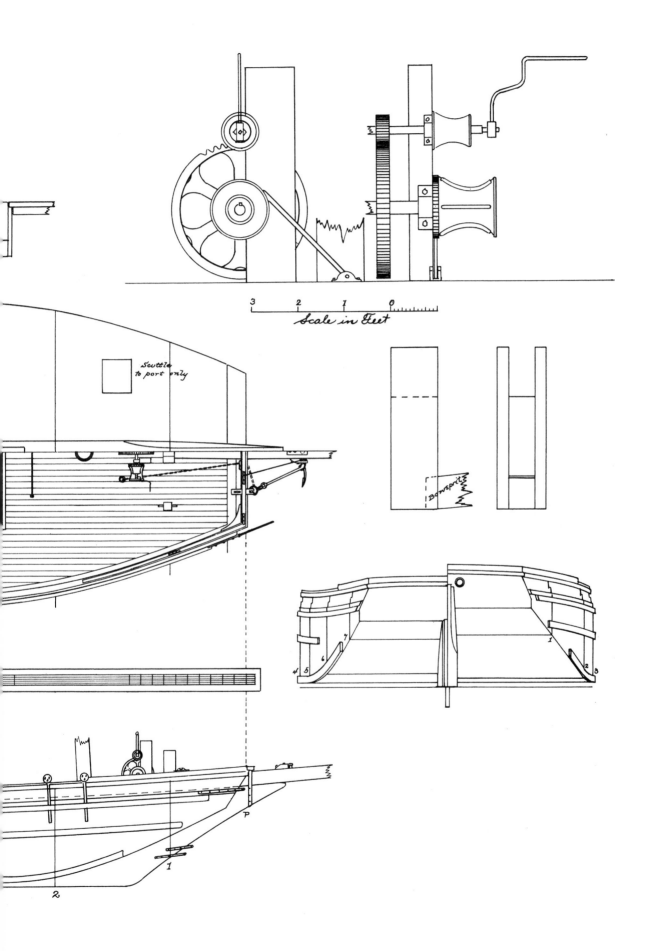

Scale in Feet

Scuttle
to port only

Bowsprit

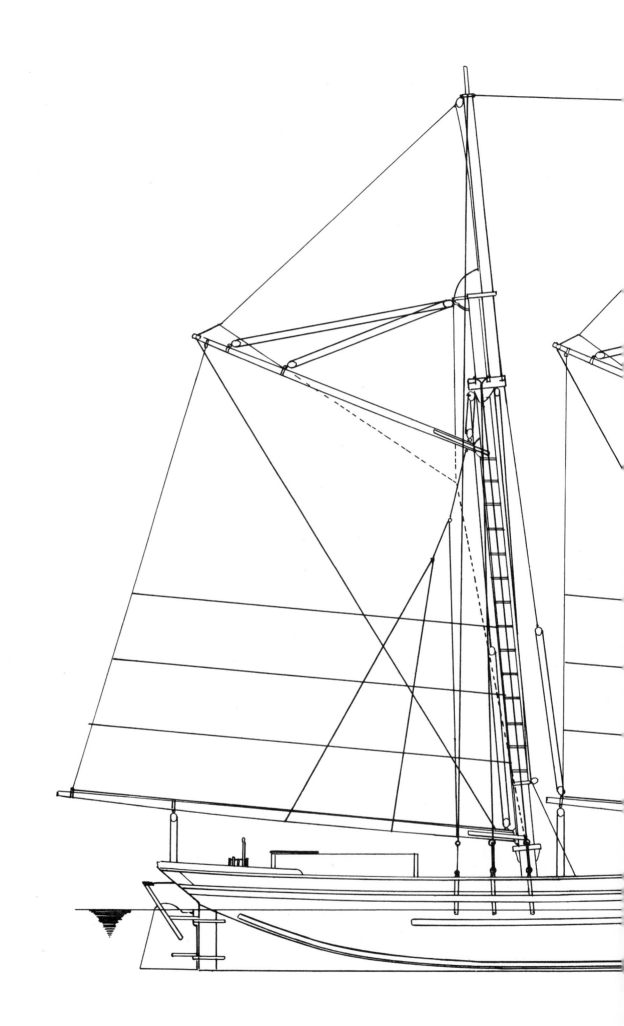

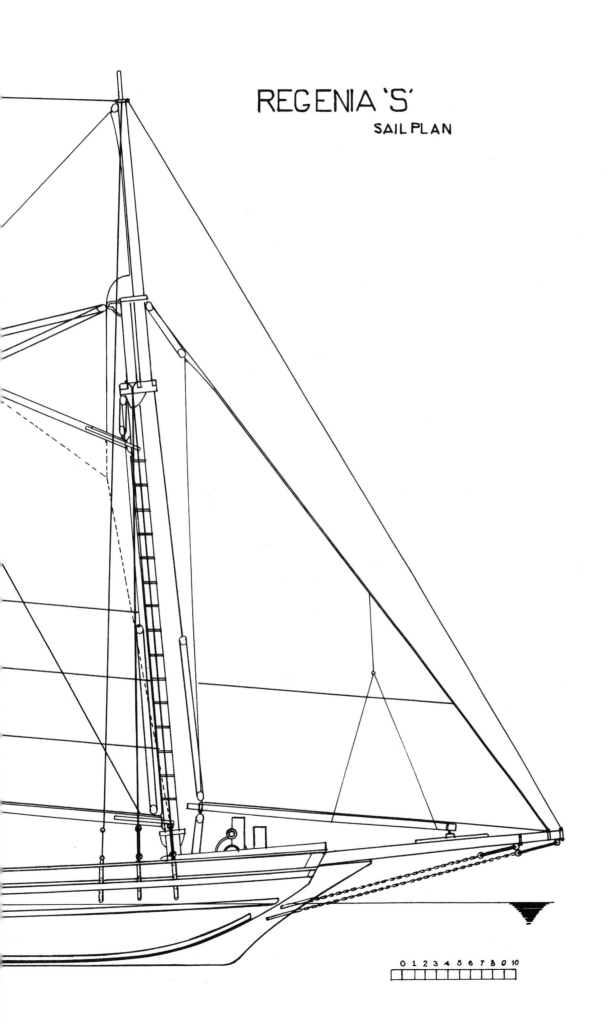

REGENIA 'S'
SAIL PLAN

0 1 2 3 4 5 6 7 8 9 10

in its outboard end for the anchor cable. Its after end is bolted between a heavy pair of bitts, that are in turn bolted to the first deck beam, just forward of the mast, and go down to and rest on and are fastened to the keelson. These bitts do not show above deck, but there is an eyebolt directly above them, driven through the floor beam, for the block of the anchor tackle. When not in use, the running block of the tackle that takes the anchor cable is hooked into a ring bolt in the waterway of the hoy opposite to the mast and just forward of the pins for her rigging, to starboard. To port are the bowsprit bitts, a pair of timbers that rise 2 feet 3 inches above the deck and between which the heel of the bowsprit passes and is held in place with a removable pin. The bowsprit is of necessity off center, as the anchor cat occupies the center of the vessel. Just aft the mast the water tank is built in. It is 26 feet 9 inches long, and its after end comes just forward of the spindle, or axle, of the after capstan. The forward capstan spindle stands in a compartment in the tank. On top of this tank is built a ball-race for the huge gears that engage the two capstans. Aft the axle of the after capstan is a bulkhead, and the after hold forms a cabin to which there is access through the companionway just forward of the tiller on deck.

It is the rig and strange appearance of the two spars forward that give to the hoy such a peculiar look; however, she is simple in construction and the model is easy to build. The first four lifts are 12½ inches long by 4¾ inches wide and they should be finished to the thicknesses shown in the plate. Lift 5 is longer, 13 by 4¾ inches, and is an inch thick.

Finish the hull to the under side of the deck as in building the skipjack, and then put on the deck, properly cambered (1 inch in 5 feet), and scored to show the deck planking. Do not paint. This model having a raised waterway, the deck-planking scores should be carried to within ⅟₁₆ inch of the edge of the deck. The low bulwark can be made a solid piece like a log rail, and should be fastened down to the deck with glue and small brads. There is a very sharp bend to this bulwark and to all pieces that go around the bows. It will be better to cut the forward ends of the bulwarks and the rails to the shape of this bend rather than to try to bend them around. Join the pieces with a scarf joint as in Figure 14, but do not make the joining at the turn nor have the joint in the rail immediately over the joint in the bulwark.

Across the stern the taffrail is closed; small knees support it, one each side, and the rails meet it at the quarters (see Plate III).

The most delicate piece of construction so far encountered comes in building the top rail with its stanchions. These are best doweled into the

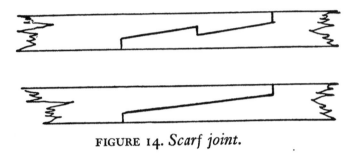

FIGURE 14. *Scarf joint.*

rails (Figure 15); due care must be used in establishing the proper rake (see Plate III). The space between the rails around the bow is filled in solid and the piece that goes between the rails may be glued and bradded in place. The bowsprit passes through a hole in this piece (washboard) and it is also cut out to allow the boom of the anchor cat to pass through it. This piece is of the same thickness as the stanchions (which are to be made square and scale 3½ inches each way). Before putting the top rail on you had better install the waterways. These are 8 inches wide and 2 inches thick. They fit on the deck, up tight against the bulwark, and go all around the vessel except at the bows where there is a breasthook across the bows (see Plate III). These waterways should be shaped around the turn of the bows and joined with a scarf, as are the other pieces here.

Paint the hull a buff yellow with a black streak at the under side of the deck. The rails are painted black and the stern is black with gold molding and stars. The inside of the bulwarks is yellow. A yellow ochre mixed with white provides the proper color for the topsides. The deck is left unpainted and oiled. The deck structures are white, as is the mainmast up to the doubling, which is black, with black caps. The anchor cat is black. The welps of the capstans are unpainted, as are the cleats and pins and capstan bars. The bowsprit and the spencer mast are unpainted, as are the other spars. Both hatch coamings and hatch covers are white. The hoy has a copper bottom; real copper strips, if put on neatly and in shipshape manner, look well on large models, but copper paint on wood gives the best appearance on all models built to a scale of ⅜ inch to the foot or smaller.

After the model is painted comes the operation of rigging. A hoy of this period was usually a vessel of sloop rig, and though there are certain

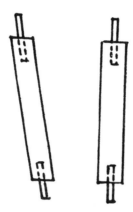

FIGURE 15. *Stanchion details for the anchor hoy.*

peculiarities of rig that fit this craft for the work for which she was designed, she nevertheless retained the general character of a sloop. Since the peculiarities affect the sparmaking we will take them up in turn, as the various spars are made and shipped. The anchor cat should be in place, as it is an integral part of the hull. Passing to the bowsprit, we find the first departure from usual sloop rig. The bowsprit, instead of being fixed in its bed, is movable, and can be run inboard like the reefing bowsprit of a cutter. Its after end is square where it passes through the bowsprit bitts. It is round where it goes out through the hole in the forward bulwarks, and it has a shoulder at the outer end. Just inboard of the shoulder a sheave hole is cut through from top to bottom. A removable iron pin, put through the bowsprit bitts and the spar, holds its after end in place. Ship the bowsprit but do not rig it now.

Step the mast. Get the shrouds over the masthead in their proper order (see Chapter Four), pass the ends through the eyes in the waterways, turn a thimble in these ends, and set them up to themselves as shown in Plate III. The anchor tackle pendant goes next over the masthead. This is a short pendant with an eye spliced in one end which goes around the mast over the shrouds; a large single block is spliced in the other end. A rope is bent to the arse of this block, passed around the sheave of a hook block, back to the first block, and down to the single block on deck; it is then taken to the fore capstan and passed around it. Fincham says that a rope messenger should be passed around the welps of a capstan three times. When not in use to support an anchor, the hook of the tackle is taken to an eyebolt in the waterways, as shown in the pinrail layout, and there made fast (see Figure 16).

Plate III shows the lead of all the rigging and where to put the blocks at the masthead. In the time of this boat there was very little iron work and rope collars were in general use to attach the various blocks to the spars; to keep stays up on the mast, wooden cleats were used.

The rigging of the bowsprit may cause the modelmaker some perplexity and it may be well to describe the attachment and lead of this gear. After the jibstay (rigged with a tackle such as is employed in rigging the backstays of a ship and which is described in Chapter Four) is in place at the side of the sloop and the forestay is in place, the eye of the jibstay is got over the masthead. The stay is then led down and rove through the sheave hole in the end of the bowsprit and a thimble is turned in the end so that it comes close up under the bowsprit. A block of a gun tackle purchase hooks in this thimble with the standing part of its tackle bent to the becket of the block. The other block of the tackle is made fast to a rope collar, or bridle, that is made fast to the stem piece by being rove through a hole in the stem. The fall of this tackle, after reeving through the blocks, is taken in through a hole or fairlead in the forward bulwarks, above the main rail, and is belayed to the starboard side of the bowsprit bitts. This tackle serves as a bobstay and it also allows the jibstay to be shortened when the bowsprit is hauled inboard.

The jib topmast stay goes over the topmast head, after the topmast stay is rigged and the suitable blocks are in place (see the sail and rigging plan, Plate III). This stay, with an eye in its end, is passed around the bowsprit,

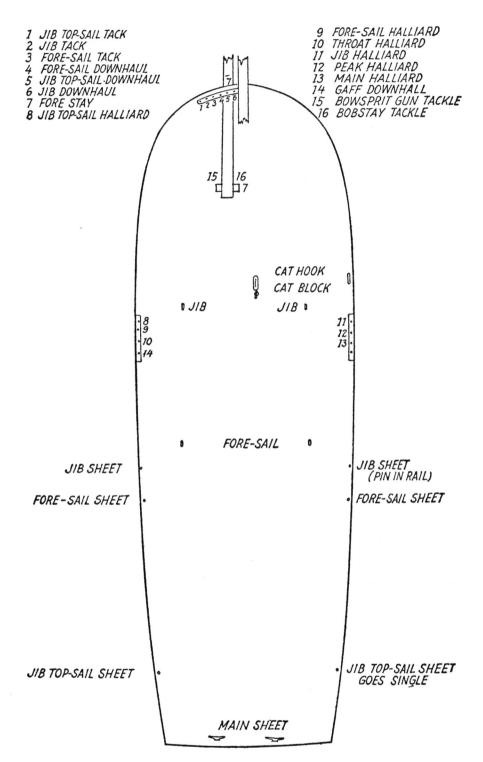

1 JIB TOP-SAIL TACK
2 JIB TACK
3 FORE-SAIL TACK
4 FORE-SAIL DOWNHAUL
5 JIB TOP-SAIL-DOWNHAUL
6 JIB DOWNHAUL
7 FORE STAY
8 JIB TOP-SAIL HALLIARD

9 FORE-SAIL HALLIARD
10 THROAT HALLIARD
11 JIB HALLIARD
12 PEAK HALLIARD
13 MAIN HALLIARD
14 GAFF DOWNHALL
15 BOWSPRIT GUN TACKLE
16 BOBSTAY TACKLE

15   16
7

CAT HOOK
CAT BLOCK
JIB   JIB

8
9
10
14

11
12
13

JIB SHEET

FORE-SAIL SHEET

FORE-SAIL

JIB SHEET
(PIN IN RAIL)

FORE-SAIL SHEET

JIB TOP-SAIL SHEET

JIB TOP-SAIL SHEET
GOES SINGLE

MAIN SHEET

FIGURE 16. *Belaying-pin diagram for the anchor boy.*

outside of the shoulder, which prevents it sliding in on the spar. The bowsprit shroud collar (see Plate XIII) is last to go over the end of the bowsprit. The pendants are very short with thimbles turned into the ends that hang on each side of the bowsprit. The block of a tackle is hooked into these thimbles and the tackle then becomes the bowsprit shrouds. The fall of this tackle leads from the outer block through a sheave in the side of the bows, above the inner block, and belays to a cleat on the inside of the bulwarks, forward of the sheave. The shrouds also can be shortened as the bowsprit is reefed. All this rigging is retained on the bowsprit with small cleats, outside of the shroud collar.

A peculiarity of the hoy's rig is the employment of a spencer mast. This mast steps on deck at the mast partners, and its upper end is held between the trestletrees with a pin. The gaff and boom are held to this mast with small rope parrals. There is a small saddle on the spencer mast that supports the boom jaws. Make the gaff and boom, complete with all cleats, sheaves, and blocks before putting them in place. Both spars have a shoulder at the outboard end, to keep the rigging in place. A small eyebolt in the end of the gaff takes the block of the flag halliard, which belays on the boom. Just forward of the shoulder there is a hole put through the spar from one side to the other for the outhaul of the head of the mainsail. The blocks for the peak and throat halliards are bent to collars with small cleats on the gaff to keep them in place. Vangs, to steady and control the gaff, may be added, in place of the flag halliard.

The boom topping lift block (single) goes outside of the shoulder on the boom. Inboard in the large end of the spar is a sheave hole and sheave for the outhaul of the mainsail. On each side of the boom just forward of the sheave hole are two pieces of wood 1½ inches thick by 4 inches wide and 16 inches long. The one to port has three ½-inch holes evenly spaced throughout its length; the one to starboard is fitted with three sheaves (see Plate III). These pieces are called the combs and take the reef tackle. On top of the boom, within the taffrail, is a stop or cleat for the mainsheet block collar. This is a 1½-inch piece of wood, 1 foot long, scored to take the collar and allow it some play, bolted fast to the spar. Inboard 3 feet from this there is a cleat on each side of the boom for the flag halliard, and

3 feet further in is another to starboard for the peak downhaul. The jaws of the gaff are 2 feet long and those of the boom are 3 feet. A pin in the jaws of the boom is put there to belay the reef tackle to. Rig the parral of the boom first, then the topping lift, and follow with the gaff and its gear.

The sails of the anchor hoy were mainsail, foresail, jib, and jib topsail. The jib and jib topsail are set flying. A collar with a small block at each side is put around the end of the bowsprit, between the jib and jib topmast stays, and the tacks reeve through these blocks and go inboard through the washboard. The foresail is bent with hanks to the forestay; its tack is bent to an eye just aft the stay. A downhaul is bent to the cringle at the head of the sail, comes down through the hanks, reeves through a block at the washboard, and is belayed forward.

The mainsail is laced to the gaff. The lacing is bent to the peak cringle, is rove through a hole in the gaff end, back to the cringle, and then taken around the gaff. It is half-hitched above the spar at each turn to hold it in place. Its forward end is made fast at the forward or throat cringle in the head of the sail.

The mainsail's outhaul is bent to the after cringle in the foot of the sail, reeves through a sheave in the boom end, and has a block turned in the fall. This block sets up to a gun tackle that belays to a pin in the jaws of the boom. A metal ring is put over the outer end of the boom and rides over the outhaul, just forward of the sheave hole. The top of the ring is lashed to the cringle. The ring serves to keep the outhaul and clew of the sail down to the boom, and in diameter it should be little larger than the spar.

The reef tackle is made with a stopper knot in one end, while the other end is rove upward through a hole in the port comb. When the stopper knot jams, the tackle is passed through a cringle in the reef band of the sail. It then reeves through a sheave hole in the starboard comb and belays to a cleat on the boom. A gun tackle is rigged between the cringle in the tack and an eyebolt in the deck just aft the spencer mast, its fall belaying to a cleat on the partners.

A belaying-pin diagram (Figure 16) shows plainly the position of the pinrails and where each rope belays.

PLATE IV: COLONIAL FISHING SCHOONER

No labor of man is conducted under more arduous, exacting and dangerous conditions than deep-sea fishing. Neither does any class of ships encounter trials to match the daily experience of the fishermen's vessels. To cope successfully with the conditions that prevail on the Grand and the Georges Banks and the stormy North Atlantic requires fine crews and able ships. The thrilling tales of Connolly and Kipling paint none too vividly the hazards and dangers that are their daily meed. Gloucester, Massachusetts, has been our great fishing port and through her enviable history runs the story of famous schooners and the men that sailed them. It is a saga of high adventure and heroic deeds, often of hardship and death and all too seldom of financial reward.

We know that Gloucestermen were fishing off shore during the early years of that settlement's history. We also have some knowledge of the craft they employed. The first of the fishermen, that is, the first type that gained recognition as such, was a small open two-masted boat without headsails or shrouds, called a Chebacco boat. These were followed by the bigger and more able dogbodies, pinkies, and heeltappers. The heeltapper was the progenitor of the modern fishing schooner, and prevailed with slight modifications as the favored type from colonial times until about 1850, when it was replaced by schooners built somewhat on the lines of the pilot boats. These were nicknamed "sharpshooters" or "filebottoms" because of the sharpness of their lines and their great deadrise, which was in such contrast to the rounder bottoms of the earlier boats. The *Romp*, built by Andrew Story at Essex, Massachusetts, in 1847, was the first of this new type. Her success and the reputation she established for speed earned general approval for the design and many schooners were built on similar lines. This model soon lost favor as the demand for fast boats led to faults in design, resulting in schooners that were too beamy and shallow, and prone to capsize.

To improve on this type, Captain Joseph Collins and Dennison J. Lawlor of Boston designed the *Grampus* for the United States Fish Commission. She was given a deeper hull and improved rig, and was a great success.

Schooners from the boards of Edward Burgess, Dennison J. Lawlor, and other notable designers were a great improvement over the earlier examples. The new boats were large, fast, handsome vessels, weatherly and able. The big fisherman's jib was done away with and the present-day arrangement of headsails was adopted. The schooners' lines were sweetened and improved, the bows cleared of headrails, and the clipper bow transformed into a straight stem. These were fine craft but better were to come.

In the late nineties, Thomas McManus of Boston, a skilled designer, came out with a schooner in which he introduced the modern curved stem and keel line. The knockabout type of fishing schooner was also his contribution, made in the interests of the safety of the fishermen. The loss of life caused by men being swept off the bowsprit or lost because of faulty foot ropes prompted him to design a model with a long overhanging bow and no bowsprit. This change vastly increased the hull length, and since cost of construction was figured per linear foot the type was expensive to build, though there were several very successful examples. Probably the most famous was the beautiful *Helen B. Thomas*, first of this type. She was a very fast and able schooner and defeated the speedy *Phillip B. Manta* in one of the early fishermen's races. Probably sailing-ship design reached its highest degree of perfection in the Gloucester fishing schooner. Such designers as Crowninshield, W. Starling Burgess, George "Mel" McClain, Frank C. Paine, and others all earned great reputations for their fine schooners.

Throughout their development these schooners have shown an increase in length with the introduction of each new type. The cost of building increased even more rapidly, until it reached a point where one of these modern big fishermen cost a small fortune, and a new type more economical to build and to operate will supersede them. Steam, which drove most wind-propelled ships from the seas, never affected them; but the internal-combustion engine is now found in every hull, and the trend is to smaller boats of the motor-sailer type. An example of this new design is the ketch-rigged *Niantic*, a Diesel-engined motor-sailer 71 feet long, from the board of H. I. Chapelle. She was built at Ipswich, Massachusetts, by Robinson for

Russell Grinnell of New Bedford. She was one of the smallest vessels to fish on Georges Bank throughout the winter and proved most successful.

The model builder who wishes to recreate one of the great modern fishing schooners will find many complete plans at his disposal and such a ship makes a most picturesque and interesting model. Like the whaling ships, they are decidedly individual in line and gear. It is an older type vessel, however, whose plans are the subject of Plate IV. She is a heel-tapper of the period 1765–1780, and is a reconstruction made after intensive study of recorded dimensions, pictures, and prints of the period, of descriptions, and of models. I am indebted to Mr. Howard I. Chapelle for permission to reproduce the plan of this schooner and to reprint the very amusing descriptions of the painting of these old vessels.

The first commissioned vessel of the United States Navy, under Washington, the heeltapper *Hannah*, was probably very much like this one, as is indicated by models of the *Hannah* at the Smithsonian Institution and in the Peabody Museum at Salem, Massachusetts.

To build this model, six lifts are required to form the block to the under side of the deck lines. The lifts vary in thickness, so be careful to get them finished according to the plan. Put on a temporary keel and finish the hull to shape. Next put on the main deck, properly scored and cambered. These schooners did not have raised waterways—they set flush with the deck planking and should be represented by scoring the outline of them on both decks. At the forward end of the break of the poop deck, face the end of the block with a thin strip of wood scored athwartships to represent planks. Let its upper edge rise above the poop deck until that deck is put on; then finish it flush with the top of the deck to simulate the narrow athwartship waterway at the break of the poop. The poop deck goes on now. It will be found more convenient to cut out the holes for the hatches, mast, rudder, and bowsprit bits before fastening the decks in place. The bowsprit bits should go down through the deck and rest on the top of lift 1 if you have hollowed out the block. The decks should be made narrower than the hull all around by the thickness of the bulwark, thus creating a shoulder on which the bulwark rests, and should also be cut out to fit around the stanchions (Figure 17).

Make and fit all the pieces of deck furniture and put on the bowsprit while you can work at them without the bulwarks to interfere, painting them as you go. At the bow, flush on the deck under the bowsprit, fitted around the knightheads and stanchions, fit a breasthook (see the plate). Its purpose is to strengthen the bows. The galley stack shows in the plan on the port side, but should be directly athwartship on the starboard side. It is made of wood, four-square, and tapered and capped over like a spark arrester with openings under the cap on all four sides. These stacks and the galley stove were originally made of wood and plastered over inside.

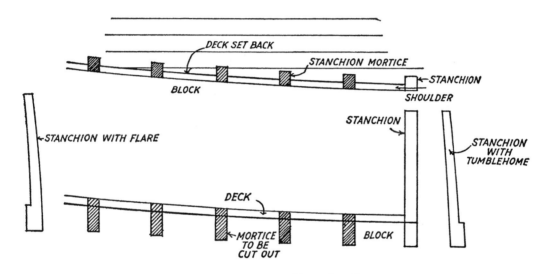

FIGURE 17. *Stanchion details.*

Now comes a most difficult piece of construction, making and fitting the timber heads or stanchions. The difficulty lies in aligning them properly when fitting them in place; therefore be careful to shape them accurately with their inner and outer faces properly beveled. It is almost impossible to correct any inaccuracies to the inboard faces after they are in place but a certain amount of fairing up can be done to the outboard sides. A light batten bent around the curves will serve to show the proper alignment both inside and out.

In a real ship these timber heads or stanchions are part of the frames that mold the contours of the hull and the ship's planking is fastened to them. Their shapes are represented in the lines by the station lines. It is shipbuilding practice to fashion a frame in two sections or halves, the center line being the station line in the plan. Each section is made in pieces called futtocks. The pieces that compose the after half of the frame overlap those of the forward half. It is the practice of ship designers in drawing the lines to omit some station lines (generally every other line) in the draught as being unnecessary when showing the ship's shape. In construction plans, which are developed from the lines, all frames are drawn in, each station being shown. For this reason we find in draughts of lines that the stations are numbered or lettered *B-D-F*, or 2-4-6, to show that frames *A-C-E* and 1-3-5 have been intentionally omitted. The distance between centers of the frames, which is the distance between station lines in fully developed construction plans, is called the room and space, and is constant between all frames that are placed at right angles to the keel. Forward and aft, where the ship's sides curve sharply inward, the frames are placed at right angles to the ship's side until, at the bows, they come very close together, the room and space diminishing. Here they parallel the keel, and form an almost solid wall of wood for a short distance each side of the stem. These frames are called the cant frames and in our plan begin at station *H* forward and at station 14 aft. The first frame on each side of the stem is carried up full size above the deck to form the knightheads, the heavy timbers that show above the bulwarks each side of the bowsprit. The next frame to be carried up above the deck should be in this model about ¼ inch aft the knightheads on each side, and the room and space should increase progressively around the bows until it reaches ½ inch at station *H* (assuming a scale of ¼ inch to the foot). Mark out the positions of the frames on the deck and be sure each frame on the port side is directly opposite a frame to starboard. When framing a real ship, only one-half of the frame is carried above the deck to form the stanchion. Usually this is the forward half forward of the dead-flat and the after half aft. For that reason the frames are shown immediately adjoining the station lines in this plate. But in all cases they are aft those lines to preserve even spacing between all pairs of stanchions on the model.

Should we shift them forward and aft, the distance between two stanchions where the change occurs would be unsightly in a model. This is a rather full description of these timbers but a knowledge of their construction is very necessary to the model builder, though he only builds them in part in making a lift model. When it becomes necessary to fashion the gun ports of an armed vessel, the understanding of the frame making comes in handy, for the gun port sills are morticed into the frames and the ports come between them, which determines the spacing of the ports. It also determines the placing of other pieces of gear that must be bolted on to something solid—for instance, the chain plates should bolt fast to frames. It is paying heed to such details that determines the worth of a model.

These exposed timber heads or stanchions, to be built into our lift model, must be solidly fastened so as to give support and shape to the bulwarks and must be stout enough to provide a substantial fastening. Fashion the outboard face of each stanchion so that it continues the upward sweep of the ship's side at the place where it is to go. The fore and aft sides of the frames are parallel but the inboard side stands slightly more erect than the outboard face, giving each stanchion a slight taper to the top (Figure 17). In length each stanchion should be ⅜ inch longer than from the rail to the under side of the deck. Below the deck line a shoulder is formed on the stanchion's outer face to correspond with the shoulder formed by the deck edge and the side of the block.

Below each notch cut in the deck to take the timbers, cut a mortice in the side of the block as deep and as wide as the notch in the deck and ⅜ inch in length. The lower end of the frame fits into this mortice with its outer face flush with the side of the block. Glue the timbers in place and fasten with treenails (make them from round toothpicks). Use the batten to fair them out and dub them off until the side of the block is a smooth and fair sweep.

The bulwarks come next. Across the stern put on the knees that support the transom and then build the transom as shown in the plan. The bulwarks for the main deck go on next, resting on the shoulder on the block, fastening to the timbers and being morticed into the side of the block at the forward end of lift 5; the mortice goes aft to station 4. Then place the poop-deck bulwarks, joining the transom squarely at the turn of the stern. The joint will be concealed under the side badges. Fit in the shelf clamp across the inside of the transom and fit a block into a ringbolt just inside the bulwarks on each side of this clamp, for the mainsheet block, which belays to the big cleat on the bulwarks. The arch board had best be made in pieces, putting on the side badges first, lower ends resting on the top of the wales, and then the curved molding across the stern. From here on the finishing up is simple. The lengths of the masts are figured from the top of lift 1.

Almost any color scheme can be employed when you come to paint the hull, but in any case the bottom should be white. Here are some items from contemporary newspapers that shed some light on this matter.

1767. November 16. *Boston Gazette.*

"We hear from the Isle of Sholes that last Wednesday Sen'night two Men, one named Richard Clark, and the other John Wardell ran away from that place with a small Schooner of about 16 tons; she is Pink Stern [this refers to the shape, not the color of the stern] painted light blue and yellow, old Sails, one new Cable, the other almost new. She had in her 25 Quintals of Fish, and some Woolen Goods, and 't is supposed they are gone to Carolina."

1761. August 24, Monday. *Boston Gazette.*

"A description of several French Privateers who sailed from Martinieco, to Cruize on the Northern Coasts. . . .

"A Sloop of 12 Guns, formerly a Marblehead Fisherman, one side lampblack and Tallow, the other Lead and Tallow. Looks like a Northern Sloop and sails fast.

"A Schooner of 12 Guns, formerly a Marblehead Fisherman, one side of her upper works Black and the other Yellow and White Streaks; a Seahorse on her Hase-holes, and looks very much like a Fisherman on the painted side."

1767. March 9, Monday. *Boston Country and Gazette Journal.*

"Two Hundred Pounds, O. T. Reward. Whereas on the 20th of July last, the Crew of two fishing schooners set on fire and totally destroyed a new schooner of 60 tons burthen at the Island of St. John's in the Gulph of St. Lawrence, The property of David Higgins and others of said Island for the Benefit of the Iron Work. Who ever will discover the Perpetrators of the above Villany so as they may be brought to Justice, shall be entitled to Two Hundred Pounds of Old Tenor from said Higgins or John Spooner of Boston. One of the Schooners was about 50 Tons, quite new, bright sides with a short quarter deck, Painted pale Blue and White with a long stump forward. The other about 40 or 50 Tons, quite Black and a short Stump."

It was quite the usual thing to paint the topsides in variegated stripes. I would suggest that the wales and the poop-deck bulwarks be painted the same color, all rails white, the sides striped above the wales and a solid color below to the waterline. It was quite usual to paint the stern in contrast to the sides. A solid color was common inside the arch board, sometimes with false windows painted here, or a decoration like a gilt sun. The inside of the bulwarks and the deck furniture may be painted to suit your taste. The inboard end of the bowsprit and the tops of the mast had better be made white, as well as the first and last quarters of the gaffs and booms. Stanchions may be white or a light color.

An anchor for each side, wooden-stocked, is lashed to the rail over the padding that shows just aft the cathead (see Plate XIV). A round-bottomed small boat is stowed upside down on deck, against the port rail in the waist.

Start to rig the model only after the painting is finished. For details of her rig refer to the sail plan and follow it carefully.

The schooner's dimensions, as given in the plans, are:

Length, overall........................60'   5"
Length, between *PP*....................58'   2"
Beam, molded...........................16'   10"
Beam, extreme..........................17'   3"
Depth in hold.......................... 7'   3"

Draught at post...................... 8'

Bowsprit............................25'   2"

   outboard..........................21'

Foremast...........................54'   6"

Fore gaff, to inside of throat...........20'

Fore boom, to inside of throat...........24'   6"

Main gaff, to inside of throat.............21'

Main boom, to inside of throat...........35'

Mainmast, to top of cap.................59'   9"

Pole topmast......................... 9'   9"

Doubling............................ 4'   6"

I wish to call your attention to the fact that you are to rig a model of a ship of about 1750 and you must not put on any modern gear. Little iron work was employed at the time and hemp and rawhide took its place aloft as well as below. See that the blocks are so stropped with the caps of wood. Masts are measured from the upper side of lift 1, and should step on this lift.

The bobstay reeves through a hole in the cutwater and sets up on itself, with a deadeye turned in its outer end. A bobstay collar with deadeye passes around the nose of the bowsprit and the stay is set up with a laniard rove through the hearts or small deadeyes.

The fore and jib stays reeve through bee holes on opposite sides of the bowsprit, come inboard through the forward bulwarks, and set up with hearts to the bowsprit bitts.

The jib sheets are in pairs, one to each side, and are led from an eyebolt in the deck just forward of the fore rigging, through the sheet block at the clew and back to a block just abaft the eyebolt, and then belay at pinrail. The jib downhaul reeves through a small block on the stay and comes in through the bulwarks and belays to a pin on the inside of the bulwark.

The foremast is bald-headed, and both foresail and mainsail are loose-footed. The outhauls go through sheaves in the spars but the boom has two sheaves which are offset slightly, one just aft of the other at the

PLATE VII
EDITH F TODD

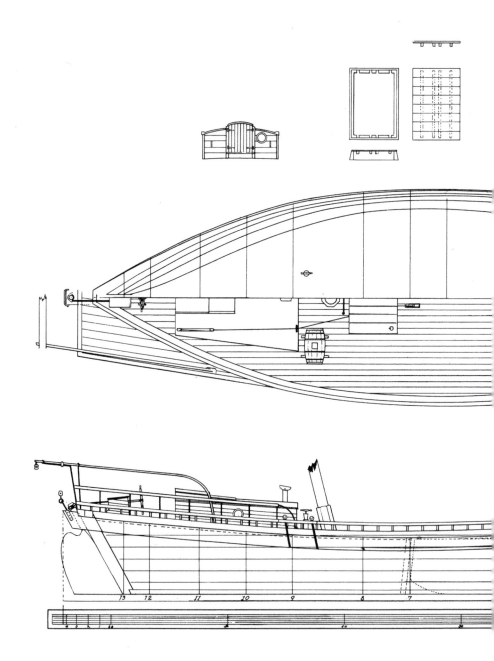

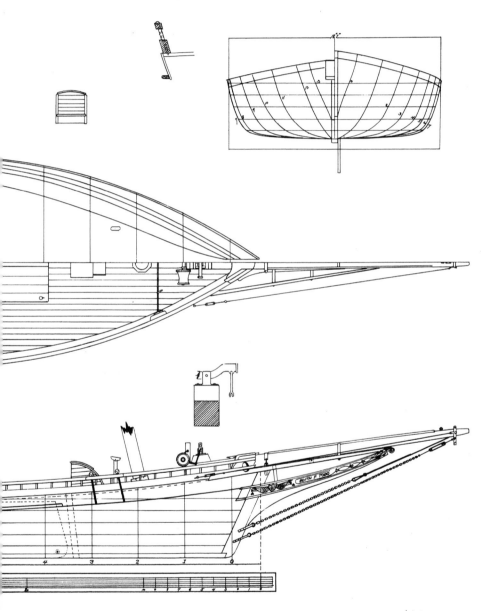

EDITH F TODD

Victor Grimwood

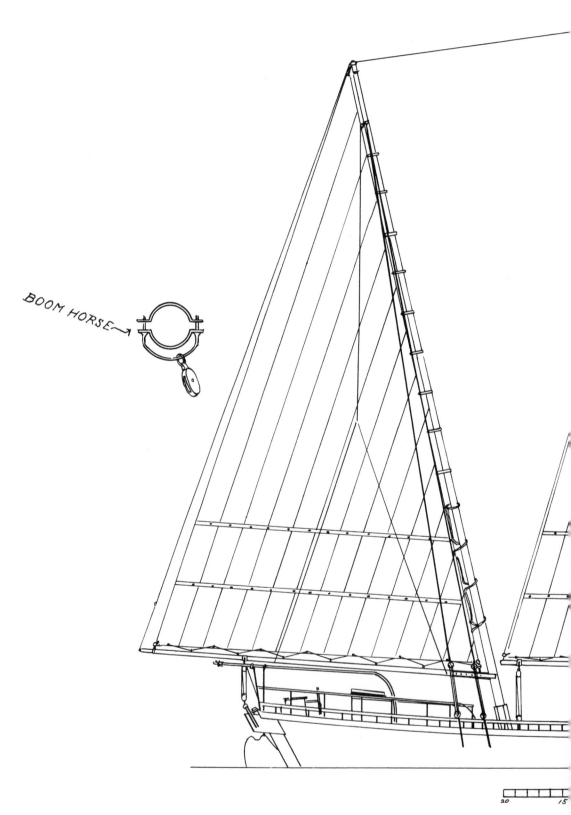

BOOM HORSE→

20   15

EDIT

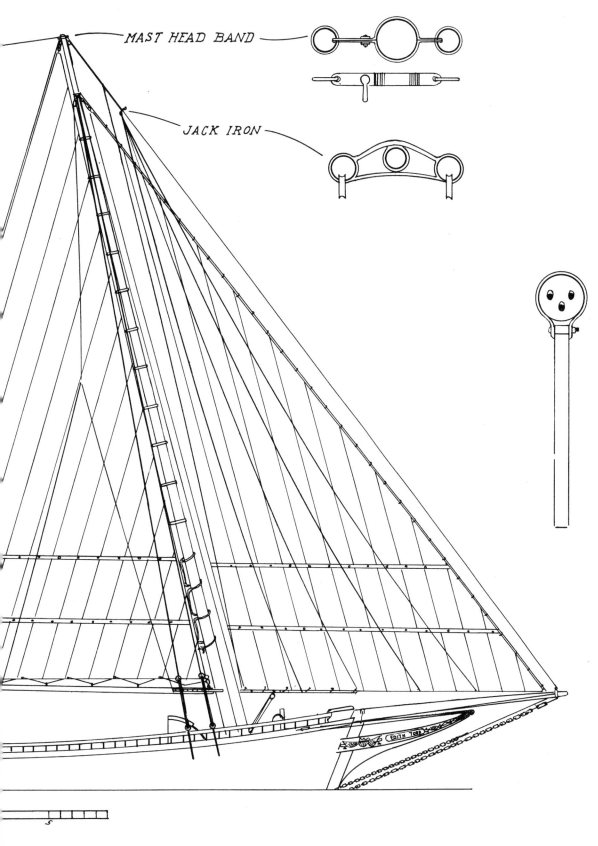

MAST HEAD BAND

JACK IRON

EDITH TODD

DD. *Sail plan.*

end of the spar, one for the topping lift and the inboard one for the out-haul. There is a single foresheet for the foresail that leads from a block in an eyebolt on the main deck, through a block at the boom, back to the deck block, and belays to the gallows frame, serving also as a belfry. The mainsheet leads from an eyebolt in the deck to a block on the boom, back to a block fastened to the eyebolt, and belays to the cleat on the inside of the bulwark. This sheet is double; there are two blocks on the boom in a rope collar, held in place by a cleat or batten with a score, a sheet leading to blocks on each side of the schooner. There are combs on the booms for the reef tackle and the peak downhaul, reef tackle, and outhaul are belayed to the boom. The cleat for the peak downhaul is on the boom jaws.

The mainstay leads from the cap of the mainmast to the cap of the foremast, then reeves through a pendant block on the mainmast under the trestletrees and sets up to the gallows frame or belfry. A heart is turned into this end of the stay and a laniard is passed from it around the center of the gallows frame, thus permitting the stay to be tautened.

The main topmast stay sets up to an eyebolt in the after side of the fore-mast. The mast caps are square. Some of these Marblehead schooners had bowsprit caps and could at will run out a jib boom on which a light head-sail could be set.

The first and last thirds of the booms and gaffs are painted white; the middle part is black or oil-rubbed. The mastheads are white, as is the bowsprit.

PLATE V: NEW ENGLAND WHALING SCHOONER *AGATE*

The old-time whaling ship with her highly specialized gear is a real marine curiosity today. The whaling industry is still carried on, but the ships and methods have been modernized out of all semblance to those of the old-timers. The only thing in the industry that remains constant is the value of some of the products derived from whales or kindred marine mammals.

Killing whales from the safety of the decks of a modern whale ship is very different from pursuing and killing these monsters while afloat in such fragile whaleboats as were used by the old-timers. In them, men had to approach the great creatures closely—in fact the boat was in actual contact with a whale when it was first struck and again when the finishing stroke was delivered with the lance. Extreme danger for boat and crew existed at either time.

Boats, tryworks, cutting-in stage and tackle, and the huge wooden davits all set the whale ship apart from other ships, and marked her as a participant in the whale fishery. The terms fish and fishery as applied to the taking and rendering of these mammals were used by the whalemen themselves, and are not misnomers.

Modelmakers are only concerned with the physical aspects of the whale ships. A history and account of whaling is beyond the scope of this book and should the modelmaker be (as he properly should be) curious as to the details of the methods employed, a vast number of informative books is available, both fictional and technical. The modelmaker should read some of these books before attempting a whale-ship model. The photographs of Albert Cook Church have been made into a book ("Whale Ships and Whaling"—see the Recommended Reading in the Appendix.) The building and equipping of the ships and the form and use of the gear are all there for us to see. Mr. Church's book is an invaluable record of the industry and is a boon to the modelmaker.

Square-rigged ships have long been the modelmaker's delight, and there is a plethora of square-rigged models. Vessels of this rig were by no means the only types employed in whaling. Vessels of fore and aft rig were used extensively, so why not make a model of one of these? Plate V shows the lines and plans of a whaling schooner, a three-boat ship. Schooner whalers were used almost entirely in the Atlantic whale fishery.

Whale ships were classified by the number of boats they carried on the davits. A ship that carried five boats was known as a five-boat whaler. The schooners were generally three-boat ships. All ships, of course, carried spare boats, sometimes stowed on deck and sometimes knocked down and stowed below. We do not show the whaleboats swung from the davits in our plate, but the *Agate* carried a boat on each quarter and one at the stern.

Whaleboats were from 26 to 30 feet in length, marvels of design and of fine construction and wonderful sea boats. Their build and equipment became standardized and the *Agate* carried the standard 28-foot New Bedford whaleboat. The gear carried in one of these whaleboats consisted of many indispensable items, stowed with great precision. All whaleboats were equipped alike and followed the same procedure in stowing the equipment, which consisted of the following items:

2 live irons (harpoons), complete with handles, the first iron bent to the line.

3 spare irons.

3 lances.

1 boat spade.

6 oars.

3 paddles.

2 tubs (large and small) of line.

An odd number of wooden buckets.

Canvas bucket.†

Mast and sail (complete with boom and gaff or sprit).

Tiller.

Rudder.

Strap for steering oar.

Lantern keg (for matches, bread, tobacco, etc.).

Compass.*

Fresh-water keg lashed to chocks.

Piggin.*

Waif.

Lantern.*

Tub oar crotch.

Double oar lock.

Rowlock.†

Knife.

Hatchet.

Grapnel.

Drag.

Canvas nipper to protect hands.†
Boat hook.

All the irons were kept in a chock at the bow. There were lockers astern in which were kept the articles marked *; the articles marked † were stowed in a space under the bow box. The hatchet was often carried on the port side with the blade thrust between the ceiling and the outside planking. The knife was often slipped into a metal sheath nailed onto the clumsy cleat, with its handle pointing aft.

No whale ship would look complete without a grindstone somewhere about the deck, generally adjacent to the cooper's bench built on the after side of the tryworks. The cooper was a most important member of the crew. He did the coopering, carpentry, and blacksmithing, sharpened tools, and kept ship when the captain went in pursuit of a whale. A five-boat whaler would have as crew the captain, four mates, four boatsteerers, a cooper, a steward, a cabin boy, a cook, and four shipkeepers or extra hands. Sometimes a carpenter and a blacksmith were carried as well. A three-boat ship would carry a proportionately smaller crew.

Since a whaling voyage often lasted as long as three years, during which time a vessel was entirely dependent on self-contained resources, the amount of stores and replacement material these ships had to carry was enormous. Trade goods were included as well, and the bulk of cargo at setting out was so great that every bit of available space was made use of. However, the ships were bulky carriers. Speed was no object with them at any time, since there was no destination. They wandered over the sea poking along wherever a whale might swim.

Ships, barks, brigs, or schooners used for whaling might be old vessels converted or might be vessels especially constructed for the whale fishing. In either case the construction had to be of the best, for experienced whalemen would not put to sea in poor vessels.

The *Agate* was built at Essex, Massachusetts, in 1853, and was designed as a whaler. Her home port was Provincetown, now more famous for its little theater than for whale oil.

New Bedford was the leading whaling port during the boom days of the industry. Further south, Sag Harbor on Long Island was also a great whaling center. Nantucket was another noted whaling port. Whale ships were built in yards all along the seaboard of New England and as far south as Maryland. Drawings of the *Agate* were made by H. I. Chapelle from the builder's half model and the deck arrangement from contemporary pictures, from which drawings the illustrations in this book were copied.

The dimensions of the *Agate* were:

Length	79′	10″
Load waterline	74′	
Beam, molded	19′	8½″
Beam, extreme	20′	1″
Depth in hold	8′	6″
Draught at post	10′	
Room and space		24″
Bowsprit	23′	9″
Bowsprit, outboard	15′	
Jib boom	28′	
Jib boom, outboard	15′	
Foremast (deck to cap)	60′	
Fore topmast	40′	
Fore gaff	24′	
Fore boom	24′	
Mainmast	64′	
Main topmast	41′	
Main gaff	29′	
Main boom	49′	

The masts of the model are stepped on lift 1 and will be that much longer (from deck to top of lift 1) than the given dimensions call for.

A whale-ship model should be built to a scale of at least ¼ inch to 1 foot. Using any smaller scale will make it difficult to fashion the deck furniture in proper scale and proportion.

Build up the block to the under side of the main and quarter decks

(Figure 19). Lift 5 is finished to the outside of planking (Figure 18 shows its contour at the side). The main deck is built to the inside of planking, setting in from the edge of the block 3 inches by scale to make a shoulder for the bulwarks 3 inches wide, from the forward end of lift 5 to the stem. Look at Figure 17.

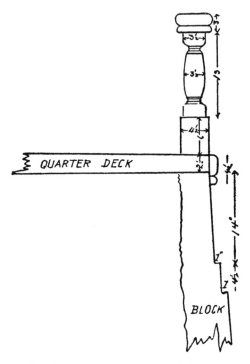

FIGURE 18. *Stanchion details and contour outside of planking for the* Agate.

Camber and score the deck and fill the scores of the deck pieces with umber, and then scrape them white, leaving the umber in the scores to look like caulking. The decks have a camber of ¼ inch to the foot. Put on these deck pieces when fashioned. Cut out the mortices for the timber heads (Figure 17). Make and put on all deck furniture and waterways, starting with the bowsprit. Details of the tryworks are to be seen in Figure 20. Carve out and put on the stanchions for the main-deck bulwarks as in Figure 17, omitting stanchions 16, 17, and 18 on the starboard side and all stanchions on both sides from No. 4 forward to the stem.

Fit the two blocks at the bows each side of the bowsprit. These should

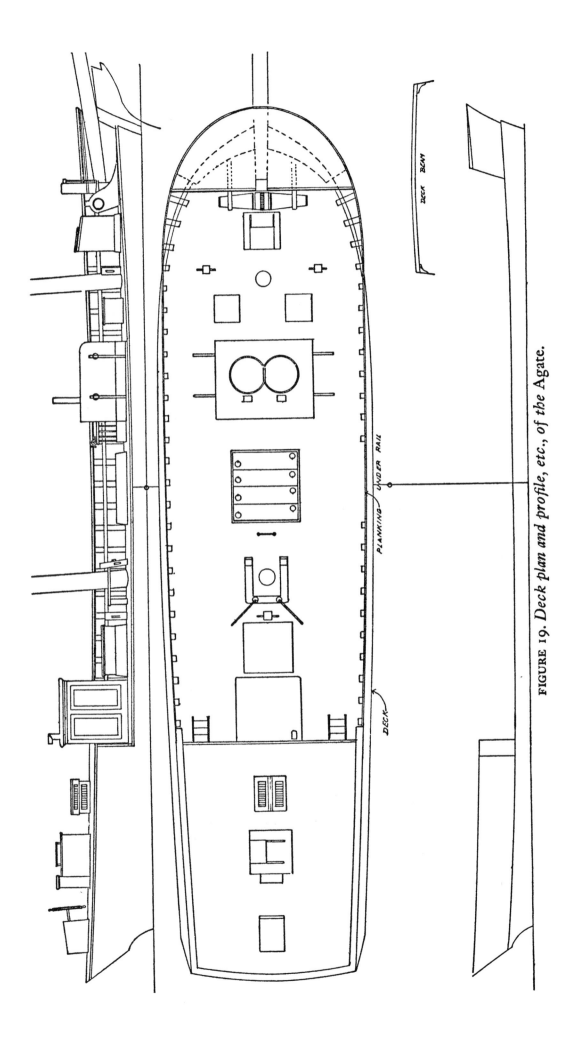

DECK PLAN

PLANKING UNDER RAIL

DECK

FIGURE 19. *Deck plan and profile, etc., of the Agate.*

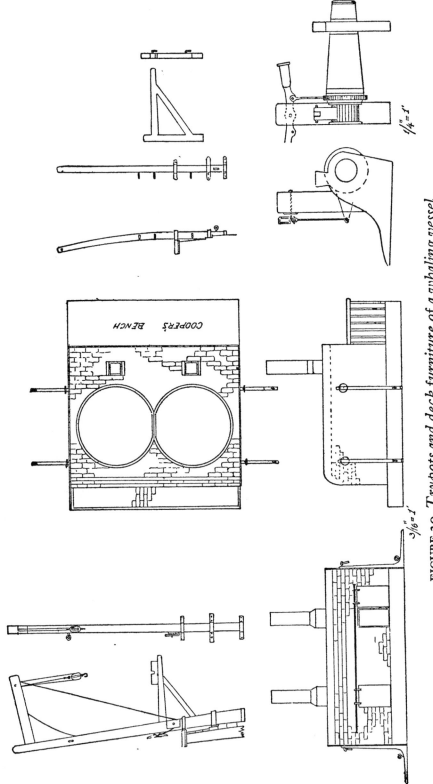

Whaling Schooner

COOPER'S BENCH

$\frac{3}{16}" = 1'$

$\frac{1}{4}" = 1'$

FIGURE 20. Trypots and deck furniture of a whaling vessel.

be cambered on the top like the deck, as the deck piece for the forecastle head is not cambered. The outer sides of these pieces are shaped like stanchions and they are made to the inside of planking and actually serve as the forward stanchions and timbers of the ship.

Put on the bulwarks as you did those on the heeltapper. They should be rabbeted into the stem. Build in the deck beam for the forward end of the forecastle head (Figure 19) and put on the last deck piece. Paint all the deck furniture now, and the inside of the bulwarks. Put on the lashing rail, inside the bulwarks, and the main rail.

Figure 18 is a cross section at station 15 of the quarter deck and shows how it should appear. The rails and the stanchions, as well as the monkey rail, should be painted white now.

FIGURE 21. *Fashion pieces.*

Turn to the outside of the hull and build on the padding shown in the plate, around the cutting-in platform on the starboard side only. Put on the fashion pieces (Figure 21), both sides, at the extreme stern, from the line of the deck up to the under side of the main rail. Leave all davits and boats until after the vessel is rigged. Paint the hull now.

Figure 22 is a detail drawing of the head of the schooner. The basic part of all heads is the head knee, which projects out from the stem to where it is cut to receive the scroll or billet head. We called this the longhead when discussing the skipjack, for that is a local term, but ship builders know it as the knee of the head. With this in place, put on the cheek knees. These are knee timbers bolted to the bows of the ship and the head knee that curve upward to the billet head. Some ships fill in the space between the cheek knees with a trail board, which we show in Figure 22. The lines of the *Agate*, however, do not show a trail board but pad out the space on the

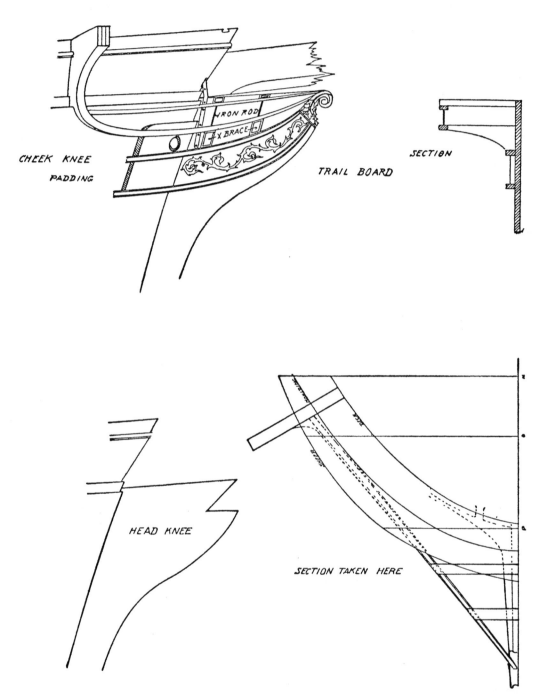

CHEEK KNEE

PADDING

IRON ROD

X BRACE

TRAIL BOARD

SECTION

HEAD KNEE

SECTION TAKEN HERE

FIGURE 22. *Detail for the head of the schooner* Agate.

hull between the cheek knees with a 1¼-inch wood pad. A carved trail board should go between the cheek knees from the pad out. Above the cheek knees there is another pad around the hawse hole, 2½ inches thick (Figure 22). The outer ends of the cheek knees seem to melt into the carved decoration of the scroll and you should make them so.

Also you will have to carve out the curving knee that supports the cathead and is bolted fast to the hull. It is better also to shape the head rail, as its upward curve is very rank and it curves horizontally to the scroll. The cross braces that support this rail are shown and are most important in strengthening the head. Paint the billet head white and run a fine white stripe along the top and bottom edges of the cheek knees and stripe the head rail. The head knee is painted like the hull. There was a useful purpose for these heads other than pure ornamentation. They were seats of ease for the crew, and the various rails were so arranged as to provide proper support for the men. While the timbers that comprise the head were more or less massive, the assembled parts must appear as a light and delicate fixture. Shipbuilders attained this end by careful proportioning and tapering and bringing the parts to a common end at the billet with a rare bit of fitting, and you must do the same. A poorly made head looks very awkward and is lubberly. Holly is good wood for making head rails and cheek knees.

Aloft, the vessel is rigged like any other fore-and-aft schooner. Figure 23 shows the cutting-in tackle and the only new problems come in rigging and making the jib boom and dolphin striker. These are shown in detail on the sail plan. The masthead assembly is also shown. This schooner had no hoops to guard the masthead man; he stood on the trees without any such aid.

The upper blocks of the cutting-in tackle are pendant from the mainmast head and hang to starboard.

Plate XIV shows a whaleboat's lines; you should make three of them and put one on the after davits and hang one on each quarter aft. If you wish to show the cutting-in stage rigged out, turn to Figure 24. It is rigged to the main rigging aft and to a removable davit at the forward end of the removable bulkwark. The sail plan also shows the cutting-in tackle rigged

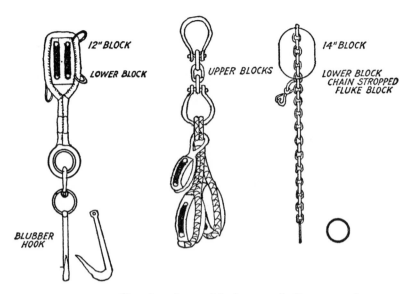

FIGURE 23. *Cutting-in tackle for a whaling vessel.*

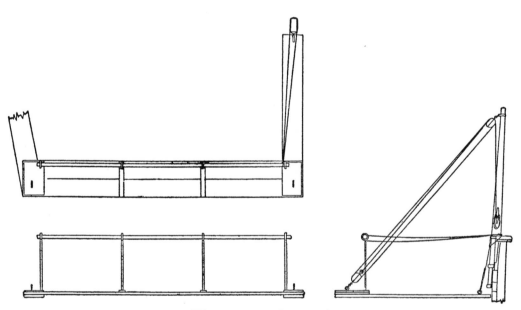

FIGURE 24. *Rigging for the cutting-in stage.*

and guyed out as though a whale were alongside and fastened with fluke chains, tail forward. The hawse to the tail or flukes comes in through one of the hawse holes and makes fast to the fluke bitts.

As a rule, black was a standard color with these whaling vessels, so we will use it on the outside of the hull above the copper. The rails are white, as is the deck furniture and the mastheads. The name is lettered in white and the billet head and rails are picked out as directed.

PLATE VI: A WEST COAST SCOW SCHOONER, *REGENIA S.*

Watermen, in seeking the most suitable types of boats to meet particular conditions, have adapted to their needs many strange types, none so divergent from the ordinary concept of sailing-vessel hull form as the scow. Somehow, one never associates such a boxlike shallow hull with sails. But when the need was to navigate the very shallow waters of bays and rivers and to combine great carrying capacity with extremely low-cost construction, the scow type offered many advantages and came quite generally into use. It does seem that the element of speed would be entirely lacking in a hull of this design, but boats of such boxlike construction have often showed a surprising ability to sail fast.

If the *Monitor* suggested a cheese box on a raft, the scow schooner bears a startling resemblance to a shallow cigar box with spars and sails. In spite of this strange appearance there is something about the scow schooner intriguing to the model builder. It may be that the straight lines, decidedly uncommon in sailboat design, lend a sort of novelty and that this queerness of form tempts one to try the construction of a miniature scow. I have seen a model of a sloop-rigged scow, and it is decidedly interesting and excites the curiosity of all beholders. In Plate VI we reproduce the plan of the scow schooner *Regenia S.*, a modern vessel whose home port is San Francisco, California.

Do not get snooty about this type and think that western sailors were responsible for what seems to be an unseamanlike craft, for as a matter of fact she is an adaptation of an East Coast type that was common to New

England waters only a few years ago. It is thought that the type originated there.

New England boatmen used scows for the transportation of ice and stone and other heavy and bulky commodities. Rockport, Massachusetts, was the home of the Rockport Granite Company that quarried granite and shipped it to all ports along the eastern seaboard. Vessels employed in this stone freighting came to be called granite sloops, some of which were sharp bowed while others were blunt-bowed scows. There is a picture of one of these eastern stone scows in the *Mariner* for April, 1931, and a most interesting article about the granite sloops by E. D. Walen and H. I. Chapelle. Unfortunately for those interested in the scow, it deals more with the sharp-ended sloops, though it does say that Quincy, Massachusetts, led in building and using scows. It states that these granite sloops were built with very flat floors to facilitate the moving and stowing of ponderous freight. Also that some of these boats were equipped with narrow-gauge railroad track below to aid in moving the heavy cargo. It adds that stone sloops are a thing of the past in New England waters, where such shipments now go by rail.

Conditions on the West Coast are somewhat different, and vessels of the scow type are still found useful around San Francisco Bay and nearby waters. Shipments of hay, grain, brick, timber, farm produce, and stone provide gainful employment for these boats. It is true, however, that many sailing scows have suffered the ignominy of having their spars removed and have been converted into motor-driven barges.

It is hard to conceive of these vessels venturing into deep water. Nevertheless, they do, and have acquitted themselves remarkably well. They have made voyages to Alaska and other northern ports and often sail as far south as Southern California. The scow type, however, is fundamentally unsuited for deep-sea use, and such voyages must be extremely hazardous undertakings.

The Historic American Merchant Marine Survey lists the lines and plans of the *Regenia S.* as survey number 16–59, and there is also on file in Washington a complete description of the vessel that is available to anyone interested.

The plan of the *Regenia S.* in the American Merchant Marine Survey shows the pumps, of diaphragm type, placed well aft of the deepest part of the hull, apparently where the hull would drain itself. In making the model, the pumps should be placed as in the plan, though this would render them somewhat inefficient. Where we have good authority for such placing, there may be an undisclosed reason for a seeming incongruity.

The greatest difficulty confronting the modelmaker comes in constructing the winch. Gears of the proper size can be turned and cut from wood or base metal on a small lathe. If such a lathe is not available, have the gears made, or try dealers in watchmakers' hardware, like Thomas Dixon & Son of Newark, New Jersey, who may have similar clock gears in stock.

Paint the hull almost any color. The model I saw was painted Indian red inside and out, and it looked very well. The deck was natural wood, scored, and the spars of course were unpainted. Chain of the proper size can be purchased, but anchors of the right pattern will have to be made. The model has raised waterways that should be painted like the hull, and the roof of the deck house and hatch covers are a slate gray.

There is a spar and sail plan given and this model looks well with sails set. As the *Regenia S.* is modern, use wire rope for standing rigging, chain bobstays, and iron bands or wythes on her bowsprit and at her masthead; blocks are metal stropped. The running rigging is rope.

The *Regenia S.* measures:

Length overall	73′	8″
Extreme beam	25′	8″
Draught, board up	5′	7″

Spar and sail dimensions to be taken from spar plan, which can be scaled.

PLATE VII: A CHESAPEAKE BAY BUGEYE, *EDITH F. TODD*

The story of the origin of the bugeye might be appropriately entitled "How the Oyster Built a Boat." Just as the whale was responsible for the creation and perfection of the New England whaleboat and its gear, so the oyster was responsible for the evolution of the bugeye. The only matter with which the oyster was not concerned was the choice of the name bugeye for this type of craft.

Many are the local tales concerning the derivation of the name, but none are plausible or susceptible of substantiation. The etymologically inclined believe it to be a derivation from buckeye and this seems to be a logical conception, for when boats of the type first appeared they were officially called buckeyes, and this name might easily have been corrupted into the more picturesque form. Be that as it may, bugeye is an intriguing name for a very exotic type of sailing craft.

The sharp shell of the oyster induced the adoption of the log bottom construction; the oyster's habitat and the methods of garnering him affected the hull form, while economic considerations dictated the proper hull size (averaging 60 feet in length) and the type of rig. The desirable log construction has been abandoned in the construction of the most recently built boats, owing to the difficulty of procuring logs of suitable dimensions, in favor of conventional frame construction, though no cant frames are used. All frames set square to the keel.

The oyster, at first but a beneficent addition to the fare of the early settlers along Chesapeake Bay, rapidly spread its renown as a desirable item of food to the rest of the country, and was soon being exported to less fortunate areas. An industry of considerable commercial importance gradually developed, which by the time of the Civil War was giving employment to a considerable portion of the local population and to a large fleet of vessels. These boats were of all types, though none were entirely suitable for the purpose. The need for an efficient vessel led to the creation of the bugeye, the brain child of a local boatbuilding genius.

The advent of the bugeye occurred in the late sixties, exact date unknown. The identity of the originator and the place where it was built are matters of conjecture. However, we do know that the underlying motif was the Chesapeake Bay log canoe.

This vessel, the hull of which was fashioned from several huge logs bolted together, was hewn to shape and hollowed out. In length the canoe averaged between 25 and 40 feet. A later type that came to be known as a "standing rig" canoe was longer and reached a length of 50 feet. The rig

PLATE VIII

U.S.N. Training Brig "Boxer."

built at Portsmouth N.H. 1904.

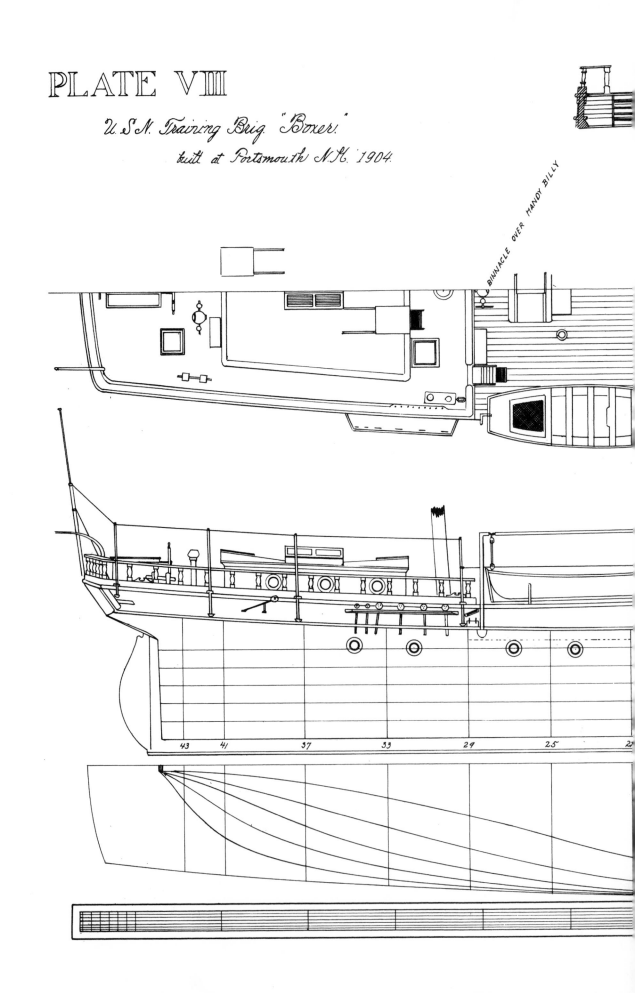

BINNACLE OVER HANDY BILLY

43   41   37   33   29   25   21

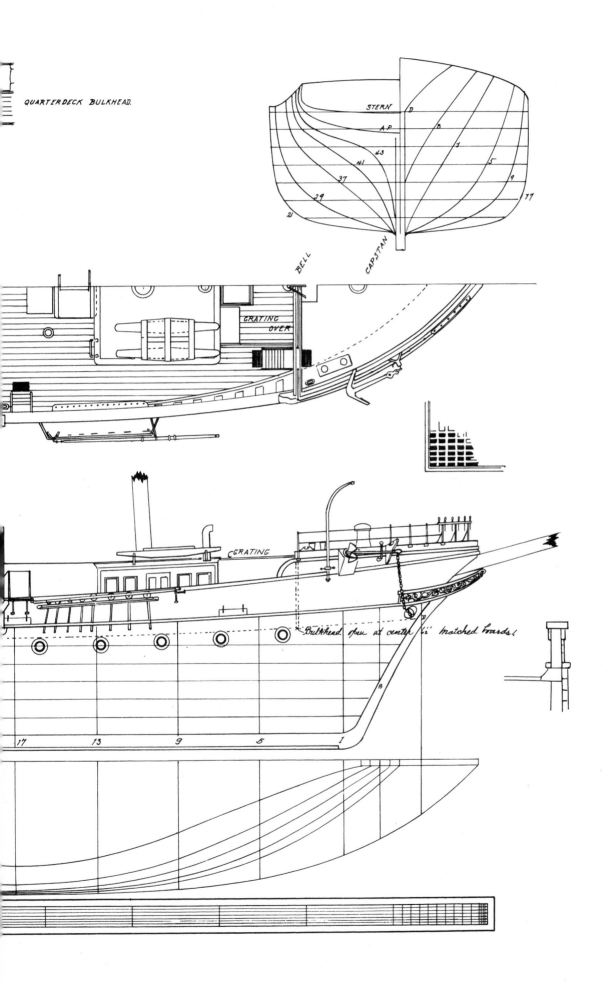

QUARTERDECK BULKHEAD.

STERN

D

A.P.

B

43

41

37

1

5

29

9

21

77

BELL

CAPSTAN

GRATING
OVER

GRATING

Bulkhead open at centre 1½" matched boards.

17

13

9

5

1

3

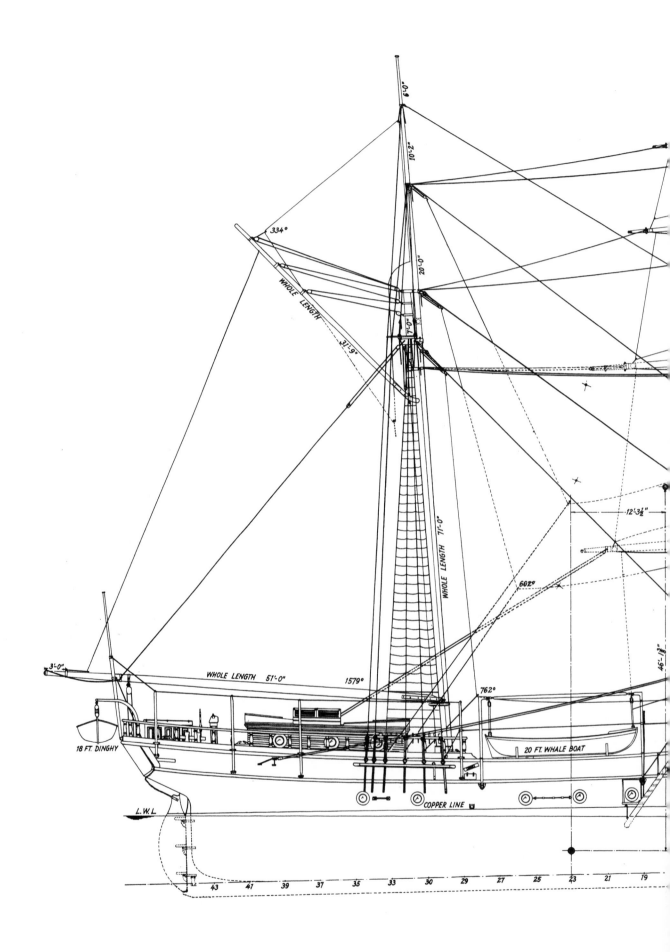

334°

WHOLE LENGTH

31'-9"

6'-0"

10'-2"

20'-0"

7'-0"

WHOLE LENGTH 71'-0"

12'-3½"

46'-1⅜"

605°

3'-0"

WHOLE LENGTH   51'-0"

1579°

762°

18 FT. DINGHY

20 FT. WHALE BOAT

L.W.L.

COPPER LINE

43   41   39   37   35   33   30   29   27   25   23   21   19

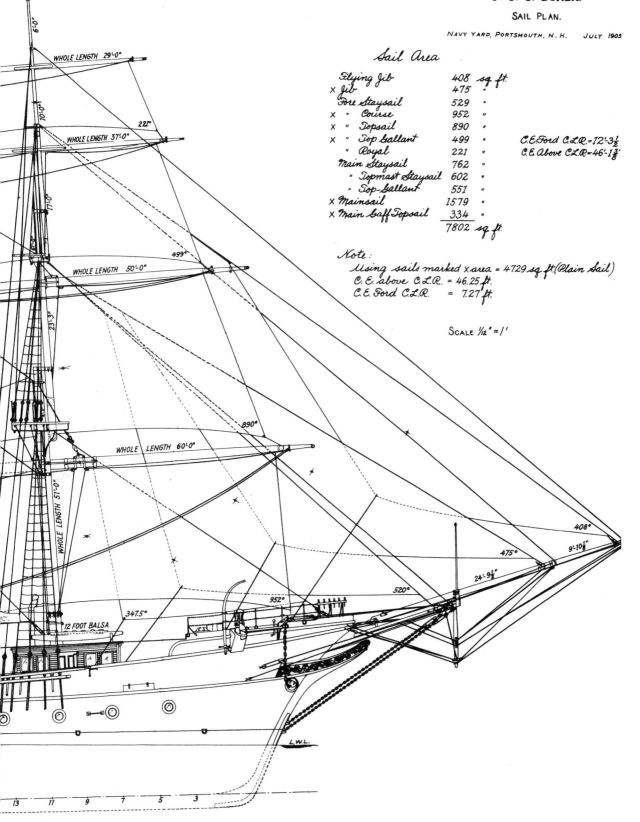

U. S. S. BOXER.

SAIL PLAN.

NAVY YARD, PORTSMOUTH, N. H.   JULY 1903

Sail Area

Flying Jib	408	sq ft.
× Jib	475	"
Fore Staysail	529	"
× " Course	952	"
× " Topsail	890	"
× " Top Gallant	499	"
" Royal	221	"
Main Staysail	762	"
" Topmast Staysail	602	"
" Top-Gallant	551	"
× Mainsail	1579	"
× Main Gaff Topsail	334	"
	7802	sq ft.

$C.E.$ Ford $C.L.R. = 12'\text{-}3\frac{1}{2}'$
$C.E.$ Above $C.L.R. = 46'\text{-}1\frac{3}{8}'$

Note:
Using sails marked × area = 4729 sq ft (Plain Sail)
$C.E.$ above $C.L.R.$ = 46.25 ft.
$C.E.$ Ford $C.L.R.$ = 7.27 ft.

SCALE $\frac{1}{12}'' = 1'$

PLATE IX

U.S.N. Sloop-of-War "Wasp"

Length   105' 7"   on dec
Beam extreme 30' 11"
Depth of hold   14' 1"
Crew   138
Carronades   16   32 ⌀ do

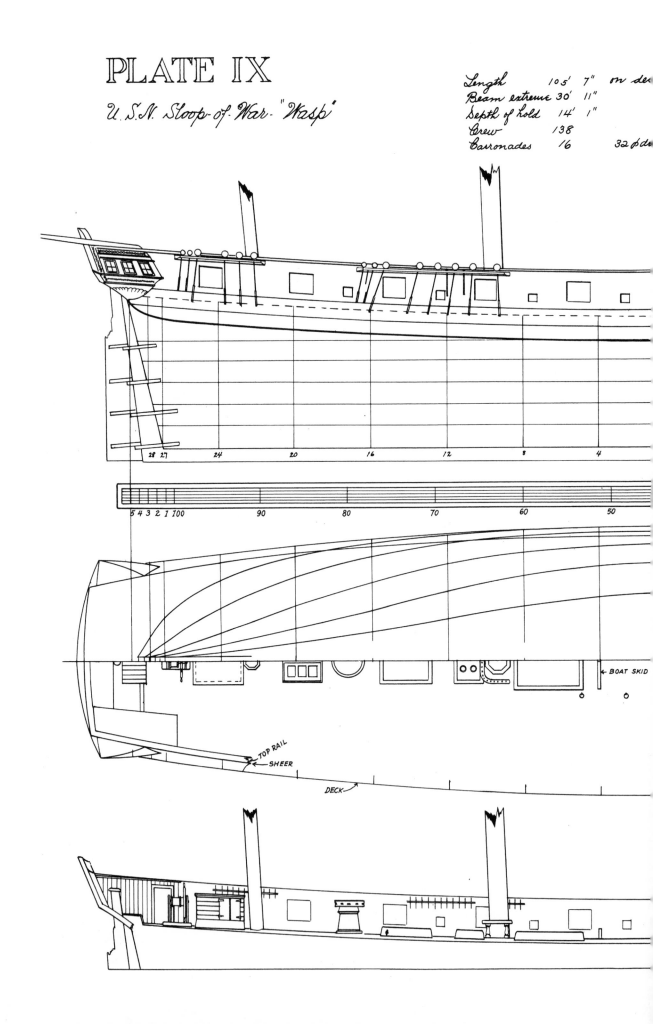

28 27   24   20   16   12   8   4

5 4 3 2 1 100   90   80   70   60   50

← BOAT SKID

TOP RAIL
SHEER

DECK

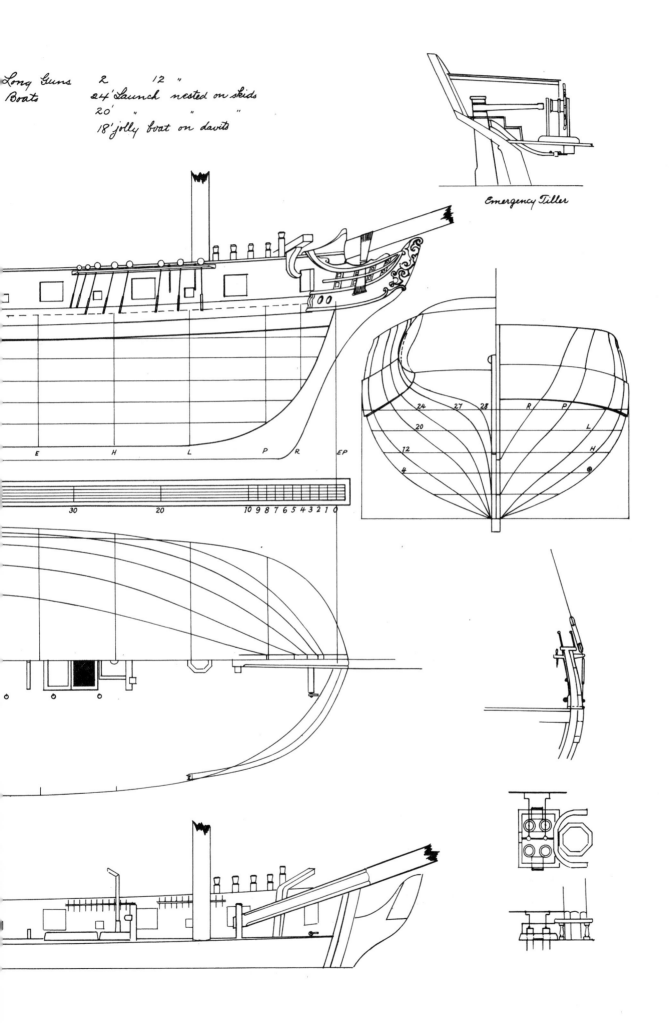

Long Guns   2   12 "
Boats   24' Launch nested on skids
               20'   "   "   "
               18' jolly boat on davits

Emergency Tiller

24   27   28   R   P
20   L
12   H
4

30   20   10 9 8 7 6 5 4 3 2 1 0

E   H   L   P   R   EP

U.S.N. Sloop-of-War "Wasp"
Rigging Sail and Outboard Profile Plan
1807

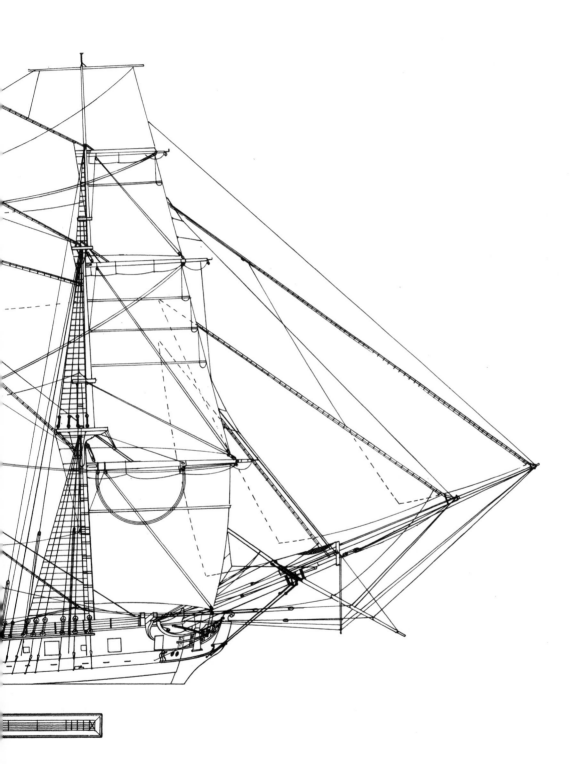

as a rule consisted of a jib and a leg-of-mutton fore and main sail, the foresail being the larger and set on a permanent mast, whereas the mainmast was removable for the purpose of shortening sail. Such boats were well adapted to negotiate the shallow water over the tonging beds, or to make landings at waterside farms to load farm produce, in the transportation of which they found employment during the seasons when oystering was prohibited.

The canoes lacked the carrying capacity to fit them exactly for this purpose or for the transportation of pay loads of oysters to distant markets. Since these trips were made when weather conditions were not good, and since the canoes were open boats, the crew had no protection from wind and cold and such trips were hazardous undertakings.

When the use of the dredge was legalized, the rig of these boats was found not powerful enough to propel the boat and pull the dredge or "scrape." The larger and conventional schooners, sloops, and pungeys in use had the power and capacity needed, but drew too much water to operate on the many shoal-water "rocks" or oyster beds. What was wanted was a hull of little draught and suitable capacity, log bottomed for durability, and with a simple rig, powerful enough to pull the dredge, a boat that would be able and steady under all conditions of wind and water. Such a vessel would of necessity be of greater freeboard and greater width than the canoe, but all-log construction did not lend itself to the construction of such a model. Length could readily be gained, but not the required height of side, or breadth.

To overcome this difficulty a boatbuilding genius resorted to the expedient of lengthening the log bottom and superimposing a framed and planked topside on what had been the sheer log of the canoe. The three top planks were fashioned to extend outward beyond the sides of the hull about an inch and formed the bends, so-called. The modelmakers' attention is directed to this, for these bends are a feature of all bugeye construction.

Like the canoe, this craft was sharp-ended, bow and stern. The hull was decked over and there was the necessary arrangement of hatchways and cabins. The rig of the canoe was adopted, but owing to its increased size certain modifications and changes became necessary. Both masts were permanently stepped and were usually supported with stays and shrouds. Booms instead of sprits were used to extend the feet of the sails. A feature of the rig is the extremely heavy bowsprit, apparently badly hogged. This hogging, however, is deliberately achieved. The top line of the spar follows a natural taper, while the under side is cut to produce an illusion, and the spar appears to bend downward toward the outboard end.

Both the bugeye and the skipjack models feature the longhead, which terminates in an embryo figurehead, and both show the typical knightheads; but only the bugeye utilizes these timbers as hawse pieces. The bugeye design as first conceived proved eminently satisfactory and, in lines, bugeyes of today follow the original. As in all sharp-sterned vessels, deck room aft was at a premium, and if the bugeye had any defect it was in the contracted space about the wheel. This fault was remedied by an invention of Captain Joseph E. Robbins of Cambridge, Maryland, who patented his device in 1908. His application called for the installation of a davit-supporting means for sharp-sterned boats. In effect it was a platform extended at the stern that gave to the bugeye the look of a boat with a back piazza. But since it not only provided support for the davits but also furnished the necessary deck space about the wheel, it was quickly installed on almost all bugeyes and has become a structural feature. With the introduction of patented wheels, the duck tail extending aft in continuation of the bends was added to give support to the rudder stock, and a bugeye whose after end does not terminate in a duck tail is now a rarity.

From the stern davits hangs the push boat. These little craft (about 10 feet long) are of every conceivable shape, round-bottomed or flat. The engine with which they are fitted is out of all proportion to their size. Generally, these are old automobile engines converted to marine duty; they make the push boat a useful auxiliary to the oyster boats. Conservation laws prohibit dredging with power-propelled vessels; therefore the oyster boat must rely on the wind, and when the wind fails over goes the push boat to take the skipjack or bugeye to port. How these push boats manage to stay afloat, weighted down as they are, is a mystery, but their great weight dictates the construction of the boat falls. Treble blocks at the davit end with double blocks below are none too powerful.

The *Edith F. Todd* was built in 1901 at Oriole, Maryland. She was of log-bottom construction and of a type similar to boats built earlier. Plate VII gives her plan, and a spar and sail plan is appended. The body plan is to the inside of the bends and the modelmaker should follow these lines in building the hull up to the under side of the deck, adding the bends to the outside later. These bends can be fashioned from a thin pine batten, which will bend to the curve of the hull. The sweep of the sheer and the lower edge of the bends must be cut to shape. Make a pattern from thin cardboard, obtaining the required shape by first bending it around the hull and then cutting it to fit. When taken off and laid out flat on the batten it will assume a surprising shape. The pattern taken for one side should serve for both, and will compel uniformity. At the stem and sternpost the bends should come to a knife edge. They should not appear to be rabbeted into the posts, as no rabbet was employed in the construction of the bugeye hull.

Paint the hull before rigging. Here the modelmaker can choose either the practically standardized coloration employed today, or can paint the model in the manner used at the time the *Edith F. Todd* was launched. Nowadays it is the practice to paint the hulls, deck houses, rails, and stanchions pure white. The underbody is generally red copper paint, while the decks and hatch covers are slate gray or a grayish blue. Mastheads, boom jaws, and bowsprit are all white, while the rest of the spars are unpainted.

When the paint scheme in vogue during the earlier days is employed, there is a greater latitude in the choice of color and the finished model may appear more interesting. Above the waterline the sides may be white or flesh colored, with the bends painted in contrasting green, gray, or some subdued color. The rails usually were white, while the deck houses and hatch coamings were darker blue or green. Often the decks were unpainted, but if paint was employed it was of the same color as the bends.

The decoration of the longhead was painted on and employed all colors as necessary, including a liberal amount of gold. The only carving was the figurehead, and as a rule this was painted Indian red. Whatever color scheme is chosen, it should be low in tone, and a garish appearance should be avoided.

Probably no other sailing vessel of her length is as easy to manage under sail as the bugeye. The rig has been so developed that this is easily accomplished by one man, releasing other members of the crew for duty elsewhere. During dredging, he sails the craft back and forth over the indicated area, frequently coming about, a matter requiring more than one man's attention in vessels of more complicated rig. A glance at the plan will show that the fore and main sheets and the centerboard pendant are belayed conveniently to the helmsman's reach.

The lift for the jib club is bent to the forestay about 2 feet above the hoist of the jack iron. Before being bent to the club it leads through the cringle of the jib clew. The standing rigging is of wire rope, and a wire-rope pendant with a large hook turned in its lower end goes over the foremast head with an eye, above the rigging (a Spanish burton) to which a tackle is hooked for catting the anchor. When not in use it is lashed to the fore starboard shroud. The centerboard pendant leads through the after hatch coaming, then over the cabin top to a tackle which belays on a cleat on the after end of the cabin, to starboard. The binnacle was placed in the cabin where it could be seen through the small window in the cabin's after end, so do not omit this feature!

In the fore rigging, just above the sheer poles, fasten the light boards to the shrouds. The shrouds should pass through metal staples on the backs of the boards. It will be noted that there is an unusually great drift between the deadeyes on the hull and those on the shrouds. This is intentionally contrived to permit the use of exceptionally long laniards which counteract the effect of rigidity in the wire-rope shrouds.

The anchors are iron-stocked, with chain cables, and are lashed to the rail forward. Lead the cable from the anchor to starboard, forward to the hook in the wythe at the outboard end of the bowsprit, back to the winch, taking two turns around the drum, and coil the bitter end down on deck. The port cable leads direct from the anchor to the winch. Later bugeyes had a cable tier below deck, and the bitter end led through small scuttles aft the winch.

Belay the running rigging as follows:

Jib lazyjack halliard to port shroud at sheer pole.
Jib downhauler to cleat on bowsprit.
Jib halliard to mast cleat to port.
Jib sheet to mast cleat forward.
Fore halliard to mast cleat to starboard.
Fore topping lift to fore shroud to starboard.
Fore lazyjack to fore after shroud to port.
Fore throat lift to fore after shroud to starboard.
Main halliard to mainmast cleat to port.
Main lazyjack to mainmast cleat to starboard.
Main throat lift to forward main shroud to starboard.
Main topping lift to cleat on boom.
Foresheet to cleat on deck house to port.
Centerboard pendant to cleat on deck house to starboard.
Mainsheet to cleat on wheelbox to port.

The modelmaker will have to make the foresheet block, as blocks of this pattern are unknown beyond the Chesapeake, and only a block of this kind should be used here, since it is a characteristic feature.

Both the skipjack and the bugeye are unusual types of sailing craft in design and rig. The appearance of either is somewhat improved by the addition of sails, as these lend character to the model. All in all, the miniature bugeye should make a highly colorful and interesting model.

The *Edith F. Todd* measured:

Length overall	64′	3″
Beam, extreme	18′	2″
Draught	4′	6″

PLATE VIII: UNITED STATES NAVY TRAINING
BRIG *BOXER*

The United States Navy's building program for the year 1903 called for the construction of three wooden sailing ships. This seems somewhat strange in view of the fact that forty years earlier the naval engagements of the Civil War had established without peradventure of doubt the value of the steam-driven ironclad and forecast the further development of highly mechanized warships.

The last sailing ships for the Navy were built in the decade 1840 to 1850, and developments in naval ship construction during the intervening years emphasized the fact that for combat use such vessels were decidedly obsolete. There were still some of these old-timers afloat—and there still are today—but they were carried on the Navy list chiefly as objects of historical interest or as relics of earlier naval glory. Some of them, with added superstructures, were serving as receiving ships, some as armories for the Naval Reserve. None were considered seaworthy or fit for active duty. Yet with full knowledge of this obsolescence, the Navy's Department of Construction and Design was authorized to design and build three sailing ships of apparently outmoded type. Two were to be bark-rigged vessels and one a brig. The barks were large ships authorized to cost not more than $240,000. One, the *Cumberland*, was to be built at the Mare Island yard, while the other, the *Chesapeake*, was laid down in the East. The brig to be named the *Boxer* was built at Portsmouth, New Hampshire, and was not to exceed $50,000 in cost.

The *Boxer* was built during 1903 and launched the following year. None of these vessels were armed; though the barks were designed to carry guns, none, apparently, were ever mounted. The *Boxer* was designed as an unarmed vessel. All these vessels were destined to serve as school ships for the training of seamen and apprentices, and served in that capacity until the outbreak of World War I, when they were transferred to other duties. The *Boxer* was at Norfolk in 1913, being refitted for Coast Guard service.

The officers who formulated the course of training for seamen and apprentices for the naval forces and also for ensigns at the Naval Academy, where the *Severn* served as a training ship, were imbued with the idea that it took a sailing ship to make a sailor. While knowledge of steamfitting, electricity, and mechanics was obviously imperative for service aboard our mechanized naval ships, still it was felt that training voyages in sail were better programs for imparting a knowledge of how to combat the elements, for teaching self-reliance, and for grounding men in the fundamentals of seamanship. This theory presupposed a faculty of naval men brought up in sail, both to command these ships and to impart instruction, but it soon became evident that the course of instruction at Annapolis and later service in the units of our Navy did not and could not train officers in sail; thus competent instructors were not being created and therefore this course of training was of necessity abandoned.

It was most fitting that one of these training ships should have been a brig, for as a class the brigs always enjoyed great popularity with Navy personnel. They offered opportunities for active service, their duties being similar to those of the modern light cruisers. Of necessity they had to be fast and their designers incorporated in their draughts the best and most advanced elements of construction to make them speedy, able little ships. Many followed the precepts of the Baltimore builders, whose Baltimore clippers were world-renowned, and the Navy's brigs showed the rake of keel and raking ends that featured those ships. In addition to the renown won for the speed, brigs won enviable fame for their victorious achievements in naval engagements. The officers and crews took great pride in the appearance of these vessels and much effort was made in their upkeep, the result being a vessel resplendent in paint and brightwork. Often at personal expense the officers and crews would install some furnishing or piece of gear that enhanced the ship's appearance.

The training brig *Boxer* of 1903 embodied many of these attributes and was a credit to her designers and her predecessors. She was designed to be fast and able and handsome. The name is traditional with the Navy, the first *Boxer* having been a British naval brig that fell a prize to our *Enterprise*, and the United States Navy kept both ship and name.

As an example of brig design, more properly in this case a hermaphrodite brig, it is a pleasure to produce the *Boxer's* plan in Plate VIII. This was re-drawn from the original plan.

Strangely, while the *Boxer* was of modern construction, the standing rigging was set up in the old-fashioned way. This type of rigging was no doubt used in order to provide lessons in rope work. However, the rest of her gear is modern. The lower yards are slung by cranse irons, as shown in the spar plan. The anchors are of modern type, while the old picturesque wooden catheads are replaced with metal fixtures of the new type.

The year 1903 was in the era of the "Great White Fleet," and the *Boxer* therefore is to be painted white above the waterline, coppered below. Her decorations and name were in gold and her rail was varnished. The metal around her port holes and deadlights was brass, kept highly polished.

The decks reflected the constant use of holystones. The insides of the bulwarks and the waterways were white. The deck houses and hatch coamings and gratings were varnished. The balsa-wood catamarans and the whaleboat were white, while the gig on the stern davits was varnished.

From the forecastle, extending to the roof of the forward deck house, was a varnished grating. The boat ladder and horse block were varnished and had brass stanchions with white rope hand lines. The boat boom was also varnished. The low stanchions forward were black, as were all chains. The tall stanchions, davits, and staff were painted white.

In the model, the lower foremast is painted white, but the mainmast on which the gaff slides is unpainted. The foreyard should be fitted with an iron jack yard to bend the sail to (see Chapter Four). All belaying pins were polished brass in varnished racks. The belaying-pin plan (Figure 32) does not apply to this model.

Rigging a brig, either modern or old, provides the modelmaker with a lesson in rigging full-rigged ships, for the rig combines features of both fore-and-aft and square-rigged ships.

The finished model should reflect the appearance of care that was lavished on the older brigs. Paint and varnish should be pristine, and the rigging may have a look of newness and not be out of keeping. Make the model handsome.

The *Boxer* measured:

> Length overall.......................125′ 6″
> Beam, molded........................ 28′ 3″
> Draught, at post..................... 10′ 5″
> Draught, forward.................... 8′

The spar measurements are given in the sail plan.

PLATE IX: UNITED STATES SLOOP OF WAR *WASP*

The ship sloop was the darling of the Navy, considered to be the war vessel *par excellence* for general service.

We go back a hundred years from the *Boxer* (to the year 1803 to be exact) and again find the Navy building brigs, the *Wasp* and a sister vessel, the *Hornet*. The life of the *Wasp* as a brig was short, for the ship-sloop enthusiasts got her soon after her launch and she was a ship sloop when commissioned. The *Hornet*, however, did get to sea under a brig rig, but in the end she had to succumb and was converted to the ship rig at the age of eight (1811).

Strange to say, both these United States warships were designed by a former English naval constructor. They were the brain children of Josiah Fox, later Naval Constructor for the United States Navy. Fox was authorized by the War Office to prepare the draughts for two large 18-gun brigs, to be fast and weatherly, comparable in size to the corresponding class of the Royal Navy. It is thought that he based his design to some extent on that of the American naval constructor B. Hutton, Jr., for the *Syren*, as both the *Wasp* and *Hornet* seemed very like her.

The career of the *Wasp* in the United States Navy lasted only until October 17, 1812, when she defeated H.M.S. *Frolic* in her sole engagement fought under the Stars and Stripes. Shortly after the fight, while repairing the damage suffered in the battle and being in no condition to fly or fight, she was forced to surrender to the British *Poictiers* (74 guns), which came up at this inopportune minute. So the *Wasp* lost both herself and her prize. After being sent to England she was taken into the Royal Navy as the *Loup Cervier*, only to be lost at sea in 1814. At the time of her engagement with the *Frolic* and her subsequent surrender to the *Poictiers* she was under the command of Master-Commandant Jacob Jones.

Leading up to the building of models of ship-rigged vessels which now follow, there is no better type to be found for modeling than the ship sloop. While the rigging of a vessel of this class is as complicated as if she were a line-of-battle ship, her hull construction is much simpler, since she was usually flush-decked. All vessels of the class carried fewer than 24 guns

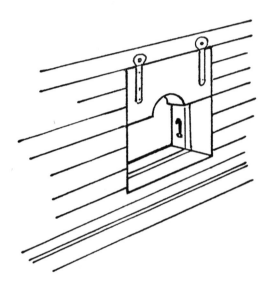

FIGURE 25. Wasp *gun port, lower lid in place.*

on one deck only, and all vessels so armed and with flush gun decks are properly called ship sloops or corvettes, whether propelled by wind or by engines. The present war has introduced a modern vessel called a corvette because it is of the flush-deck type, but in no other way does it resemble the old-time ship sloop.

There is very little in the hull construction of the *Wasp* that is complicated or presents the modelist with difficulties in the building. The *Wasp* and the *Oliver Cromwell* (Plate XI) had gun ports. The *Wasp* had ports with double lids, an upper and lower lid like an old-fashioned door. Figures 25 and 26 show how the lids were made. The upper half was a removable piece that was held in its place with hooks and eyes on the sides of the port, inside. It was also secured with a short piece of rope. The lower half of the lid was hinged at the bottom. Bridle ports had the lid made all in one piece and it was hinged at the top.

Josiah Fox's original plan shows a timber head immediately above the second port hole, and the plan in Plate IX copies the original. These timbers were very useful for belaying warps and other lines.

The bulwarks of warships were sealed up on the inside and the stanchions did not show inboard. They were called solid or closed bulwarks. This

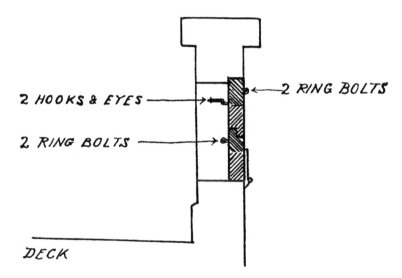

FIGURE 26. *Section of* Wasp *gun port, showing the manner of fitting and fastening the lids.*

inside planking had two purposes: it served to make a breastwork of the bulwark for the protection of the men and also strengthened the structure. It was thus that the bulwarks of the *Wasp* were built. The main or cap rail, of course, went on top of these. A closed bulwark is much easier for the modelist to make, as he can omit the timber heads in building lift models. The only difficulty occurs when there is considerable tumblehome to the bulwark. Above the deck and pinned down to it put on a narrow strip of wood all around. Do not make it all in one piece, but of short lengths, and butt the ends together. This piece should be thick enough to come up just under the port sills. Put in the port sills or mark them on this piece. Resting upon this piece go short lengths that build the bulwark up between

the openings for the ports. Cap the whole with another strake that will
build the bulwark to the under side of the rail. These pieces are as wide
as the bulwark is thick, they are staggered and in fact somewhat resemble
the lifts that build the model (Figure 27). Care must be observed in this

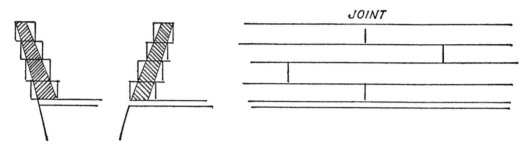

FIGURE 27. *Construction of a solid bulwark: strakes with flare, strakes with
tumblehome; method of laying.*

construction at the bows where the tumblehome changes to an outward
flare. Here the process of staggering is reversed. The curved pieces around
the bows had better be cut to shape. See that the lower lift makes a close
fit on the deck, since any gap here would be fatal and would spoil the looks
of the model. The upper strake should be cut to the sheer of the under
side of the rail.

After the rail is on, fashion from black hairpin wire the iron stanchions
for the hammock netting (Figure 28). Fit them in place on the rails and
rig the lines as shown in the sail plan, just before the process of rigging is
started.

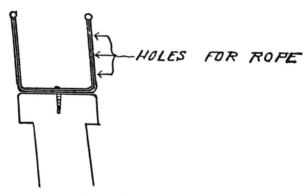

FIGURE 28. *Stanchions for hammock netting.*

Also before the model is rigged aloft, put the eyebolts around the ports and in the deck for the gun tackle rigging. Figure 29 shows how to rig a gun, while the place for the eyebolts in the deck is shown on the deck plan.

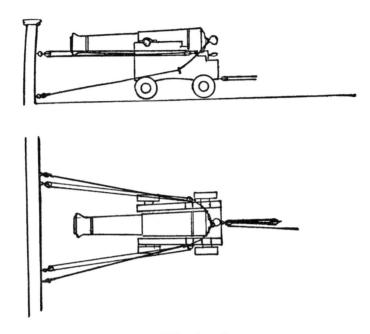

FIGURE 29. *Rigging for a gun.*

The sail plan is most complete in details of rigging. Snake the stays as shown in the plan, as this is a feature of all war vessels. Figure 30 shows a stay properly snaked.

The *Wasp* measurements and armament are given below. Since the spars are drawn to scale in the spar plan, their measurements are not given.

Length on deck...........................105′ 7″
Beam, molded......................... 30′
Beam, extreme......................... 30′ 11″
Depth of hold......................... 14′ 1″
Crew ....138 men
Carronades, 32-pounders............... 16
Long guns, 12-pounders................ 2

The rigging plan clearly shows the lead of all the rigging. If you try to put on the sails, you will involve yourself in a tremendous undertaking. Furthermore, the sails will not look well. I would only put on enough of the rigging to control the bare yards.

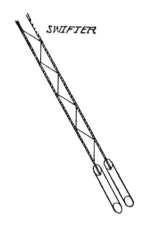

FIGURE 30. *Snaked stay.*

Figure 31 shows a ship's bowsprit of the time of the *Wasp;* the bowsprits of the *Republican* and the *Oliver Cromwell* are similar. The springstay and the forestay come down to collars on the bowsprit. They set up with hearts and are snaked together. The bobstays (two on the *Wasp*) set up to collars immediately ahead of the stay collars, with the shroud collar next. All this rigging is kept from coming inboard by a cleat on the spar. The mainstay leads past the foremast to starboard. A cleat or batten (Figure 32) on the foremast keeps it in place. A heart is turned in the lower end of the stay. It sets up to an eyebolt on deck at the bows. Make a small eye in the end of the springstay, pass the stay around the foremast, through the eye, and lead it up to the mainmast head under the mainstay. This end has two legs with a small eye in each, between which a laniard reeves back of the masthead. The fore topmast stays reeve through bee holes at the end of the bowsprit, and have either a deadeye or block turned in the ends to set them up, with a luff and luff tackle to eyebolts in the bows. The main topmast stay reeves through a block or thimble in a collar at the foremast head, leads down on deck aft the foremast through the trestletrees, and sets up with a heart to an eyebolt in the deck aft the mast. The springstay leads to a thimble strapped around the foremast head under the bibbs, leads up through this thimble to another strapped around the foremast head above the rigging, where it sets up.

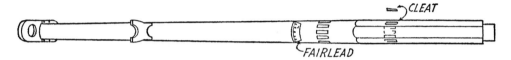

BOWSPRIT WITH SADDLE FOR JIBBOOM

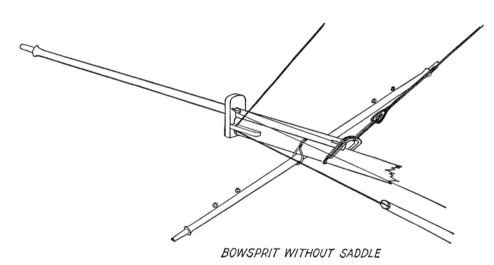

BOWSPRIT WITHOUT SADDLE

FIGURE 31. *Bowsprit of a ship contemporary with the* Wasp.

A large thimble or small heart is lashed in a collar around the mainmast. The mizzen stay leads through this down on deck, a heart is turned in at the end of the stay, and it sets up to an eyebolt on deck.

Plate XIII shows a yard all rigged and also slings and jeers, while Figure 32 is a belaying-pin layout.

The *Wasp* carried two launches, one 24 feet long and one 20 feet long, nested amidships, and an 18-foot jolly boat on the davits aft.

The *Wasp* is to be painted black above the waterline, with a yellow streak through her ports. This streak should be from a line about 2 inches (by scale) above the top of the ports, carried down to a line even with

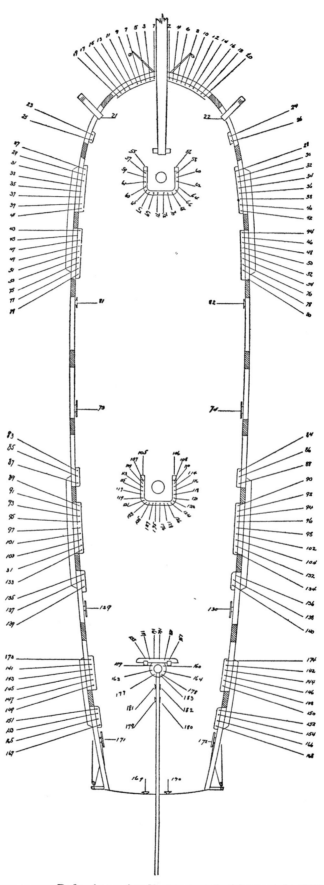

FIGURE 32. *Belaying-pin diagram suitable for the* Wasp.

PLATE X

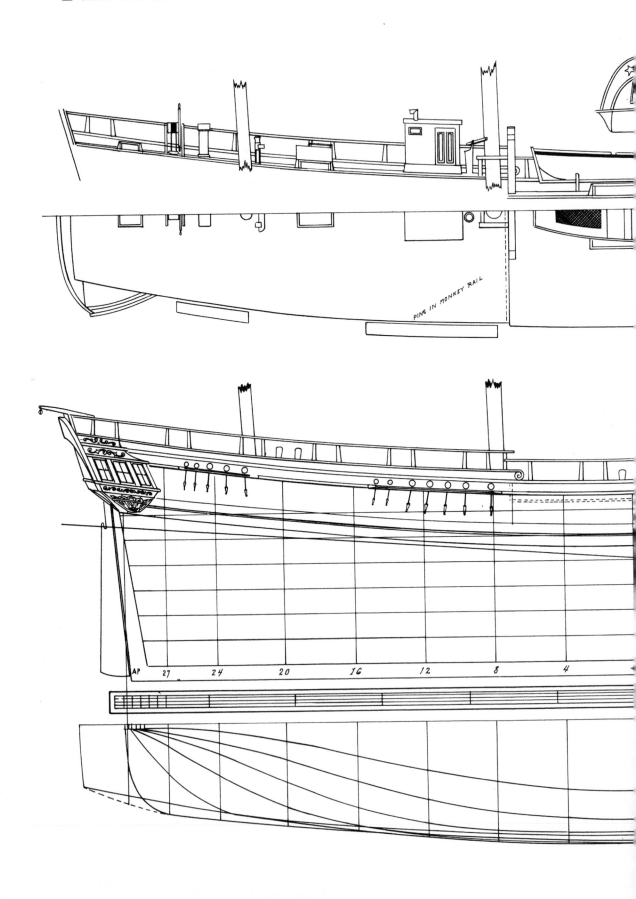

PINS IN MONKEY RAIL

AP   27   24   20   16   12   8   4

Merchant ship "Republican"

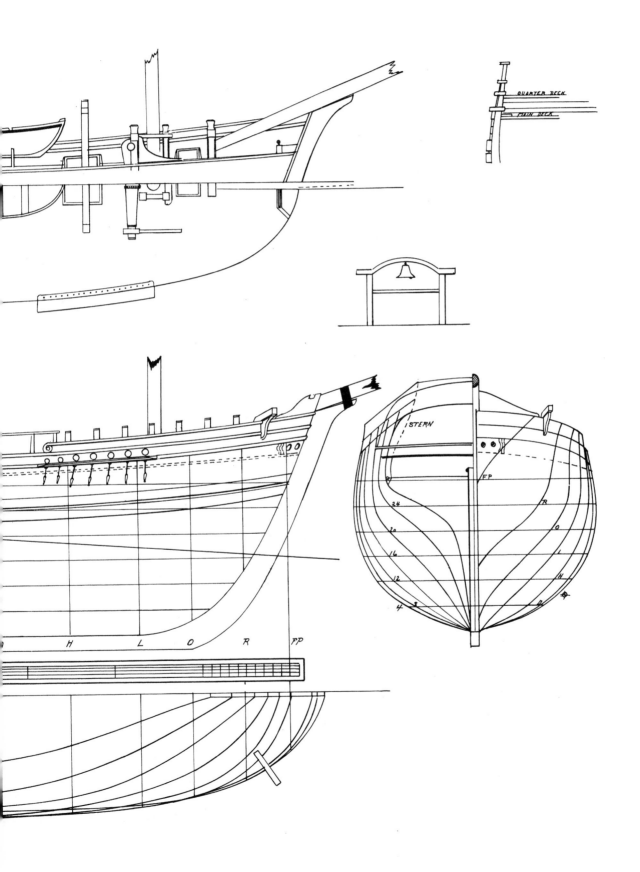

QUARTER DECK

MAIN DECK

STERN

FP

24
20
16
12
4

R
O
L
H

H   L   O   R   FP

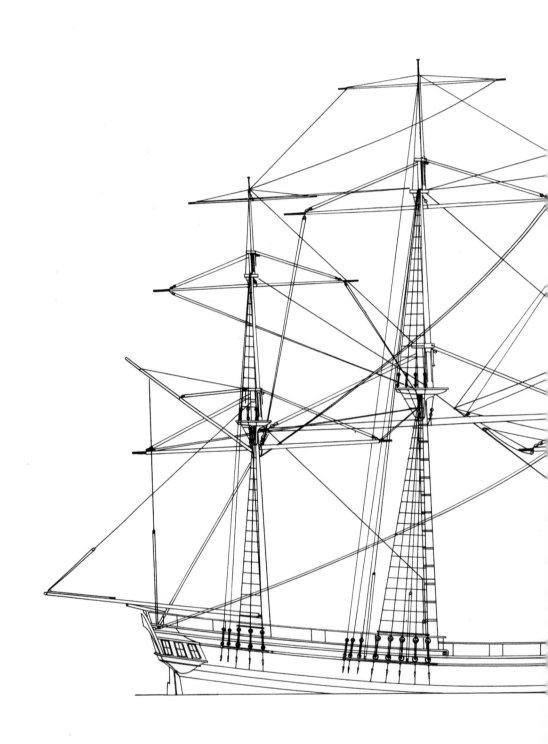

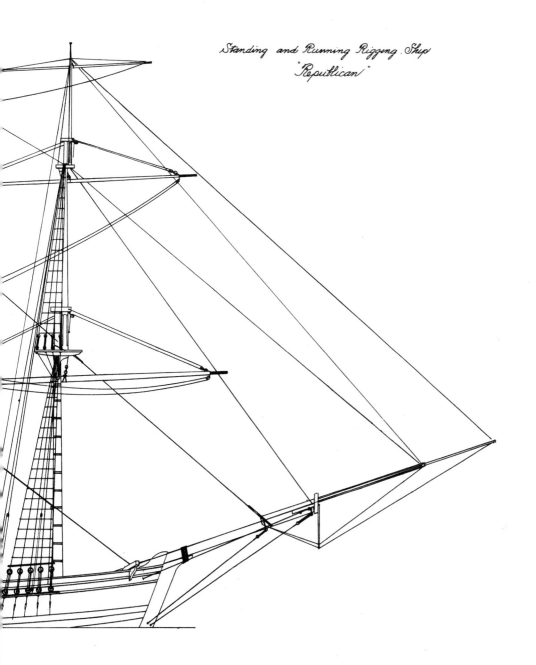

Standing and Running Rigging. Ship
"Republican"

PLATE XI

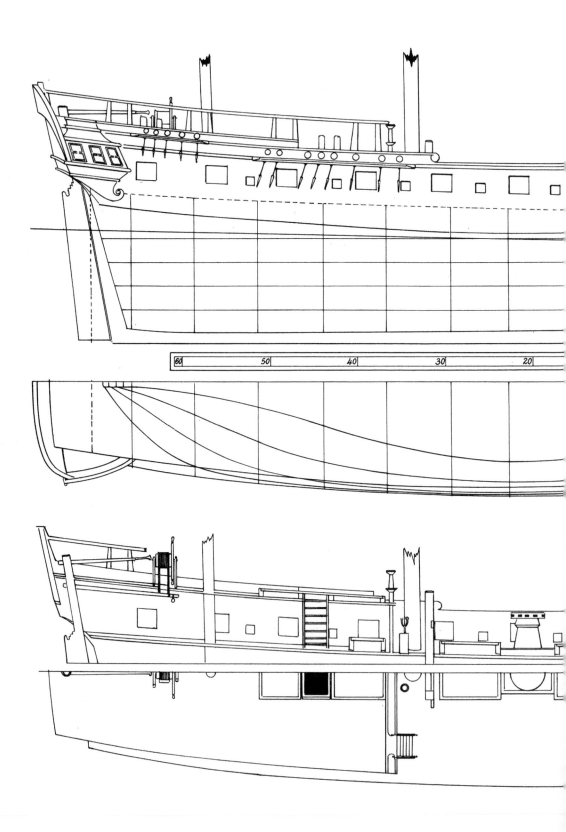

OLIVER CROMWELL

87 6 5 4 3 2 1 0

LWL

LIFT

| 60 | 50 | 40 | 30 |

OLIVER CROMWELL. *Ri*

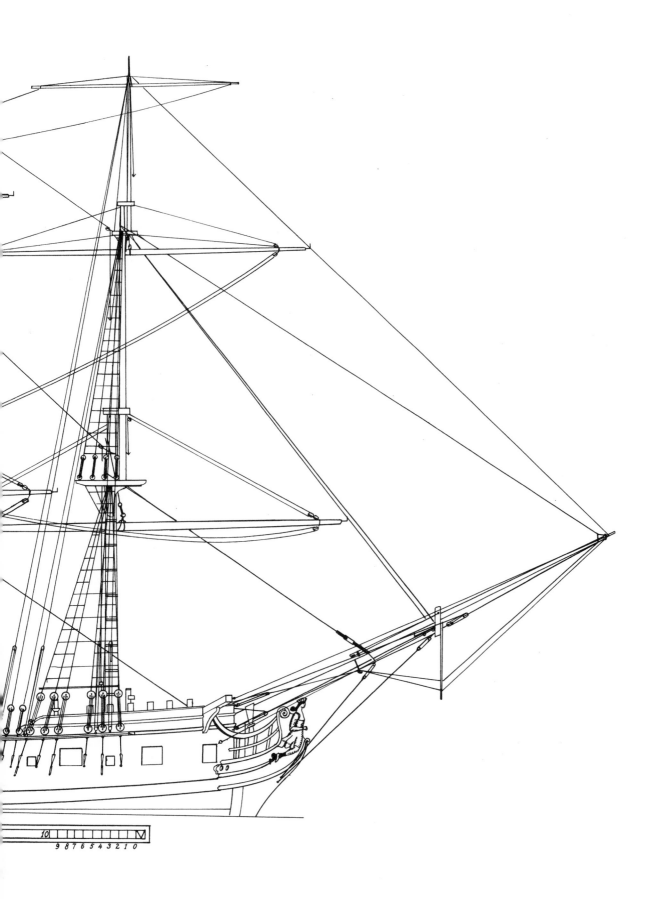

10 ║║║║║║║║║║ ░
9 8 7 6 5 4 3 2 1 0

KEY: 1, 2, fore buntline; 3, flying jib downhaul; 4, jib downhaul; 5, fore top-mast staysail downhaul; 6, dolphin-striker outhaul; 7, 8, spritsail lift; 9, 10, fore tack; 11, 12, fore bowline; 13, 14, fore topsail bowline; 15, 16, dolphin-striker backrope; 17, 18, fore topgallant bowline; 19, 20, fore royal bowline; 21, 22, jib sheet; 23, 24, fore topmast staysail sheet; 25, 26, flying-jib sheet; 27, 28, fore lift; 29, 30, fore forward leech line; 31, 32, fore after leech line; 33, 34, fore topsail buntline; 35, 36, fore topgallant clew line; 37, 38; 39, fore topgallant buntline; 40, jib halliard buntline; 41, fore topmast staysail halliard; 42, flying-jib halliard; 43, 44, fore royal clew line; 45, 46, fore royal sheet; 47, 48; 49, 50, fore topgallant sheet; 51, fore topgallant halliards; 52, fore royal halliards; 53, 54, main bowline hauling part; 55, 56, fore topsail sheet; 57, 58, fore topsail halliards (small ships belayed on the fife rail generally, but halliards often be-layed at the pinrail as described in the text); 59, 60, fore clew garnets; 61, 62, spritsail brace; 63, 64, fore lower reef tackle; 65, 66, fore topsail clew line; 67, 68, fore topsail reef tackle; 69, 70, truss tackle; 71, 72, jeer falls; 73, 74, fore-sheet belays on cavil or cleat; 75, 76, main royal bowline; 77, 78, main topgal-lant bowline; 79, 80, main topsail bowline; 81, 82, main tack belays to cleat; 83, 84, main forward leech line; 85, 86, main after leech line; 87, 88, main top-sail buntline; 89, 90, main topgallant clew line; 91; 92, main topgallant bunt-line; 93, 94, main lift; 95, 96, main royal clew line; 97, 98, main royal sheet; 99, 100; 101, 102, main topgallant sheet; 103, main royal halliard; 104, main top-gallant halliards; 105, 106, main topsail sheets; 107, 108, main topsail halliards (same as fore halliards); 109, 110, main clew garnets; 111, 112; 113, 114, main lower reef tackle; 115, 116, main topsail clew line; 117, 118, main topsail reef tackle; 119, 120, main truss tackle; 121, 122, fore royal brace; 123, 124, main topgallant brace; 125, 126, main topsail brace; 127, 128, main brace; 129, 130, mainsheet; 131, 132, cross-jack brace; 133, 134, mizzen topsail brace; 135, 136, main topgallant brace; 137, 138, main topsail bowline; 139, 140, main topgallant bowline; 141, 142, cross-jack truss tackle; 143, 144, mizzen topsail clew line; 145, 146, mizzen topsail reef tackle; 147, 148, mizzen topsail buntline; 149, 150, mizzen topgallant sheet; 151, 152, mizzen topgallant clew line; 153, mizzen top-gallant halliard; 154, mizzen topgallant buntline; 155, 156, mizzen topsail sheet; 157, mizzen topsail halliard; 158; 159, 160, main topsail brace; 161, 162, main royal brace; 163, 164, main topgallant brace; 165, 166, spanker-gaff throat hal-liard; 167, 168, spanker-boom topping lift; 169, 170, spanker sheet; 171, 172, main brace; 173, 174, cross-jack lift; 175, 176, main jeer tackle; 177, 178, cross-jack jeer tackle; 179, spanker outhaul; 180, spanker inhaul; 181, gaff topsail tack; 182, gaff topsail sheet; 183, gaff topsail halliard.

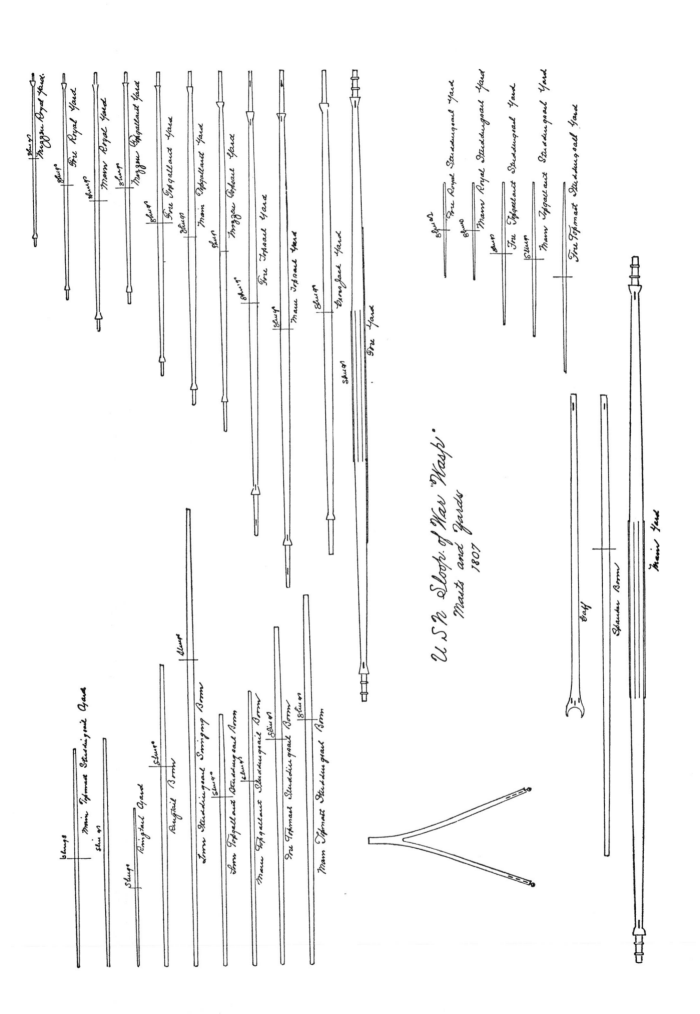

U.S. Sloop of War "Wasp".
Masts and Yards
1807

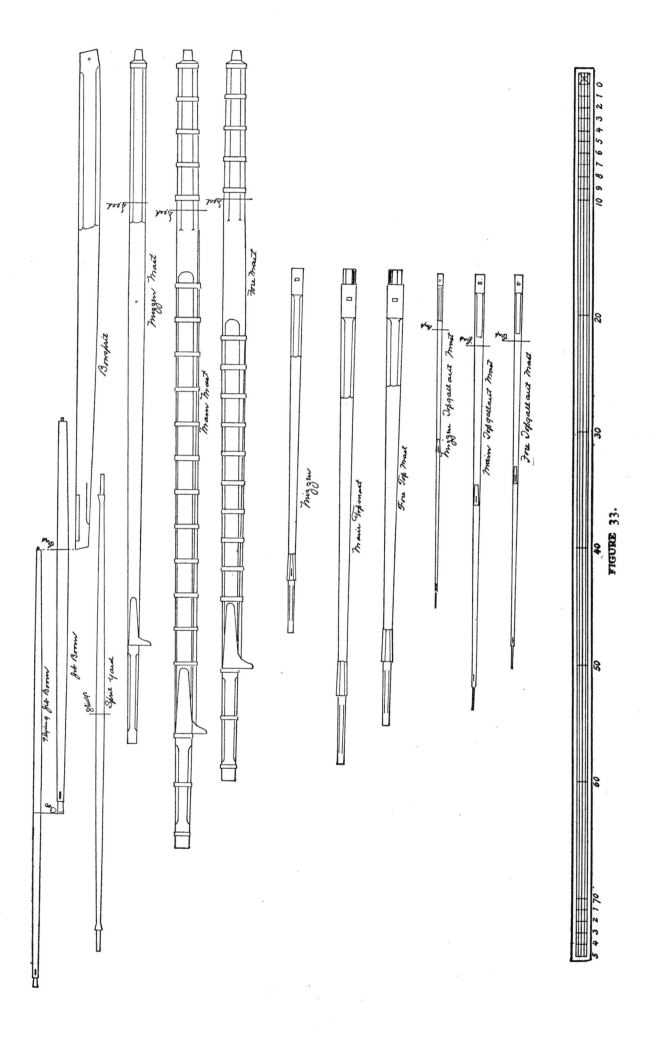

FIGURE 33.

the lower part of the quarter galleries. Port sills and lids should be black. The boats may be white or black. The guns are black. Either yellow or buff is proper for the head rail, billet, and cheek knees. Paint white stripes on the stern, with white window frames. Decorate the trail board in black, white, and gold. The main rail is black. Have the inside of the bulwarks and the hatch coamings a lightish red. The bowsprit is black. Black is used for the lower masts, tops, and caps; leave them unpainted aloft.

PLATE X: AMERICAN MERCHANT SHIP *REPUBLICAN*

It was only natural that a young country, such as ours was around the year 1800, should have depended on comparatively small ships for the transportation of its merchandise. For many reasons, small ships were best suited to the needs of the times. Small ships could be built for a comparatively small sum and in a reasonably short time. They required only small crews to operate them, making them economically desirable. While these early American merchant ships were exceedingly well built and were by no means unseaworthy vessels, every voyage was nevertheless a hazardous undertaking; and should it result in the loss of a small ship, such a loss was not necessarily crippling to the owners.

Yankee ingenuity and Yankee seamanship got the best out of these ships and the custom-house records of the times report many successful voyages. In fact, it was these successful and profitable voyages that were the foundation of many great American fortunes and firmly established some of our great shipping houses.

"Old Time Ships of Salem," published by the Essex Institute of Salem (1922), lists a large fleet of small merchant vessels that were notable in the history of that port. No doubt each American coastal city could evolve as long a list and as notable, for the small ships sailed from every port along our seaboard. It is neither the list of ships nor the annals of their voyages that make this book such a delight to the ship lover; rather it is the fine color reproductions of old ship portraits that are of such great interest to the student or the modelmaker. From the illustrations in this book one can make himself familiar with the appearance of the ships that constituted a large part of the American merchant marine of the early part of the nineteenth century.

It must not be imagined, because we concern ourselves with the small merchantman, that the United States did not at the time have large ships also. This was the period of the establishment of our great transoceanic shipping lines—the Black Ball Line, the first to inaugurate regular sailings; the Dramatic Line; the Red Cross Line, and others. Rivalry and competition between the transatlantic lines was responsible for the development of the packet ship, thought by many to be the finest example of American shipbuilding.

Most ships, either large or small, at the turn of the century were constructed with elaborate heads and quarter galleries, but there was in use at the time a type of small vessel whose outboard sides were clean of these extraneous features. Most books give the credit to the designers and builders of the clipper ship for doing away with these features that had survived for centuries, but the designers of the small merchant ship antedated their ideas by many years. Some retained the quarter galleries and had bald heads, and some were built in semblance of the older accepted type. Other construction features of the small merchant ship were practically flush decks, there being no forecastle or quarter deck, but beginning just forward of the mainmast the deck was raised about 8 inches continuing all the way to the taffrail; the galley was in a movable small structure just aft the mainmast; and there was a gallows frame for stowing the long boat between the fore and the main.

On the deck of the *Republican* under the bowsprit is a manger running from bulwark to bulwark. The hawse pipes opened into this manger from the outside of the ship and the muck and slime brought inboard on the cables was deposited in this trap before it could foul the decks. Most ships have mangers, but they are generally hidden from view by other construction. Put in this feature; it is of interest. One can safely omit the waistcloths, but the spare spars and the pinnace should be included. The davit at the stern rests on the monkey rail and the small boat hangs with her keel about on the level of the deck.

As a rule the small merchant ships did not cross royal yards and were altogether simple in rig and construction. "Old Time Ships of Salem" gives pictures of two vessels of this type that are wonderfully replete with detail, and as we have selected a vessel of this kind to be the subject of Plate X these pictures have supplied any missing detail that is not shown in the original draught. Yes, the plans given in Plate X are from a rare original draught made shortly before 1800 by a notable American ship designer.

Samuel Humphries, the able son of an accomplished father, learned the intricacies of ship design while apprenticed to his father—Joshua Humphries, our first Chief Naval Constructor and designer of the famous *Constitution*. Like Joshua, Samuel Humphries is chiefly notable for his work as a naval constructor. He entered the employ of the government in this capacity in 1815 and became Chief Naval Constructor about 1825. To his credit are the designs of the line-of-battle ship *Pennsylvania*, the ship sloops *Vincennes, Warren, Lexington,* and others of this class, and the store ship *Relief*.

While working as an apprentice for his father, Samuel designed ships for non-naval purposes, and among the papers that he left are to be found the most complete lines of a small merchant ship. As she is named *Republican* in the draught, it is logical to assume she was built, but records do not disclose where or for whom or what became of her.

Her lines reflect Samuel Humphries' ability, for they show that he designed a vessel of maximum carrying capacity and at the same time introduced elements of design that must have made her notably fast.

Again from the Salem portraits, we can learn how these ships were painted. A tallowed (white) underbody and from the waterline to the wales a dark reddish yellow was common. Wales were darker, or painted in a contrasting color, then yellow again to the main rail; the rails were painted like the wales, while a streak of the color ran between the rails from the mainmast aft. The stern was dark, with colored stars and decoration. Inboard the ship was painted throughout, there being no brightwork (varnish). Her low bulwarks were light yellow ochre, her house and coamings darker, with moldings in color. White was little employed at the time, so paint the longboat like the bulwark, with a dark streak of contrasting color under the gunwale. The lower masts were painted like the sides (not white), and they had dark hoops. Mastheads were dark but not black, and had lighter caps. Construction of the gallows frame is shown in the last plate. The manger at the bow had a roller on the manger board over which the cable passed.

All vessels of the period carried an armament of sorts, and the *Republican* will not be out of character if she shows a battery of long guns of small bore, probably four- or six-pounders. Merchant ships more often than not did not fill the ports with guns, but there should be enough to fill all ports on one side. It was the custom to move the guns across the deck in order to fire a broadside. The guns were rigged at the ports of the ship's open rail in the same manner as if she had high bulwarks.

This little ship will make a model that is interesting in type and of a good size for display.

PLATE XI: AMERICAN PRIVATEER *OLIVER CROMWELL*

England at time of the American Revolution was the dominant naval and maritime nation of the world. Her naval ships of all types numbered over 500; her merchant ships were legion. To contend with this mighty armada of England, the Colonial naval strength was exactly zero when hostilities began. We did have a certain number of merchant ships and in this extremity the Continental Congress had to rely on these to perform naval duties. The first ships of our Revolutionary navy were chartered or purchased merchant ships converted to our needs. However, the needs were for ships in quantities and we had neither the time to build many nor the money to hire suitable ones, if such could have been found.

In this emergency, privateering was encouraged by the new government. Vessels of all kinds, from sloops to full-rigged ships, were encouraged to put to sea to harry England's commerce. Private owners of vessels made idle by the war saw at once the possibilities of huge profits and quickly armed their ships and put to sea in quest of prizes. The records show that these vessels were often successful and that some of them earned great amounts of money for their owners and crews.

The tales of the adventures related by the crews of the returning ships excited the minds of seafaring men of the Colonies and berths aboard privateers were eagerly sought. It was usually possible to get either a ship or crew, and the English commerce suffered greatly at the hands of the privateersmen.

In this way the Revolutionary government enjoyed the services of a supplementary navy of sorts, at small expense. The total expenditure per ship was for delivering the required letter of marque, and while the profits of privateering all went to private individuals the country at large benefited through needed goods being brought into port. All other maritime ventures at the time were under embargo, and the country was in sore need of imported goods.

However, there was another side to the picture. Everything was fine until, through some unfortunate chance, the privateer fell in with an English naval vessel; then, too often, she became a prize. The most unpleasant outcome of such an happening for the crew was the ensuing sojourn in a prison or prison ship. England regarded American privateersmen as but little better socially than pirates, and treated them accordingly Officers and crew all fared alike in the grim prisons, and the fare was horrible by all accounts.

Kenneth L. Roberts gives us a very vivid account of the romance of privateering in the tale of the *Lively Lady*, and paints a black picture of life in a wartime prison.

It was in reading "Stars on the Sea" that I came across a mention of the privateer *Oliver Cromwell*, her success in capturing prizes, and the fortune she earned for her owners. The story does not tell, however, that she was later taken a prize and—being a fine ship—was sent home to England by her captors. Here she was surveyed and her lines were taken off and her plans eventually found their way into the archives of the British Admiralty. Through the courtesy of a friend I obtained a copy of the draught, and it is with much gratification that I include her plans herein.

This vessel, before being named for the dour Oliver, was called *The Terrible Creature*—to my way of thinking, a name that creates much speculation in the mind of anyone considering her career. It must have been a change of ownership that accounts for a change of name so drastic.

At any rate there was nothing about the ship's appearance that would cause anyone to call her a terrible creature, for she is a very handsome little ship. Her home port was Newport, Rhode Island. And when she bore the name of *ye Terrible Creture*, Benjamin Moses was her sailing master. She was commanded at different times by Nathaniel West, Benjamin Cole, and James Barr. She was a ship of 150 tons burthen, 16 guns, and had a crew of 100 men. Though only 84 feet long on deck, she was frigate built or was of that persuasion during her privateering days, so she would probably have solid bulwarks, like the *Wasp* of later date. She had a quarter deck and forecastle. There were ports under these on the gun deck; you will keep them closed in the model so as not to show the block construction used in making it. The quarter-deck rail was open, with open ports, except across the stern; the carved arch board here partially closed the rail. The stern ports on the quarter deck opened through the arch board. The ports were made like those of the *Wasp*. Between the *Oliver Cromwell's* gun ports were sweep ports, which had lids called bucklers that fitted into rabbets at the bottom of each port. At the fore end of her quarter deck there was an athwartship rail on carved stanchions and this was duplicated at the after end of the forecastle deck. Incorporated in this forward rail was the belfry.

Build the hull all complete with the exception of the quarter galleries and the arch board. This includes, of course, the head knee. Be sure you cut the hole for the gammoning in this piece; you will find it convenient to put on the rope gammoning now while you can get at it. See Plate XIII and Chapter Four for a description of how to rig the gammoning. After the hull is finished put on the quarter galleries which project outward at the stern.

If you will look at Plate XI you will see that there is what looks like a molding just under the windows of the gallery. Make a block to fit between this molding and the one above the windows. This block will be wide in the after part and will curve in to meet the hull at its forward end. In the sides of this block countersink window spaces. Paint the flat surfaces a very dark blue and when the paint is dry fit in window lights of celluloid; then over the lights put a window framing to fit in the window openings snugly. This framing is hard to fashion out of wood if the model is small, so I advise that you cut it out of a fine quality white card, stiles and all. Glue the cardboard frames in on top of the celluloid window lights. When painted, these frames will appear as well as if made of wood. Make the windows at the stern in the same way, cutting the openings in the block. The lower molding is actually a floor; it continues around the stern as a wide molding under the stern windows. Glue and brad to the under side of the small block and put the assembled pieces on the hull, hiding any nails. The after end of the block should continue the curved sweep of the stern of the main block, and the floor should project enough to form a seat for the arch board. Under the floor put on a second block to fill the space down to the lower molding. Treat this as a floor at the sides and as a molding across the stern. Under this floor at the side comes still a third block, heavily carved in a classical pattern, that melts into the hull at the heavy wale. Above the windows put another floor piece, whose outboard edge is a continuation of the main rail. Above this flooring comes the roof of the structure. Study the plan in the Plate XI and get the shapes of the various pieces of the structure well in mind before shaping the pieces. The after ends or faces of all the pieces are continuous with the contour of the stern of the block, and actually widen the stern by the width of the pieces. The arch board is a separate piece. For ease in carving, it should be made of pine. Also, to avoid cross-grained wood, make it in three sections: two upright pieces and a piece across the top. It has a rounded surface of the same contour as the ship's stern. If you nail it in place use wooden treenails reinforced with glue; if you use iron brads, countersink the heads deeply and fill the holes with plastic wood.

Paint the hull white or gray-green below the waterline and yellow above, with black or very dark blue wale. Between the main rail and the second rail on the quarter deck and forecastle, use the same color used for the wale. The lids of the gun ports and the sweep ports are to be buff. Paint the stern inside the arch board dark with buff moldings, and the arch board buff. Paint the rails buff and the quarter galleries below the floor under the windows dark, the head dark, picked out with buff up to the top cheek knee, with the upper rails and brace pieces buff. Paint the figurehead to your fancy. Paint the inside of the bulwarks red or light green. Leave unpainted the hardwood rails and belfry athwartship. Paint the bowsprit dark.

The *Oliver Cromwell*, a small ship, measured:

Length on deck.......................85′ 9″
Beam, extreme.......................26′
Draught, at post.....................12′ 7″

The boats carried were a longboat on deck and a jolly boat astern on davits. The dimensions of the *Oliver Cromwell's* spars can be scaled from the rigging plan.

PLATE XII: INTERNATIONAL "M" CLASS
YACHT, 50–800

It was the intention to follow the plans of the earlier types of sailing craft with the plans of one of our modern cup defenders and show the ultimate development of the sloop. But instead, it was decided to present the plans of a sloop just as modern in lines and gear as Mr. Vanderbilt's *Ranger*, yet having the added advantage when built that she can be taken to the nearest water and sailed and raced. In order that the builder can find competition to try out his boat's abilities, Plate XII gives the plans of an International "M" Class miniature yacht, popularly known as a 50–800. The model derives its name from the fact that it is 50 inches long and has 800 square inches sail area.

Each summer offers owners of these small racing craft plenty of competition, and when war and its alarums do not hamper, there are international races. The contestants in these events have to prove their superiority and the competing boats are selected by the American Committee of the International Yacht Racing Association.

It may also give added zest to the pleasure of creation to see that the result of your craftsmanship is an able boat. Two 50–800's were built in my workshop and were sailed in adjacent Great South Bay under conditions that were a test for any boat, and they acquitted themselves well.

There may be a model yacht club near your home that will welcome you as a member and your boat as a competitor. From it you can obtain the rules and regulations that govern this class.

Do not deviate from the specifications as given in the plan. All necessary gear which has the approval of the I.Y.R.A. can be purchased from dealers in model boat fittings if you do not feel like making it. The dealers are also prepared to make suits of sails of the correct dimensions for these little racers and they are cut to enhance the speed of the model.

In general, the specifications for these boats call for an overall length of 50 inches (with a ¼-inch tolerance) and a sail area of 800 square inches. The area of the fore triangle is not restricted, only the total sail area being taken into consideration. There are certain prohibitions, so do not get over-ambitious. You cannot use movable keels, metal fins, or fins without hollow garboards, and no centerboards, lee boards, or the like. The roach of sails must not exceed 2 inches and the battens of the mainsail shall not number more than four, 4 inches long. In the head sail, 2-inch battens are allowed, of which there shall not be more than three that divide the leech into approximately equal parts.

There is no limit to the height of masts, but spars shall not exceed ¾ inch in diameter. The masts and the spars may be hollow or bent; masts may rotate or be of bipod construction.

There are other factors in the rules that chiefly concern the designer and some that concern the setting of sails and extra sails that the model yacht racer must know so as to keep within the racing rules.

The making of all small parts of the gear is hardly worthwhile when excellent items for rigging can be purchased. Sheaved and swivel blocks, miniature turnbuckles, and proper cleats all come exceedingly well made. The Braine steering gear is, I believe, a patented device, but it is invaluable and should be bought and installed. The boat will sail better with it.

Wire for stays comes in single strands; I prefer a twisted wire, as described in Chapter Six. It is just as strong, is more flexible, and can be spliced, so make this yourself. Where you splice it into turnbuckles, serve the splices with linen thread and paint the servings with white paint. Build the paint up thick and smooth.

The choice of color for the hull is optional. In such large boats every conceivable color is found. For the underbody use a regulation marine paint well rubbed down. A contrasting color boot-top and a narrow gold stripe along the sides just under the deck sets the vessel off. Paint her inside as well as out to preserve the hull. Have the hatch covers removable so that air can reach the interior and aid in drying out. A dry boat sails faster.

Speed has to be built into a boat, and nobody can tell you how it is done. It is the touch of the master that produces fast boats—and I hope you have it.

CHAPTER FOUR

RIGGING

I T IS not within the scope of this book to describe in detail the rigging of all the models as shown in the plates. The sail plan of each vessel shows clearly the lead of the ropes, and in most cases the gear employed to make the rigging operative is also shown in the plans or explained in the text. This chapter deals with the rigging in a general way and aims to be explanatory in cases where the plans are obscure regarding some way of achieving an end. Plate XIII is designed to show such adjuncts to the rigging as were used when their form is not clearly shown in the other plates and plans.

Rigging on ships is of two distinct types, standing and running. The standing rigging of a ship is devised to support the various spars. It is fixed in place and does not function in a mobile way. The running rigging, as the name implies, is mobile; it reeves through the blocks and controls the movement of sails and spars. Therefore the standing rigging that supports the fixed spars must be in place before the running rigging is rove. All sailing vessels are rigged in that order.

To a sailorman, the way a rope is made is important, and determines its place and use aboard ship. In general three kinds of rope were used in rigging: Hawser-laid, cable-laid, and shroud-laid. Hawser-laid rope is composed of three single strands of rope yarn and is laid, or twisted, right-handed (with the sun). Shroud-laid rope has four strands laid in the same way, with the sun, while cable-laid rope is of nine strands, three strands of three strands each, which is laid left-handed (against the sun). These twists govern the manner of the employment of the ropes. The riggers so arranged that the strain put upon the ropes will tend to tighten the twists and strengthen the ropes. The way an eye splice is made, a deadeye turned in, or the way a rope is seized to itself is all governed by the twist or lay.

THE STANDING RIGGING

Ropes are treated to protect them from wear caused by chafing, by being wormed, parceled and served. Worming means filling the interstices of a twisted rope with spun yarn to give the rope an even surface. Parceling is wrapping over the worming with narrow strips of tarred canvas. Serving is winding small stuff (spun yarn) closely over the parceling, heaving it tight with a serving mallet. The old rule should be followed here:

"Worm and parcel with the lay;
Turn and serve the other way."

Ropes of the standing rigging are always served in places of wear and exposure, shrouds and stays where they go around the masthead and where eyes or hearts are turned in. Modelmakers find that linen cord of small diameter does not lend itself well to this treatment; the resulting job is cumbersome so they usually put up the rigging without serving, particularly on small models. I recommend, unless the model is built to a scale of at least ¼ inch to 1 foot, that you abandon serving—but you should turn in the deadeyes, thimbles, etc., and make the seizing to accord with the ropes. You can buy properly laid rope from tackle dealers or dealers in model findings for use where indicated.

Great care should be exercised in making and setting up the shrouds of the models, if for no other reason than looks. Of all the rigging, the shrouds appear most prominently to the eye of the beholder.

Shrouds in many old vessels were made of cable-laid rope, and such rope should be employed to fashion them for models. While it is out of sequence, we will describe the making and rigging of the shrouds and you can perform the operation in its proper order later, with a knowledge of how to do it.

Generally shrouds are made in pairs. A single strand of the proper length is doubled in the bight just below the bend; the two legs are seized together to form an eye that will fit over the masthead snugly; a deadeye is turned in the lower end of each log, that eventually is made fast to the lower deadeye on the hull. A shroud of a ship is served where it goes around the masthead and where the eye is turned in. If there is an odd number of shrouds (on port or starboard) the odd shroud is eye-spliced at the masthead.

Measure the distance from the bolster on the trestletrees at the masthead to the partners on the hull, and drive two heavy pins in a board at points this distance apart. Beginning at one pin, lay a coil of the cordage around both pins. Continue this operation with the rope or cord, and lay a coil for each pair of shrouds in turn. The first turn will be the first pair of shrouds to starboard. The second coil will be the first pair to port, followed by the second pair to starboard. The shrouds alternate in this manner until enough coils have been laid for all the pairs of shrouds. If there are six shrouds to each side of the ship that means three pairs to a side. It is obvious that, as laid in the coils, each succeeding coil will make a slightly longer pair of shrouds than the preceding pair. Mark each coil for identification as to sequence. Cut the coils straight across at the starting point and you will have the required number of pairs of the proper lengths. The variation in length is deliberately achieved, and will be taken up as the shrouds are set up. It is also obvious that the after shrouds must be much longer than the forward pair if we are to keep the deadeyes in a straight line horizontally.

In rigging a ship it is customary to get the shrouds over the mastheads first, then the stays on the lower masts, and then the fore and aft stays. There are deviations from this rule and exceptions to it, but we do not have occasion to discuss them here. Form the eye in the bight of the shortest pair of shrouds and put it over the masthead; shove it well down until the eye rides on the bolster of the trestletrees. Bring the legs down to starboard through the lubber hole of the top and turn in the deadeyes left-handed as shown in Plate XIII. After turning around the deadeye the short end of the shroud is seized to itself with a round seizing immediately above the

PLATE XII   *Sailing M...*

JIB HOOK RACK

International M Class
Length overall   50"   ¼" tolerance
Sail Area   800 sq.
Headboard. not to exceed ¾" at base.
Jib stay   "   "   "   80% of height of headboard.
Height of mast   unlimited.
Battens   4 main-sail   evenly spaced
    "   3 jib   "   "

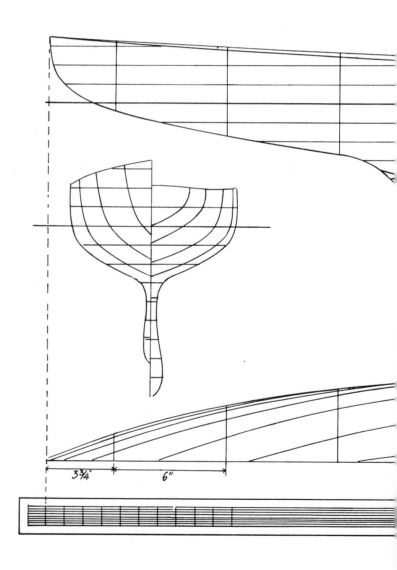

3¾"   6"

Class 50-800.

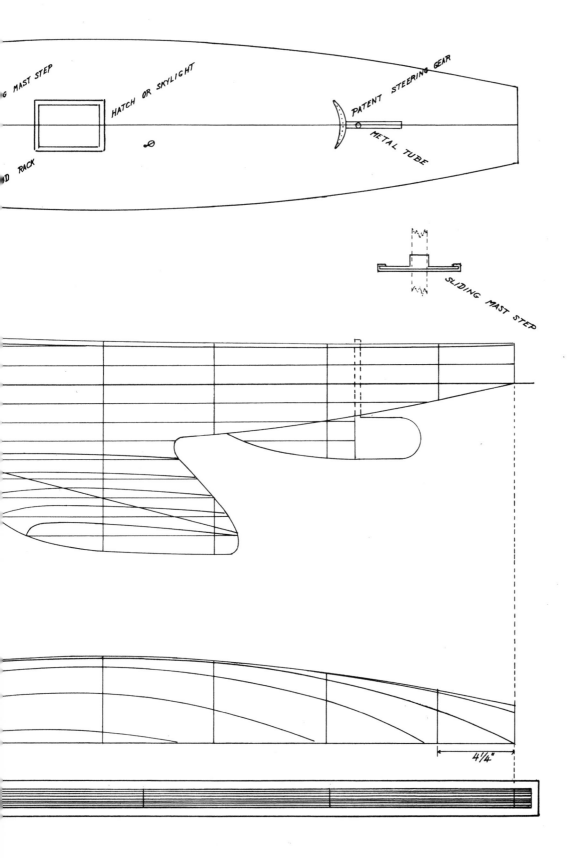

ING MAST STEP

HATCH OR SKYLIGHT

PATENT STEERING GEAR

METAL TUBE

D RACK

SLIDING MAST STEP

4¼"

SCREW EYE

HOOK

WIRE JACKSTAY

MAST

deadeye, with another seizing above that close up to the bitter end. The eye of the second pair of shrouds rests on the eye of the first pair at the masthead, and the shrouds lead down to port. The other pairs follow in order, first to starboard and then to port, until all are over the masts. The port shrouds should lie with the short end aft and this end is forward to starboard when the shrouds are set up.

The laniards that connect the deadeyes of the shrouds to the deadeyes in the channels should be about one-third the diameter of the shroud, while the deadeyes should be apart a distance equal to four diameters of the deadeye unless plans show otherwise. This rule will give the approximate length needed for the laniards. Cast a stopper knot on one end of the laniard and reeve the laniard through the deadeye from the inside out. On the starboard side with cable-laid shrouds you begin at the after hole and reeve forward, but when you cross the ship you begin with the forward hole and reeve aft. The end of the laniard, after reeving through the last hole, which will be in the lower deadeye, is brought up and taken around one part of the shroud above the upper deadeye and then around both parts of the shroud until the end is expended. It is then stopped to the shroud.

A piece of wood or pole, called a stretcher or squaring staff (now called a sheer pole) is seized to the shrouds athwart all shrouds and just above the deadeyes. It should parallel the top of the rail or sheer of the vessel when in place.

To make a ladder for the men to go aloft on, ratlines are employed. They are evenly spaced as they go aloft, at convenient stepping intervals. An eye is spliced in each end of the ratline by which it is made fast, first to the forward shroud (seized). It is then clove hitched around the intervening shrouds and is seized fast to the after shroud. A common spacing of ratlines is 15 or 16 inches.

All the standing rigging is well tarred and so has a blackened look. To obtain this appearance rub the cord with black flytier's wax or brown or black shoemaker's wax and then rub it down smooth. Do not give the rigging the appearance of being painted, which will result from using black paint or varnish.

Plate XIII shows supplementary rope work which the modelmaker should practice in order properly to make fast the various ropes. It is the neatness of the eyes, collars, stropping of blocks, etc., that makes well-rigged models.

The spar plan of the *Wasp* is applicable to small ships of the period and can be used for making the spars of the *Republican* and the *Cromwell*, though the dimensions may change.

Many of the models have wire-rope rigging, and it has long been the bane of the modelmaker to fashion an imitation of the rope found aboard sailing craft. I hit upon a way to make this wire rope so that it is a more than good imitation. Rope of any diameter can be made by starting with strands of wire of proper dimensions.

Picture wire, as found in packages in the five-and-ten-cent store, forms the stock for making it. Pull out three strands of this wire from a coil. Fasten the ends together in the eye of a small screw eye and hold the screw eye by its shank in a vise. Pull the other ends of the strands through a second screw eye, and when they lay taut make them fast. Put the shank of this screw eye in the jaws of a bit stock. Now draw the strands taut between the eye in the vise and the eye in the bit stock. Rotate the bit stock and it will twist the strands into a proper-looking rope. The wire rope can be given a right or left hand twist and any number of strands can be used. Wire rope so made can be spliced properly to form eyes, and turned in for deadeyes or turnbuckles.

Fittings of various kinds—which include deadeyes, bullseyes, and hearts —all had their place aboard ship, and a properly made and properly rigged model will employ them in the right places.

All the masts above the lower ones are supported by standing backstays as well as by the shrouds. These backstays reach from the tops of their respective masts to the channels. The topgallant backstay is the after leg of the after pair of topgallant shrouds. The backstays set up to small deadeyes in the channels.

After the standing rigging, the next consideration is the running rigging. How much of this it is necessary to show depends upon the model. If you put sails on a square-rigger then you must rig her completely. If you show her as she would be in port with her sails sent down, you can then eliminate over half the number of ropes shown in the plate as running rigging, and yet show the model in correct condition.

One could fill pages in describing the running rigging of the yards, and limited space prevents our doing so. Yet a model, to be worthwhile, must be correctly rigged. We hope that the figures of yards and their rigging, as shown in Plate XIII, will be more explanatory than any written description. Combined with the rigging plan and the small figures of Plate XIII that show how the rigger accomplished his ends, all needed information is there. There are many rigging books that give detailed instruction for rigging ships (see the Bibliography).

It is not necessary to determine the exact sizes of rope used for the rigging. We can be sure, however, that rope of larger circumference was used to rig the lower fore and main masts than was used to rig the comparatively light mizzen or royal masts. For any rigging, get hard-twisted linen cord. Three-strand can be used for the running rigging and can be had in several diameters. Linen fishing line has the right twist, and is available in many diameters, but it is hard to find it dyed a rope color. Buy the linen cord white and dye it to need. There is a table of rope dimensions that gives the proportionate sizes of ropes for each rigging operation, and a great variety of dimensions are given. Lay out your rigging to diminish in size as you rig aloft, strike a general average for size at each mast, and your model will be well-rigged. There is, of course, a differentiation made in the rope sizes on each mast, and this is more apparent in the standing rigging than in the running rigging. Get the stays and shrouds of the right proportions to the spars.

Ship's iron work, for modelmakers, is a delicate job. The making of the iron bands with eyes for the mast tops and bowsprits is the most common job, especially in modern types of fore-and-afters. It is comparatively simple to make such bands in the following manner. Cut a strip of sheet metal to the desired width of the band. Bend up the metal to form the eyes (Figure 34). Shape the band to the size required. A touch of solder will hold together the pieces that form the eyes. Drill holes in the turned-up pieces of the right size for the eye, round off the corners where the eye is formed, and a band is made.

To metal strop a deadeye is quite a trick if you wish it to look well, and the easiest way I ever discovered to do the job is to start with a soft metal ring of small wire, larger than the deadeye that you are stropping. To make the connecting eye, bring the wire ring together into an eye with long-

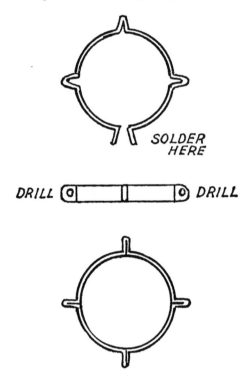

FIGURE 34. *Metal bands for the ends of spars.*

nose pliers, and draw it tight at the same time around the deadeye (Figure 35).

It would be well to bear in mind that rings of this type usually have a soldered joint and heating them will melt the solder. They can be re-soldered afterwards, of course, and it is best to have the joint come below the deadeye where the wires are squeezed together so that the solder will cover both pieces of wire, as this joint will be covered by the battens on the edge of the channels and will not show. Also brass, when heated and al-lowed to cool slowly, has a tendency to become hard, the opposite of which is true regarding iron and steel. Perhaps copper wire would be the better material for the model builder, and I have found this to be true in most cases. Steer clear of spring brass, German silver (nickel silver), or iron wire unless you have had considerable practice in soldering. Annealed brass and copper are best.

By using rings of proper diameters links for the chains can be nicely fashioned. Heat the metal rings until the metal is pliable and the ring can be bent or shaped as desired. You can make eyebolts from bank pins. Form the eye by bending the pin about a round object like the shank of a small twist drill of the proper diameter; with the pliers, adjust so that

CLOSE UP

SOLDER TWIST IF NECESSARY

FIGURE 35. *Metal-stropping a deadeye.*

the eye is properly centered on the shank of the pin; then close the eye to the shank with a small drop of solder. I have found that you can buy these eyebolts very cheaply from the dealers and that it is a waste of time to make them; resort to it only in an emergency.

There are many good books on the rigging of ships that will supply the modelist with complete rigging details. Most books deal with the rigging of definite periods. We can only give details of rigging as they apply to the vessels shown in the plates, which are by no means all-embracing.

THE RUNNING RIGGING

The running rigging of any vessel consists of those ropes that run or reeve through blocks and are used to control the various spars and sails. The running rigging of a fore-and-aft rigged vessel is comparatively simple, and the spar and sail plans of the fore-and-afters here given should guide the modelmaker correctly when it comes to rigging one of these models. This is also true of the rigging of the fore-and-aft sails of a square-rigged ship, but the rigging of a square sail and the yard becomes a more complicated matter. So that the builder may get a working knowledge of the rigging of such a ship, a general description of the rigging of the yards and the sails is here attempted. Also, a belaying-pin plan for a small ship is appended, but it must be remembered that this is a tentative plan as no belaying-pin plans exist for the ships in our plates; where ropes belayed on ships was a matter for the captain's determination and was never an arbitrary matter. This plan can be used for rigging other and larger vessels by adding additional pins to take care of additional sails and spars. The builder is cautioned to see that all ropes lead and belay in such manner that one rope will not interfere with any other.

The yard of a ship probably was at first simply a tapered and rounded spar that crossed the mast for the purpose of spreading a square sail. As ships developed, the middle of the lower and topsail yards became octagonal, and a saddle which rode against the mast was added to the after side of all yards. The ends of the spar were shouldered and thus formed the yardarms. A pair of cleats was placed on the forward side at the center of the yard. Between these cleats the slings go, and this part of the yard is called the slings of the yard. Horses (foot ropes for the men to stand on) are first rigged on the spar. An eye is spliced in the end of a rope and is put over the yardarm, the other end reeving through thimbles in stirrups at intervals along the yard, and is bent to the strap of the opposite quarter block. The sail was bent directly to the yard on old-time ships; small ropes called rovings passed from the head rope up over and around the yard. Later-day ships fitted first a rope, then an iron rod called a jackstay that passed through eyebolts in the top of the yard and reached from yardarm to yardarm, to which the sail was rove and from which the foot-rope stirrups hung.

The rigging of all yards is substantially the same, though the form of the apparatus used to achieve similar ends may differ as the weight and size of the yards change. The rigging of all yards consists of the four following parts:

1. The parrals that attach the yard to the mast.

2. The slings or tyes to which are attached the halliards (which sway the yard aloft).

3. The lifts attached to the yardarms, that steady them, and by which the men can move the ends of the yards up and down.

4. Lastly, the braces that are used to rotate the yards around the masts and brace them in position.

In one way the lower yards of a ship differ somewhat from the other yards aloft, in that they are more or less permanently fixed in position at the top of the lower masts. They are lowered only in case of need for replacement or repair, never for the purpose of shortening or taking in sail. Since the lower mast does not need to serve as a track for the yard to travel on, it can be painted, and certain parts of the rigging may be attached to it by means of straps put around the mast. The parral that holds a lower yard to a mast (see Plate XIII) is constructed somewhat differently from those parrals used aloft that have to slide up and down the upper masts. The former are made of rope and are attached to yard and truss tackles with the falls coming on deck that permit the crew to draw the spar close to the mast or allow it to move away from the mast as conditions require. The parrals of the topsail yard and often the topgallant yard, which must slide freely on the masts, consist of a series of lignum vitae balls or rollers with wooden trucks between them, a more elaborate form of the necklaces of balls that serve as parrals to hold the gaff or boom to the masts of all fore-and-afters. Generally the parrals of the topgallant yards and always of the royal yards were made of two short hide-covered ropes strapped around the yard and seized together (see Plate XIII).

Slings for the lower yards consisted of a collar with thimble turned in that went over the lower masthead above the rigging. The thimble hung down forward, coming over the forward crosstree and between the trestletrees. Another thimble was turned in a smaller collar that went around the yard, the thimble passing upward aft the yard through the bight of the collar, and a laniard was passed alternately from one thimble to the other, the end part being frapped around the whole. There was no halliard for the lower yards, but men-of-war were rigged with jeers that were used on occasion to lower the yard, at which the time slings and parrals were cast off. Later-day ships, after about 1820, had chain slings.

To sling the topsail yards, strap a block (large single) at the center of yard. Lash two single blocks, one on each side of the masthead hanging down close under the stay collar. A rope called a tye is reeved through one of the blocks at the masthead, through the single block on the yard, and then through the block on the other side of the masthead, the ends of the tye hanging down aft the mast. Double blocks, called fly blocks, are turned into the ends of the tye. The end of the halliard is made fast to a becket in the strap of a single block in the channel, reeves through the fly block, back to the single block, to the double block again, and belays to the pinrail on each side of the ship. When the halliards belay at the fife rail, as in some small ships, the single block is made fast to an eye in the top and the halliard leads down aft the mast and sets up to a tackle made fast to an eye in the deck and belays at the fife rail. Sometimes there is a sheave hole in the topmast head below the trestletrees and the tye (single) reeves through this sheave, then through a single block on the yard, and the standing part is taken up and seized around the masthead above the trestletrees. A single block is turned in the end of this tye. A runner reeves through this block and has a double block turned into each end through which the halliards reeve.

The topgallant tye is bent to a thimble in a strap put around the center of the yard, or is bent to the yard directly. It reeves through the sheave hole in the mast top and the halliard reeves like the topsail halliard, the lower block being strapped to the topsail trestletrees. The halliard belays on deck either at the pin or fife rail.

If the fore topmast halliard belays to port, the main will belay to starboard and the mizzen will again belay to port. The royal halliards go the same, but the topgallants will be belayed in reverse order.

The lifts for the lower yards, because of the size and weight of the spars, should go double, though very small ships might employ single lifts here. Double lifts are rigged in the following way. The lift reeves through a single block that is fastened to an eyebolt in the under forward end of the mast cap. It then reeves through the lift block at the yardarm and is taken up and the end is made fast to an eye in the mast cap. The other end leads down and a single block is turned into this end. A single block is hooked to an eye in the channel, just within the foremost deadeye; the standing part of a tackle is bent to the becket of this block and rove through the block in the end of the lift. It then returns and reeves through the becket block and the fall comes inboard and belays at the pinrail. When the lift goes single it reeves through blocks in the mast cap as before, and an eye spliced in the end goes over the yardarm outside of the topsail sheet block. The hauling end sets up to a tackle as before.

Topsail yard lifts are also usually double. A hook is spliced into the end of the standing part, which is hooked into an eye in the forward end of the cap. The other end then reeves through the lift block at the yardarm, goes up and reeves through the lower sheave of the sister block, which is seized in between the two foremost topmast shrouds. The hauling end of the lift is made fast with a hitch or is belayed to a cleat on one of the lower shrouds.

Topgallant lifts go single and reeve through thimbles seized in between the foremost topgallant shrouds and are hitched around or belayed to cleats on the topmast shrouds in the tops. Royal yards are rigged in the same way.

The fourth and last pieces of rigging common to all yards are the braces, but before rigging them let us see that the rigging of the yardarms is proceeding in proper sequence. Plate XIII shows a topsail yard and alternate methods of rigging the yard are shown. A yardarm may be rigged either with brace blocks or with pendants. The yardarm to your left is shown rigged with single brace blocks; the use of a pendant is shown at the opposite arm. There are other differences in the gear which seem to need explaining. Beginning to the left, the horses or foot ropes are first put on the yard. They have an eye spliced in one end that just fits over the yardarm. The other end reeves through thimbles spliced into the stirrups. These stirrups are put about the yard and hang pendant from it, but in later-day ships they hung from a rope jackstay stretched along the top of the yard, reeving through eyebolts. Later yet, the jackstay became an iron rod, but when jackstays of either kind are used the sail also is rove to this stay. A thimble is spliced into the inboard end of the horse and it is lashed by a laniard around the yard on the opposite side of the slings without the quarter block, or the slings are seized to the strap of the quarter block or to a thimble seized to the strap of the clew-garnet block.

Next over the yardarm goes the eye of the yard-tackle pendant. In its lower end a thimble is turned in, to which hooks the upper block of a long tackle, the fall of which leads on deck. This yard tackle is used for hoisting in boats and provisions, etc. A rope called a tricing line is bent to the thimble, and when the long tackle is unhooked this tricing line is used to trice the yard-tackle pendant up out of the way and secure it along the yard. It belays in the top. At the right arm the yard tackle is simply a strap around the yardarm with a thimble close up to the yard into which the long tackle block is hooked.

Then comes the brace block, either with or without a pendant, followed by the eye in the strap of the topsail sheet block. At the right yardarm the lift block is strapped above the sheet block, while at the left arm, the lift being single, it goes over the yardarm with an eye. There are no yard tackles on the yards aloft.

Now to rig the braces, starting with the fore brace. It is, of course, understood that in all cases braces go in pairs, leading to opposite ends of the yards, but one description covers the lead of both. The fore brace reeves through a block lashed to the mainstay collar, then reeves through the brace block at the yardarm, and the standing part is taken back and seized to the mainstay collar. The leading part goes down by the mainmast, reeves through a leading block strapped to an eyebolt in the deck, and belays on the main fife rail. Sometimes the brace is seized fast to the mainstay, reeves through the brace block back to a lead block on the mainstay, and then leads down the stay to belay at the fore fife rail as on the *Republican*. The fore topsail yard brace also sometimes follows this lead, but usually it reeves through a block on the mainstay above the fore hatchway, then through a block on the mainstay collar to the brace block, and the standing part is hitched around the collar of the mainstay above the block.

It leads to and is belayed on the main fife rail. At times a double block is used on the mainstay collar, one brace leading through each sheave to the opposite yardarms. This is a neat way to rig the brace in a small model, where many blocks become confusing.

The fore topgallant brace is seized to the main topmast stay collar, reeves through the brace block to a block lashed to the stay, and leads in some vessels down along the stay to a lead block lashed around the foremast head and goes down the mast to belay on the fore fife rail. A handier way is to lead the brace down by the mainmast and belay to the main fife rail. When this brace goes single it has an eye put over the yardarm and there is no brace block. The fore royal leads the same, and is generally single.

The main brace is bent to the end of the main-brace boomkin, leads through the block at the yardarm, back to a block seized to the boomkin, and comes inboard through a sheave in the ship's bulwarks and belays to a large cleat or a cavil on the inside of the bulwarks.

The main topsail brace leads like the fore topsail brace. It reeves through a block at the mizzen stay collar, then through the brace block, and the end is made fast to the mizzen stay collar. The leading part is belayed at the foot of the mizzenmast. Where there is no fife rail at the foot of the mizzenmast, there being bitts only, a spider ring is bolted around the mast somewhat like a boom saddle, the belaying pins fitting in the ring.

The main topgallant brace reeves up through a block seized to the upper part of the foremost mizzen topmast shroud, with the end made fast to the mizzen topmast stay collar. It also belays at the ring. The royal, single, leads from the yardarm to a block at the masthead or strapped to the stay, leads down on deck, and belays.

The brace block on the crossjack yard does not go over the arm with an eye, but is strapped around a thimble in an eye which in turn is strapped around the outer quarter of the yard so as not to interfere with the main backstays when the yard is braced up sharp. The standing part of the port brace is hitched to the after starboard main shroud. It leads across to the port-side brace block and back to a block strapped or seized below the end of the standing part on the starboard shroud and leads down the rigging and belays on the pinrail. The starboard brace reverses this lead and belays to the port pinrail opposite. The mizzen topsail brace, generally single, reeves through a block seized fast to the mizzen topmast stay just before the main masthead. The topgallant brace, also single, leads through a block on the after main topmast shroud. Both belay at the pinrail. These braces do not cross like the crossjack brace.

There is one other yard to rig, the spritsail yard, that is slung under the bowsprit. The slings are made like the lower forestay collar except they go without a heart. The doubled collar lies over the bowsprit, the eyes formed in the bight lying below. The yard is put through the eyes and a rope parral like those for the topgallant yard goes outside of the slings, all being retained in place by cleats nailed to the slings of the yard. The yard is round its entire length.

Horses go on first, and if the lifts are double the brace block has a pendant; if single, the brace block is close up to the yard. The standing parts of the braces are bent to the forestay collar above the mouse and eye. They reeve through the brace blocks up to blocks fast to eyes each side under the top, forward of the lubber hole, then through another block under the after part of the top and directly in line with the first block. They then lead down the mast to belay at the fore fife rail.

The lift, double, is bent to an eye in the upper side of the bowsprit cap, the hauling part reeving through the brace block, back to reeve through a block at the side of the cap below the eye and go inboard to belay at the forward pinrail. The lift, being single, goes with an eye over the yardarm, reeves through a block on the upper side of the cap, and belays the same.

Modelmakers are often perplexed in making a proper gammoning to hold the bowsprit in its bed. Take a long cord and pass it around the bowsprit close up under and forward of the gammon cleats on the bowsprit, seizing it fast to itself. Take the leading part down to starboard and pass it through the hole or slot in the knee of the head. The forward end of the hole should come just below the cleat on the bowsprit, the slot extending aft. Take the leading end back up to and over the bowsprit again, crossing the first turn, and repeat until you have taken at least nine turns. Each turn goes forward on the bowsprit and aft in the hole, and in turn crosses the others. The last turn is over the bowsprit, when the end is frapped about the whole with the same number of turns as there are in the lashing. The frapping should draw the gammoning together at the center of the lashing, so that it fans out to the bowsprit and to the hole below. Between 1815 and 1840, many men-of-war used chain gammonings, as did large merchant ships of the same period.

Plate XIII shows a fore topsail. It has four reef bands with cringles and three bowline cringles. Another cringle just below the lower reef band is for the reef tackle to hook into when the sail is hauled up for the purpose of taking a reef. The sail is bent to the yard in old-time ships or to the jack-stays of more modern vessels with short pieces of rope called rovings that pass around the yard or jackstay.

The clew-line or clew-garnet blocks, as they are called, on lower and topsail yards are stropped with two legs and are put through the clews and seized. The clew lines on each side are reeved through the clew-line blocks on the yard, then through the clew-garnet blocks at the clews; the standing part is hitched around the yard without the upper blocks, and the leading part goes down through the lubber hole and belays.

The sheet, with end stoppered, is put through the clew with the stopper lying aft, rove through the sheet or shoulder block on the lower yard, through the quarter block lying under this yard, down through a sheave in the topsail bibbs, and belays to the bibbs.

The buntline blocks are strapped to the tye block or lashed to the under side of the crosstrees on each side. The buntline is bent to a cringle in the foot of the sail, passes up over the forward side of the sail, reeves through the buntline blocks and comes down on deck to belay. Monkey blocks are placed on the yard near the slings for the buntlines to reeve through as fairleaders before going to the blocks above. There are similar monkey blocks for the leech lines, which reeve through blocks at the outer under side of the top, through the buntline blocks on the yard, and then are made fast to the upper reef cringle. The leech lines belay on deck.

A line called an earing is spliced into the head clew and two turns are taken with it around the yard without the stop cleats at the yardarms and through the clew each time, and then as many turns are taken around the yard within the arm as will expend the earing, the end being seized to itself. This serves to stretch the top of the yard and to help sustain its weight.

A wood batten with several holes through it extends down forward from the top for a few feet and its lower end is seized to the lower stay. A rope netting or crowsfoot is formed by passing a rope alternately through holes around the forward edges of the tops and through alternate holes in the batten or euphroe. This crowsfoot prevents the bolt rope of the topsail from catching under the top or chafing the stays. This was a feature of the rig of men-of-war.

CHAPTER FIVE

GEAR *and* FURNITURE

MOST of the plates show the models without anchors at the catheads. Where they are shown, they are anchors of special design and we must supply the missing anchors for the others. Our
three square-riggers should have wood-stocked anchors about 9 feet 6
inches long. The whaler's should be 9 feet and the fishing schooner's 8 feet
6 inches long. The anchor hoy should use a smaller size, wood-stocked,
5 feet 6 inches long, while that carried by the gundalow can be iron-
stocked, 4 feet 6 inches in length.

Two of our models should have guns, and the armament of the *Wasp*
is given. A privateer of the American Revolution would be unlikely to
have carronades, so her gun equipment would be carriage guns, and we
are told that the *Oliver Cromwell* carried sixteen 6-pounders. The tables
show the length of a 6-pounder and give the information for making the
gun carriages. However, Figure 29 shows guns and carriages both.

How about small boats? We know what the boat equipment was of
the *Wasp* and we can see in detail that of the *Republican,* but the *Oliver
Cromwell* and the fishing schooner do not show their boats in the plates.
The *Oliver Crowell* no doubt carried two boats, nested right side up on
gallows frames amidship, while the fishing schooner carried a small boat
at the stern. The anchor hoy also carried a small round-bottom boat on
stern davits; the scow schooner and the gundalow, which wanted the deck
clear to carry deck loads, would also carry small boats of nondescript type

on stern davits. The lines of some small boats are given in Plate XIV.

Take my advice and buy steering wheels already made. The old-fashioned wheel with its delicately carved spokes, wooden rim, inlayed and decorated, is a jeweler's job to construct. There is no short cut and model wheels must be built as the original wheels were. Plate X shows a single wheel, but if the ship were bigger, say a 44-gun frigate, she would have a double wheel. That is, there would be two wheels, with the drum for the tiller rope between two stanchions. The fore stanchion is made single, while the after stanchion has two legs. Sometimes the tiller comes on deck and the tiller ropes are rove from side to side of the ship above the deck. In other vessels the tiller comes below the quarter deck and the tiller ropes go down through sheaves to the deck below. The gundalow has a wheel with tiller and tiller ropes all above the deck. Plate XIV shows a tiller under the quarter deck, and the *Wasp* had an emergency or extra tiller above the deck while the operating tiller was under the gun deck (see Plate IX).

The gear of a ship comprises such a great variety of articles that it is hard to tell whether it is more properly rigging or furniture.

The sheathing of ships' bottoms with copper was first tried about 1760 and after that the practice soon became general. Sheet copper of different weights was used, but generally 28-ounce copper was used at the bows and as it went aft lighter sheathing was used, coming down at the stern to 20- or 22-ounce gauge. A sheet of copper sheathing measured 14 inches by 4 feet and the process of putting it on was quite intricate. When a ship was to be coppered the bottom required some preliminary preparation. After the bottom of a ship had been well caulked it was then sheathed with heavy felt laid in hot pitch, and over that the sheets of copper were laid on. From the keel up, the copper was laid on in parallel belts. In order to maintain this evenness in laying, where the shape of the ship's body calls for it the copper is gored, as it were, so the bands of copper sheets come out correctly at the waterline. To copper small models is beyond the average modelmaker, and the bottoms of all models scaled less than ⅜ inch to the foot should be painted. Larger models can be coppered and shim copper in sheets can be used. Cut strips 14 inches wide by scale. Every 4 feet by

PLATE XIII

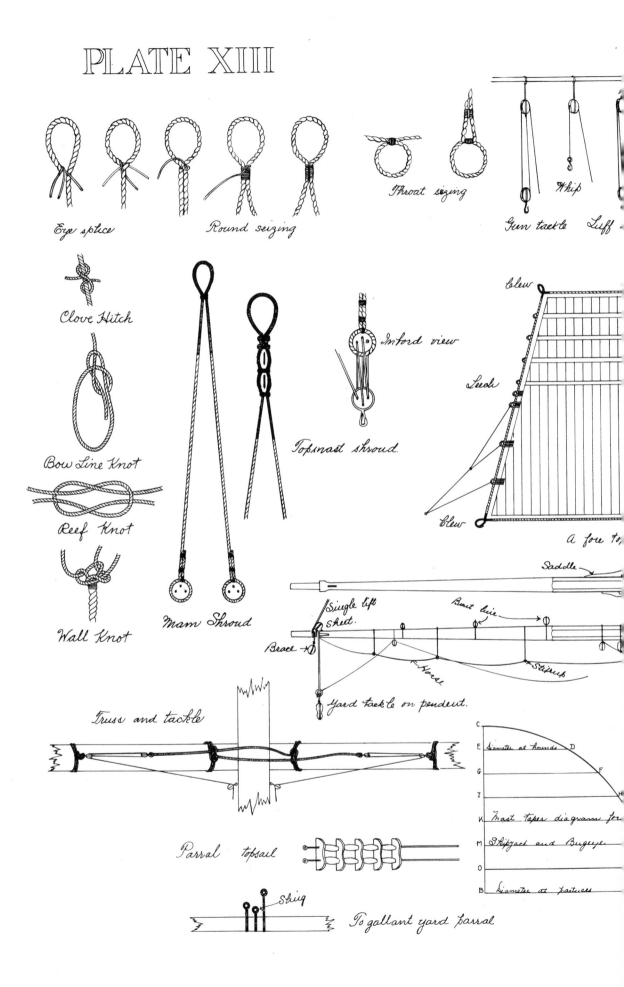

Eye splice

Round seizing

Throat seizing

Gun tackle   Luff

Whip

Clove Hitch

Bow Line Knot

Reef Knot

Wall Knot

Main Shroud

Topmast shroud.

Inford view

Clew

Leech

Clew

A fore to

Saddle

Single lift
Sheet.

Bent line

Brace

Horse

Stirrup

Yard tackle on pendent.

Truss and tackle

Diameter at hounds

Mast taper diagram for

Skipjack and Bugeye

Diameter at partners

Parral   topsail

Sling

To gallant yard parral

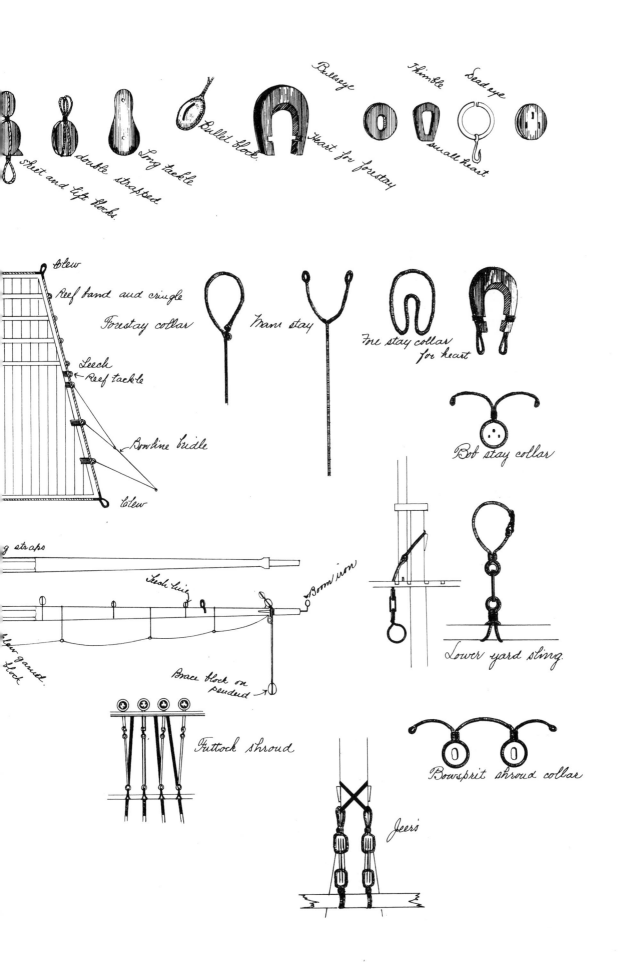

Sheet and lift blocks.

double strapped

Snug tackle

Bullet block.

Bulleeye

Heart for forestay

Thimble

small heart

Dead eye

Clew

Reef band and cringle

Forestay collar

Mane stay

Fore stay collar for heart

Leech

Reef tackle

Bob stay collar

Bowline bridle

Clew

g straps

Leech line

Boom iron

Lower yard sling.

Brace block on pendent

Futtock shroud

Bowsprit shroud collar

Jeers

scale bend the sheathing, or strip, back on itself so that the strips show seams 4 feet apart, as though the copper were in separate sheets. The sheets are laid brick-fashion, the joints of one row coming in the middle of the sheets of the row above. You will have to drill holes for the nails and do not drive the nails home hard. Let the heads stand up a bit and file them down at last, leaving something to hold them fast to the hull.

I know that gun ports are an integral part of the hull, but we will consider them as gear, just so that we may say something about them here. They are governed as to size by the guns, and tables giving proper sizes for the respective guns will be found at the back of the book. Something that we do not have to consider in building a lift model is the placing of the ports in proper relation to the ship's timbers. Were we building a built-up model we would have to be meticulous about placing them between the frames. Actually, in framing the ports, the timbers of the ship entered into the construction, and while we can disregard that matter to a slight degree, still we must not place them in foolish or impossible positions. We must consider to some extent where the timbers come and while we need not be governed exactly by the structural layout we must keep the matter in mind. The lids and the method of hinging the lids varied. Some three different types were in use at different periods and a vessel might have ports of different kinds in her sides. The most common lid was a single cover hinged at the top. A chain bridle, rigged to the outside of the lid with a short chain coming inboard through the side above the port, was used to open the port and hold the cover in place. Next most common in use were ports of the buckler type, such as the *Wasp* had in her sides. The third type, less frequently seen, had lids in two parts divided vertically, like a double house door. These were hinged at the sides with two hinges to a shutter.

Mr. Chapelle, in writing of this feature in the *Mariner* for July, 1934, regrets that most plans do not show the type of lid used on the particular vessels. He also states that "up to 1800 one-piece hinged lids were common for American vessels; the bow, or chase ports, may be in two parts, to lift out. Between 1760 and 1810, however, many vessels had gun-port lids like the doors of a cupboard. A few plans show this feature. . . . I think this form of port lid was commonly used for bow ports, and less commonly for other gun ports. . . . In the American service, a great many small craft had both portions of horizontally-divided lids hinged, at the top and bottom."

Guns themselves were mostly of one design, that is, long guns were all similar and carronades were alike. If any difference occurred in the form of the gun it was in the matter of how and where the trunnion was placed, how the gun was hung. Some had the trunnions on center and some had them at the lower quarter. Guns are referred to as being hung by the centers or hung by the quarters. This would make quite a great deal of difference in the construction of ports and carriages, as it would make a difference in the height above deck of the muzzle of the piece. In the making of guns for models, two methods are open to the constructor: the guns can be turned or cast. If they are turned, it is easy to work bronze or brass, and all details can be sharpened up. If it is intended to simulate iron guns, brass or copper must be colored. Brass guns were in use, however, and many ships carried a mixed battery of brass and iron guns; hence it is not necessary to paint all brass guns to imitate iron. If you do paint your guns, be sure to use a flat black paint, not a gloss—or better yet, have the guns oxidized if convenient; a jeweler or silversmith can probably do this job for you.

Warships and merchantmen in pictures seem much alike, but actually there was a great difference between the two types of ships and it was found difficult to convert a ship designed for one purpose to the other use. The designer was confronted with the problem of weight distribution. A merchant ship had the bulk of transported weight in the cargo she carried, and this was stowed below decks, with the greatest weight below the waterline, a condition that made for stability. Armed ships had to be designed to meet conditions that were exactly opposite: the greatest weight carried was in the guns and it was placed high above the water and made for instability. These opposed conditions called for vastly different hull shapes. The excessive tumblehome to the warships' topsides was an element of design calculated to bring the weight of the guns in from the sides toward the center line. The same tumblehome to the topsides of a merchant ship is achieved at the expense of cargo room and is therefore never as pronounced in these ships. This is a most patent feature of the difference between the two models as seen from outboard. When we can see the decks and observe the gear of the two ships we again see striking differences. It must be remembered that the merchant ship carried a small crew, while the number of men in the crew of a warship was at least ten times as large. Having all these men to handle her, a warship's gear could be heavier than could be managed aboard a merchant ship, and therefore ships of the same size would have gear of proportionately different size and weight. The merchant ship carried lighter and smaller boats than did the warship, and fewer. As a rule, warships carried a larger rig than merchant ships of the same size and used heavier rope in the rigging. The gear in general was both heavier and better finished in the men-of-war. Hatch coamings as a rule were of different construction, being molded so as to form a trough in which shot for the guns could be stowed. Moreover, since the hatches were not openings for the admission of freight or cargo to the hold but means of access for the crew to reach sleeping quarters and storerooms, the coamings generally were handsomely finished and in some cases varnished rather than painted. The hatch covers on merchantmen were solid wooden lids that were battened down and were cambered across ship; in the man-of-war these were replaced with gratings that were necessarily flat on top, unbattened, to give light and ventilation below. Solid, flat hatch covers were fitted in place of the gratings in men-of-war, in bad weather.

Larger anchors were carried on the fighting ships, with correspondingly great cables. There were plenty of hands to man the capstans and a heavy anchor was broken out smartly.

When we said that the spar plan of the *Wasp* would do for the *Oliver Cromwell* and the *Republican*, it was meant that the spars were in general much alike, but not in exact measurements.

With the large crews, much time was spent in keeping the warships' gear in perfect condition, and this should be reflected in the models. Paint was kept fresh as well as the brightwork. Small boats were of better construction than on merchantmen and had an elegant appearance.

Most of the deck houses on ships showed the manner of their construction through the paint. If they were made of matched boards this was apparent. They were so fashioned that the boards fitted into the general lines of the ship and tended to improve the appearance. If the hull were short, matched boards were run horizontally to give the general illusion of

FIGURE 36. *Deck houses.*

length. In making deck houses, etc., the lines made by the joining of the boards can be scored in.

The furniture and gear of most of the models is shown in the plates or on the sail plan of each ship, and what is missing or is not clearly shown will be found in Plate XIV. Once again, the scale of every part is extremely important.

CHAPTER SIX

TOOLS *and* MATERIALS

TOOLS for the modelmaker are of two kinds: the ordinary equipment of any worker in wood, plus certain special tools that experience has taught are particularly suited to the needs of miniature shipbuilders. It would be well, if the novice is to buy tools, to look at the tools of a cabinetmaker and pattern the equipment on what is found in such a kit. I am speaking now of the tools for general work—saws, planes, hammers, chisels, gouges, and an indispensable *drawknife*. You should include an *oilstone* of medium texture, if only one is to be acquired. If you are unlimited in the money you can invest in tools, get both a fast and slow stone —that is, one that is coarse and one that is very fine to finish the sharpening process with. A *jackknife* of the kind known as a carpenter's knife will be used incessantly. The large blade of this knife is pointed. A bit stock and an assortment of *twist drills*, all sizes from ⅛ inch up to ½ inch, will come in handy. Add to this a *medium-sized miter box* for rough work. Three different kinds of *saws*, cross cut, rip, and panel (which has a rigid back) are convenient to have. The equipment of *chisels* can include several sizes of blades for roughing out. *Wood rasps* should not be too coarse and should be augmented with a few fine-toothed files.

Thin glass makes the best *scraper*. Score the straight edge of a piece of thin glass with a three-cornered file diagonally across the edge of the glass, place the thumbs of both hands on the glass close up on each side of this mark, and bend the hands down and apart, exerting a breaking strain on the glass. It will break across the piece in a curved manner with an inclined edge like the cutting edge of a chisel. The edge will make a very sharp scraper, most useful in making a smooth surface on any kind of wood.

A large investment can be made in tools but it is wise to go slow and purchase only as needed. Great care should be exercised in the selection of whatever tools are bought. The ability of cutting tools to keep an edge depends on the original quality of the article. It is better to have a few good tools than a large assortment of poor ones. If you do not know who makes the best, consult a reputable hardware dealer and be guided by his judgment.

Remember you are not building a house, and when we speak of the larger phases of the work bear in mind that even this is in relation to a miniature. False cuts and mistakes on work, when working to a small scale, are fatal. Always allow plenty of margin and cut to the line only in putting on the finishing touches. All tools should be purchased with the size of the work in mind; though you will find, as your proficiency increases in the use of tools, that you are doing fine work with incredibly large tools, do not buy oversized instruments.

The special tools of the modelmaker are another matter. Here the smallness of the tool may count. You will find that you are not only working in wood but that other mediums are worked extensively. Metal work is encountered in imitating the hardware, and it is the work of a jeweler to make the small metal parts. Thomas Dixon & Son of Newark, New Jersey, specialize in jewelers' tools, and they catalogue tools for the modelmaker. Send to them for a catalogue. It is most intriguing reading. You will be surprised to find out how many kinds of hammers, alone, are in use in the various trades. The Dixon metal-working tools are without peer. No doubt there are other dealers in similar tools in the larger cities of the West, but I am not familiar with their line of goods.

Among these small tools needed by the modelmaker are, first, those used in woodworking. An absolutely indispensable (to me) article of equipment is a *miniature miter box*. This is to be absolutely accurate. You should get a small *panel saw* to go with it. These come with eighteen cutting teeth to the inch and make a smooth cut. A *jeweler's back saw* is also required, and to go with it a variety of blades for metal cutting as well as for wood. These come as fine as a hair.

You can buy a small set of *woodcarver's tools;* these come about 4 inches long and are very handy with their variety of cutting blades. Bent chisels and gouges, at least one of each, with ¼-inch blade, are in the set of wood-carving tools. A narrow straight chisel should be part of this equipment.

Small *planes* have been especially designed for the modelmaker; these come with round and flat soles. The round-soled ones are to smooth out the wood in the hollows, which they do to perfection. File equipment should be somewhat extensive. Do not fail to get a set of *diesinker's files.* These are of a variety of shapes and include three-cornered, round, and flat files, all very small. You can also buy *bent files* with both sharp and blunt ends and with cutting faces of a variety of shapes. The Nicholson File Company makes these as well as the diesinker's files, and is familiar with the needs of the modelmaker.

Small *hammers,* one with a ball pene, are required in the miniature tool equipment.

Small *twist drills* in sizes 75, 70, 65, 60, 55 and 50 are of constant use and cannot be dispensed with. They work in both wood and metal. A small bit stock with jaws that close tightly, or a set of pin vises, is required to hold them while drilling.

For general use you will need a number of *clamps*—large ones of wood for forming the block and gluing the lifts together, and smaller metal C clamps (which can be purchased in the five-and-ten-cent stores) for a variety of uses.

Here is an additional list: *carpenter's square, calipers, dividers, gauges, rule, scratch awl, pliers* (long nose), *stilletto, tweezers* (long nose), *cutting pliers, metal-cutting shears* (small), *soldering iron* (small), *wire hook* (small).

Discarded dental tools, burrs, and chisels make fine modelmaker's tools. Beg these from your dentist and sharpen them to your use.

If you can go in for power tools, a small *lathe* is the first thing to acquire.

It will do almost everything except take the place of a jig saw. It can be equipped with small circular saws for cutting, or with sanding wheels. It can be arranged to turn both wood and metal.

Lay in a good supply of *sandpaper* in all grades.

Now follow remarks on materials.

Toothpicks: These you will use for the wooden treenails. Get round ones of the best grade.

Applicators: Small round ones make excellent dowels and treenails. Purchase these in a drug store.

Copper: In thin sheets that can be folded for coppering bottoms.

Celluloid: Can be bought new in sheets of all thicknesses. Old photograph film with the emulsion washed off is good for window lights.

If you feel inclined to cast small parts, consult your dentist. He has casting equipment just suitable for the job. Make patterns of boxwood or fiber and castings of *type metal*. This metal will produce small castings with sharp detail.

Paint: Coach colors are best; use no enamel. Get umber in tubes from color man. Do not thin it out, but apply it to decks as it comes from the tube. Other paints for hull and furniture should go on very thinly. Apply varnish hot. Rust is inevitable about iron marine fittings, and all black parts should be dull and slightly rusty-looking. Do not have too much brass show about your models; paint parts to look as if made of iron. Give new wood a coat of filler, well rubbed down.

A number of *spring clothespins* can be of great use for holding small parts. Fishing-tackle dealers keep both small split *rings* and solid ones. Dealers in model parts for miniature ships can supply all *fittings* correctly made and to scale. It is best to buy such parts as *blocks* and *deadeyes* ready made. It is most monotonous work to make either in the quantities needed. Get catalogues from these dealers. Your model will look best with small articles of gear properly fashioned. The dealers carry *eyebolts, belaying pins, chain, clevises,* and *turnbuckles*—in fact everything needed by the modelmaker. The fittings for mechanical model yachts are standard.

Wood is the indispensable material. A different variety grows to fit almost any need. Avoid woods that are fuzzy in texture. The novice dotes on balsa wood because of its ease in working. For the modelmaker it may have its uses, but I have never found them. Here is a list of woods generally used to advantage by the modelmaker.

White pine: A soft wood that carves well and takes a smooth finish, of many varieties. Get clear, straight-grained, well-seasoned wood. Kiln-dried wood not as good as naturally seasoned wood. Patternmaker's pine is the best for modelists' use. Use it in lifts and spars; it takes paint finish best.

Mahogany: A cabinetmaker's wood of several degrees of hardness. It takes a beautiful finish. According to variety, the grain runs from open to close. Use it for lifts and rails and fittings; finish with paint or varnish.

Ash: A very useful wood, as it bends freely. It can be steamed without injury. Use it for bulwarks and all planking. It will take paint or varnish finish.

White holly: Close-grained and hard. This wood sands down smooth and stains well, but in original color looks too white and has to be stained or painted. It bends well, and is excellent for all small fittings, such as deck houses, ladders, hatch coamings and covers, gratings, etc. Give it a paint or varnish finish, or leave it natural.

Black walnut: Another cabinetmaker's wood of excellent finish. It does not bend. It is excellent for fittings, especially where varnish is to be used to finish.

Boxwood: A light yellow, close-grained, and very hard wood that is very strong. It stains poorly, carves excellently. It is good for small parts, blocks, cleats, stanchions, bitts, and all working gear. Finish with varnish or leave natural.

Pear: Fine in grain and extremely hard; bends freely. Use it for furniture, keels, beams, frames, planking, stem and stern posts. Give it either paint or varnish finish.

Cherry: An excellent wood for such small detail as bits, pinrails, knight-heads, gun carriages, hatch covers, etc. It has a natural dark brownish color which grows richer with age, and unless a high-gloss finish is desired, a little olive oil rubbed into the wood is all the finish needed. This color gives the appearance of age, and it is particularly suited for work on unpainted or natural finished models. Cherry is an excellent substitute for teak or walnut on yacht models, and superior to either for steaming and bending; it holds glue much better than teak.

Apple wood: A good material for catheads, sheaves, chess trees, bumpkins, bitts, windlass barrels, etc. It is dark to light brownish in color, very hard, excellent for turning, and usually available in short lengths only. Because of its unusual hardness and the fact that it does not warp, apple was the favorite wood of our early clockmakers for gears and pulleys. It is not a good wood to steam. Drill it for brads. It holds glue well.

White wood: Medium hard and fairly strong. Finish with paint.

Rosewood: A fine-quality, close-grained hardwood that takes a fine polish. Use it wherever boxwood can be used. It has good color; give it a natural or varnish finish.

Degama: A wood that does not warp freely. Use it for all small spars, in natural, paint, or varnish finish.

Linen cord: For rigging. Get it from dealers in model fittings, for example, McCutcheon and Co., Fifth Avenue, New York. Linen cord comes both cable-laid and hawser-laid, generally white, and has to be dyed rope color.

Metal: The Chase Brass Co. makes all thicknesses or gauges of sheet brass, hard or soft; soft is best for modelmaking. They also have hard and soft wire of all gauges, and small-diameter metal tubing and rods of all shapes and sizes. You will have to order through your hardware dealer.

Fiber: Comes in sheets of all gauges, has no grain and can be bent, cut, or sawed to shape. It is very strong, with smooth finished surface. Its color is a disadvantage, and it has to be used for painted parts. It is excellent for tops and caps, wheels, deck houses, etc. It makes the best templates. Buy it at hardware dealers.

Wire: Use soft brass and picture wire pleated, also black hairpins or annealed wire.

Glue: Cabinetmaker's glue comes in sheets and has to be boiled down. Apply hot and thin. Casein glue is very holding; it comes in powder and is mixed with cold water, and must be used at once. It is not good on unpainted surfaces, as it stains. The new synthetic resins such as Cascamite and Weldwood will not stain. They are mixed cold in a manner similar to casein glue and when once hardened are insoluble in water. Plywood made with these glues can be steamed without separating the plies. They are available in most hardware stores. The mixture is good for about four hours, but should be discarded when it starts to congeal.

The making of models calls for a lot of ingenuity on the part of the builder. Do not be afraid to devise new ways to do things or to introduce new materials, providing they are fitting. Have the model rigged and made in exact counterpart. Try and make every part neatly and to scale and make the model a worthwhile effort.

APPENDICES

SHIP TONNAGE

To find the tonnage of a ship, William Sutherland gives the following rule (1794):

Calculate length of keel multiplied by greatest breadth multiplied by half breadth; then divide by 94 for merchant ships, by 100 for men-of-war.

SIZE OF STANDING RIGGING FOR SHIPS (INCHES)

	1,250 tons	1,000 tons	800 tons	600 tons	450 tons	300 tons	200 tons
Bowsprit:							
Gammoning	7	7	6½	5½	5	4½	4
Shrouds	7	6½	6½	5½	5	4½	4½
Foremast, Mainmast:							
Shrouds	10½	10	9	8	7½	7	6
Deadeyes	16	16	14	11	11	10	8
Stays	16	15	14	13	12	10	8
Fore topmast, Main topmast:							
Shrouds	6½	6	5½	5	4½	4	4
Deadeyes	10	9	8	7	6	6	6
Stays	7½	7	6½	6	5½	5½	5
Backstays	7	7	6½	6	5½	5½	5
Fore topgallant mast, Main topgallant mast:							
Shrouds	4½	4	3½	3½	3	3	2½
Deadeyes				In proportion			
Backstays	4½	4½	4	3½	3	3	2½
Mizzenmast:							
Shrouds	7	6½	6	5½	5½	5	
Deadeyes	10	9	8	8	8	8	
Stays	8	7½	7	6½	6	6	

	1,250 tons	1,000 tons	800 tons	600 tons	450 tons	300 tons	200 tons
Mizzen topmast:							
Shrouds	5	5	4½	4	3½	3½	
Deadeyes	8	8	7	7	6	6	
Stays	5	5	4½	4¼	4	3½	
Backstays	5	4½	4½	4	4	3½	
Mizzen topgallant mast:							
Shrouds	3	3	3	2½	2½	2¼	
Deadeyes			In proportion				
Stays	3	3	3	2½	2½	2	
Backstays	2	2	2	1½	1¼	1¼	

SIZE OF STANDING RIGGING FOR SCHOONERS (INCHES)

	120 tons	160 tons	200 tons
Bowsprit:			
Shrouds, Bobstay	⁹⁄₁₆	⁶⁄₁₀	⅝ chain
Gammoning		Iron clamp	
Foremast:			
Shrouds	5¼	6	6¼
Stays	7	8½	9
Fore topmast:			
Shrouds	2¾	4	4
Stays	2¾	3	3¼
Mainmast:			
Shrouds	5¼	6	7½
Deadeyes	7	7½	8
Sciatic stays	5½	6	6¼

SIZE OF STANDING RIGGING FOR SLOOPS (INCHES)

	30 tons	60 tons	90 tons
Bowsprit:			
Shrouds	3	4	4½

Mast:
Shrouds 4¼   5¼   5¾
Deadeyes 5   6½   7

LONG GUNS (CIRCA 1800)

Pound	Caliber, inches
3	3.113
4	3.204
6	3.498
9	4.30
12	4.623
18	5.292
24	5.547
32	6.105
42	6.684

In making gun carriages, the bracket should be the thickness of the caliber, axle trees the size of caliber. The after side of the forward axle trees should be under the center of the trunnion. The center of the trunnion hole should be twice the diameter of the trunnion from the fore end of the bracket. The length of the bracket should equal the distance from the center of the trunnion to the end of the pomillion plus twice the diameter of the trunnion. Plan the height of the brackets to allow the center of the guns to be 3 inches below the center of the ports. The wheel diameter is 3 times the trunnion, the wheel thickness equal to the caliber of shot.

DIMENSIONS OF GUN PORTS ACCORDING TO WEIGHT OF SHOT

Shot, pounds	Height		Breadth		Distance above deck	
42	2′	10″	3′	2″	2′	4″
32	2′	8″	3′		2′	3″
24	2′	6″	2′	10″	2′	1″
18	2′	5″	2′	8″	2′	
12	2′	3″	2′	5″	1′	11″
9	1′	10″	2′		1′	9″
6	1′	4″	1′	6″	1′	6″

Key to Plate XIV

1. *Pintle and gudgeon.* Best made of 18-gauge sheet brass, bent around a solid piece and soldered.

2. *Crosstrees.* Main top of man-of-war.

3. *Top.* Main top of man-of-war. Thin diagonal battens on top. Raised rim all around. Proportion for top—breadth, ⅓ length of topmast or ½ ship's beam; width, ¾ of length.

4. *Longboat.*

5. *Trestle trees.* Profile plan. Proportion for trestle trees—depth, 25 to 26 inches per foot of length. Breadth ⁵⁄₇ of depth. Crosstrees same breadth as trestle trees and ½ as deep.

6. *Lower cap.* Proportion for caps. Breadth twice the diameter of topmast. Length twice breadth, thickness diameter of topmast.

7. *Topmast crosstrees.*

8. *Netting.* Netting with iron stanchions extends across after end of tops. Merchantmen use weather cloths made of tarred canvas.

9. *Fore topmast crosstrees.* Sheaves in after crosstree or chock.

10. *Main top.* Merchantman. Front rounds more and the top is not as deep as a man-of-war's top.

11. *Whaleboat.* Floored. Ceiled up to within 8 inches of gunwale. Frames 8 inches center to center. Thwarts at top of ceiling.

12. *Rudder.* Perspective view. Bolt with rings for chain fastening. Chain or rope, about 9 feet long and fastened to ship's stern, but must allow rudder to swing. Both sternpost and fore edge of rudder chamfered off to permit rudder to swing 45° in either direction.

13. *Anchor (catted).* A rope with end stoppered is put through a hole in the cathead. It is passed through the anchor ring to a cleat on the cathead and is made fast to a timber head.

14. *Chess tree.* Goes on the outside of the ship aft the fore rigging. The main tack reeves through a vertical sheave and then through a horizontal sheave in the bulwarks to belay on a cleat inside.

15. *Hatch and shot rack.* The sectional view of the coaming is drawn ⅜ inch to the foot. The rest of the plan ³⁄₁₆ inch to the foot. Hatch coamings as a rule vary from 9 to 12 inches in height. The coaming is rabbeted to make a ledge for the cover to rest upon. The large hatchways of merchantmen are fitted with a wooden bar through the center from fore to aft that fits into a recess cut down below the rabbet. The covers are made in sections lying athwartship, with inner ends resting on this strongback. Shot racks are removable, generally having partitions between each ball. Shot are more conveniently stowed here than piled at the pinrail, where they prevent the men from reaching the rigging.

16. *Anchor.* Large ships carry a sheet, spare, two bower, one stream and one kedge anchor. All are alike in proportion and construction but vary in size. The sheet and the bower anchors are of the same size, while the others diminish in size, the kedge anchor being smallest. Small ships carry fewer anchors. It is enough to show two anchors at the catheads, fished and stowed.

17. *Boat stowage.* Gallows frames support raised platforms over the hatchways. Spare spars are lashed on the projecting arms of the frames. Boat chocks are built on the platforms. The *Oliver Cromwell* might have carried her longboat in this way above the capstan. Steel gives the height of the frames as from 5 to 6 feet. Curved-top gallows frames go without platforms, the boat resting across them. Pictures of ships like the *Republican* show a spare spar lashed from the fore- to the mainmast above the boat to which it is griped. Small boats swing from the stern davits in port but at sea they are carried on the after deck, lashed, upside down.

18. *Curved-top gallows frame.* Also used as a belfry and bitts.

PLATE XIV

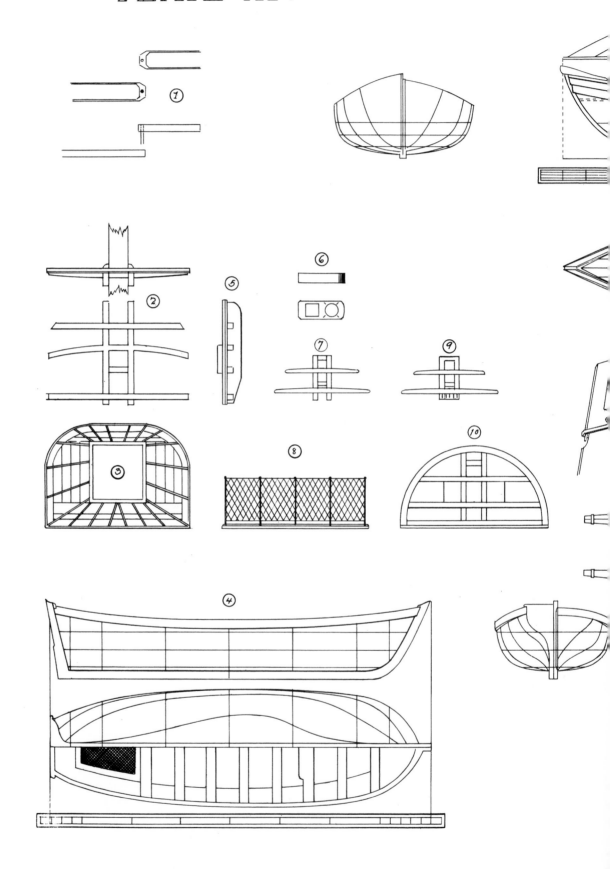

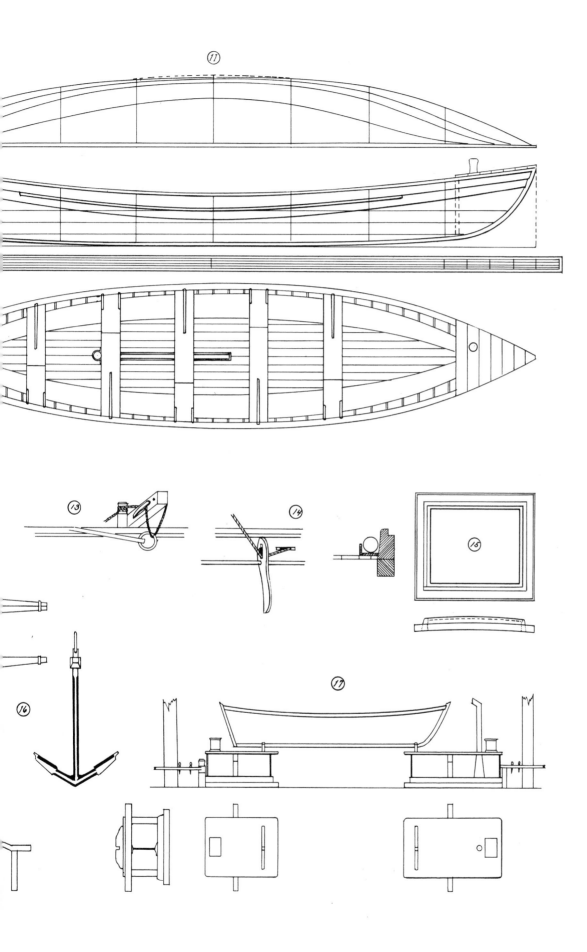

12 Pdr Long Gun and Carriage. 1800

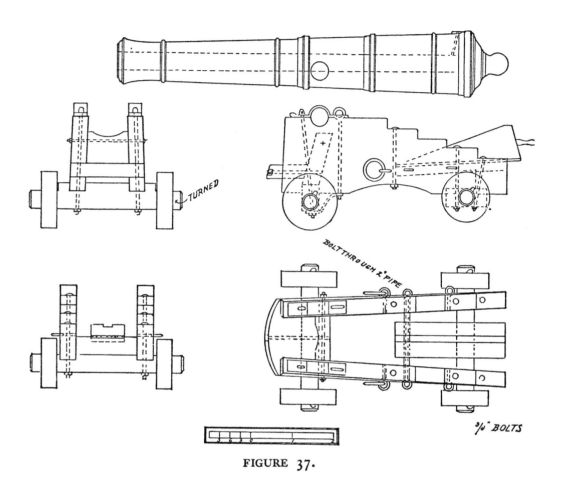

FIGURE 37.

CARRONADES (DIMENSIONS ACCORDING TO SIMMONS FOR THE YEARS 1800 TO 1816

Shot, pounds	Length	Bore
68	5′ 2″	08.2″
42	4′ 5″	06.9″
32	4′	06.2″
24	3′ 8″	05.7″
18	3′ 6″	05.2″
12	2′ 9″	04.6″

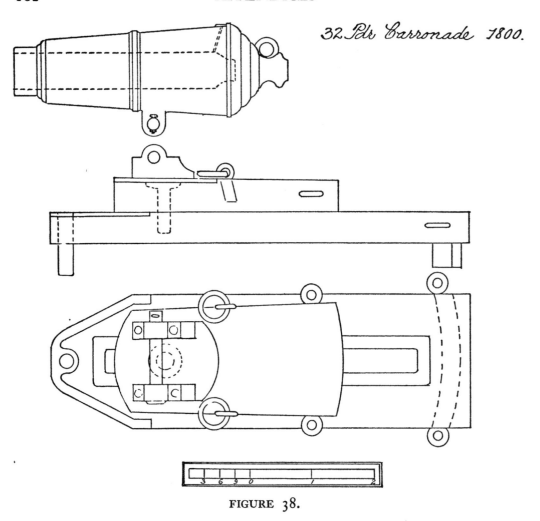

32 Pdr Carronade 1800.

FIGURE 38.

CARRONADE PORTS (FROM SIMMONS)

	32 pounders	*24 pounders*	*18 pounders*	*12 pounders* All in the clear
Length	3′ 4″	3′ 2″	3′	2′ 10″
Height	2′ 9″	2′ 7″	2′ 5″	2′ 3″

GUN EQUIPMENT

1 handspike, the length of the carriage.
1 crowbar, the length of the carriage.
1 rammer, as long as from the breech of the gun to the muzzle.
1 rammer head, in length 1¼ times the bore of the gun.

1 sponger, in length 18 inches longer than the rammer.
1 sponge head, in diameter equal to 1½ times the bore.
1 elevating quoin.
2 chocking quoins.

MASTING

In making the spars for models of merchant ships of the period around 1800, the following general proportions are applicable.

Mainmast = beam $\times$ 2 + ⅙ of the sum.

$$\textit{Example.} \quad \begin{array}{ll} \text{Beam of } 30' \times 2 & = 60' \\ \text{⅙ of sum} & = 10' \\ \hline \text{Length of mainmast} & = 70' \end{array}$$

Main topmast = $\frac{7}{12}$ of mainmast.
Main topgallant mast = ⅓ of mainmast.
Main royal mast = $\frac{5}{24}$ of mainmast.
Foremast = $\frac{11}{12}$ of mainmast.
Fore topmast = 1 foot shorter than corresponding spar on main.
Fore topgallant mast = 1 foot shorter than corresponding spar on main.
Fore royal mast = 1 foot shorter than corresponding spar on main.
Mizzenmast = ⅚ of mainmast.
Mizzen topmast = $\frac{5}{12}$ of mainmast.
Mizzen topgallant = ⅓ of mizzenmast.
Main yard = ⅚ of mainmast.
Main topsail yard = ⅔ of main yard.
Main topgallant yard = ½ of main yard.
Main royal yard = ⅓ of main yard.
Foreyard = length of main yard.
Fore topsail yard = length of main topsail yard.
Fore topgallant yard = $\frac{7}{15}$ of main yard.
Mizzen yard (crossjack) = $\frac{11}{15}$ of main yard.
Mizzen topsail yard = $\frac{8}{15}$ of main yard.
Mizzen topgallant yard = ⅓ of main yard.
Spritsail yard = ⅘ of main yard.
Gaff = ½ of main yard.
Bowsprit = beam.

Diameter of spars: For modelmakers, fractional measurements for models are unnecessary unless the model is a large one. The following proportions are general and averaged:

Diameter of masts:
    Main and fore .... 1″ at partners to 3′ of length.
    Mizzen .... 1″ at partners to 4′ of length.
    Bowsprit .... 1″ at partners to 3′ of length.
    Diameter of yards ...... 1″ to every 4′ of length.

As a rule, modelmakers are inclined to make the upper yards too heavy and the model therefore has a topheavy look. Err on the light side, if at all.

CABLES

Diameter of cable: ½ inch to 1 foot of beam. Hawse hole, 2½ times diameter of cable.

SCUPPERS

Scuppers on all vessels from schooners to 44s (frigates) should be lead-lined, 4 by 6 inches, elliptical, there being 8 scuppers on the upper and lower gun decks. Most small vessels have scuppers made by cutting slots in the bulwarks between the stanchions. This was always the practice in the Gloucester fishing schooners, for example.

RECOMMENDED READINGS FOR SHIP-MODEL BUILDERS

THE HISTORY OF AMERICAN SAILING SHIPS. Howard I. Chapelle. W. W. Norton & Co., Inc., New York, 1935. Plans of sailing ships of many types.

THE CHESAPEAKE BAY BUGEYES. Marion V. Brewington. The Mariner's Museum, Newport News, 1942. Plans of the famous bugeye type.

*THE BALTIMORE CLIPPER. Howard I. Chapelle. The Marine Research Society, Salem, Massachusetts, 1929. Plans of privateers, etc.

SHIPBUILDING, THEORETICAL AND PRACTICAL. Theodore P. Wilson. New York, 1878. Naval shipbuilding information, 1850–1870; spar proportions, hammock nettings and rails, etc.

SHIPS OF THE PAST. Charles G. Davis. The Marine Research Society, Salem, 1929. Plans of certain American ships, with photos and details of many small vessels.

*SHIP MODEL BUILDER'S ASSISTANT. Charles G. Davis. The Marine Research Society, Salem, 1926. General information on ship-model construction and details; dates of details not always given, an unfortunate omission.

AMERICAN SAILING CRAFT. Howard I. Chapelle. Dodd, Mead & Co., New York, 1936. Plans of many local types of commercial and fishing small craft, schooners.

AN INTRODUCTORY OUTLINE TO THE PRACTICE OF SHIPBUILDING. John Fincham. London, 1852. (Also called "Fincham on Shipbuilding and on Masting Ships.") Details of wooden ship construction and masting rules.

SOUVENIR DE MARINE. 6 vols., Adm. Paris. Paris, 1882–1908. Collection of ship plans, usually foreign, but a few American vessels are included.

ARCHITECTURIA MERCATORIA NAVALIS. Chapman, 1763. Plans of sailing and rowing craft, mostly European, 1740–1760 period. Reprinted in Germany prior to the present war in a cheap edition.

RIGGING AND SPARRING

ELEMENTS AND PRACTICE OF RIGGING AND SEAMANSHIP. David Steel. London, 1794. Covers rigging practice from the Revolutionary period to 1800.

*SHEET ANCHOR. Darcy Lever. Philadelphia, 1808. Rigging practice from 1800 to 1830; reprinted, 1930, by The Ship Model Society of Rhode Island, Providence.

NAUTICAL ROUTINE. Murphy and Jeffers. Reprint by The Ship Model Society of Rhode Island, Providence, in 1933, only recommended. Covers period 1830–1850.

*THE RIGGING OF SHIPS, 1600–1720. R. C. Anderson. The Marine Research Society, Salem, 1927.

*KEDGE ANCHOR. William Brady. New York, 1850–1859 (numerous editions). U.S. Naval practice, rigging, and fitting, 1840–1850 period.

SEAMANSHIP. Nares, London. Numerous editions, photos of rigging of men-of-war, 1850–1870, in editions of this period.

GENERAL INFORMATION

WHALE SHIPS AND WHALING. Albert Cook Church. W. W. Norton & Co., Inc., New York, 1938. Photos.

AMERICAN FISHERMEN. Albert Cook Church. W. W. Norton & Co., Inc., New York, 1940. Photos.

THE FORE-AND-AFT RIG IN AMERICA. E. P. Morris. New Haven, 1927.

The Mariner's Mirror. London. Quarterly dealing with nautical historical matters.

The American Neptune. Salem, Massachusetts. Quarterly devoted to marine historical subjects of American interest.

*Republished by Dover Publications, Inc. For availability and current prices log on to **www.doverpublications.com**.

GLOSSARY

Admiralty models—Models built for the Admiralty Board before ships were constructed. See Chapter One.

aft—Toward the stern of a vessel.

amidships—The center of a vessel either from the stem to the stern or athwartship.

applicator—A small wooden stick used by doctors in applying medicine; useful to the modelmaker for small spars, etc.

arch board—A large decorated frame across the stern of a ship outside of the stern planking and framing the stern windows.

arse—The bottom end of a wooden pulley block.

athwartship—Across the ship from side to side.

backstays—Stays that support the mast from aft. They lead from the mastheads to the channels on each side of a vessel, and assist the shrouds to support the mast.

badge—A carved ornament on the quarter of a vessel, containing a window or the representation of one.

batten—A strip of light wood fitted in a pocket sewed into a sail approximately at right angles to the leech, to make it set flat. A piece of wood nailed on a yard or other spar as a fairlead. An iron bar stretching and holding a tarpaulin over a hatch cover or grating. A strip of wood nailed or clamped around the covering of a hatchway to hold it in place. To apply battens.

beam—Breadth of a vessel athwartship. Extreme beam is measured to the outside of the wales or bends. Molded beam is measured to the inside of planking. Also, any of the strong timbers under the decks, bound to the sides with knees.

becket—A simple device for holding something in place: a small grommet; a loop of rope with a knot at one end to catch in an eye at the other; a ring of rope or metal; a bracket; a pocket; a handle of rope; a hook.

bee, blocks, bee holes—A pair of blocks bolted to the bowsprit on either side, their forward ends butted against the bowsprit cap, pierced by two bee holes for cordage. When excess wood was cut away the blocks shaped up like the letter B. In later practice the blocks were left rectangular and each had only a single bee hole.

belay—To make fast.

belaying pin—A pin around which ropes are belayed.

belfry—The framing from which a ship's bell is suspended.

bend—To knot or make fast. A knot.

bends—The wales, which see.

bibb—A side piece of timber bolted to the hounds of a mast to support the trestle trees.

bight—Any part of a rope between the ends.

billet head—A scroll or ornamental carving used in place of a figurehead.

binnacle—The frame or box to hold the compass.

bipod—Two-legged.

bitt—One of the vertical pieces of heavy timber, usually in pairs, extending from the keel upward above the deck, around which lines may be made fast; a metal casting firmly fastened to the deck, with the same function. Also, a small upright timber or pin with a crosspiece, to which a rope can be belayed.

bitter end—The inboard end of a cable or a rope, that is, the end to be made fast to the bitts.

block—A grooved pulley or sheave encased in a frame or shell, having a hook, eye, or strap by means of which it may be attached to an object.

boat skids—Frames of wood on which boats are stowed.

bobstays—Stays extending from the stem to the end of the bowsprit to hold the latter down.

bolt rope—Rope sewed to the edges of a sail, to which some of the rigging is made fast; it also protects the sail fabric.

boom—A large spar used to extend the studding sails and spanker of a ship and the fore-and-aft sails of other vessels.

boom iron—A ring on a stationary spar or part through which a movable spar traverses; specifically, an iron ring on a yard for a studding-sail boom. Quarter boom irons fasten to the yards with a clamp. See Plate XIII.

boom jigger—The tackle for running the studding-sail booms in or out on the yards.

boomkin—A small boom, used as an outrigger, or specifically to extend the tack of a sail. Also called bumpkin, bumkin.

bow—The forward part of a vessel.

bowsprit—A large spar projecting forward from the stem of a ship to carry sail forward and to support the masts by stays; formerly a mast, later canted forward to the now familiar position.

brace—A rope used to turn the yards about the masts.

brace block—A block carrying a brace.

brail—A rope fastened to the leech or corner of a sail, and leading to a block, by which the sail can be hauled up or in.

break—A part in a ship or deck where a partial deck ends and there is a drop to a deck on a lower level.

breasthook—A piece of timber placed across the bow of a boat to hold together the timbers of opposite sides.

breeching—A rope used to secure a gun and prevent excessive recoil.

bridle—A two-legged rope.

bridle port—The first gun port aft from the bow on either side. Guns were not usually mounted at these ports, but could be. Cables were sometimes brought through these ports to form a long loop called a bridle which was used in mooring and towing.

buckler—A block or shutter of wood or iron made to fit a hawse hole, gun port, or other opening.

built-up model—A ship model built with keel, frames, and planks, in the manner of a real ship.

bulkhead—An upright partition separating compartments.

bullseye—A wooden thimble.

bulwark—The side of a ship above the upper deck.

bumkin, bumpkin—See Boomkin.

buntline—A rope attached to the foot of a square sail to haul the sail up to the yard for furling.

burton—A tackle used to set up the topmast shrouds, support the topsail yards, etc.

cabin—Sleeping or living compartment.

cable-laid rope—Three plain-laid ropes laid together, with a left-handed twist.

cant—To turn from the square. The condition of being canted.

cant frame—A frame set at an oblique angle to the keel of a ship and at a right angle to the side.

cap—A collar used in joining spars, as the lower mast and the top mast, or the bowsprit and the jib boom. A cover of tarred canvas at the end of a rope.

cap iron—An iron cap.

capstan—A drum turning on a verti-cal axle of heavy construction, around which to wind rope or cable for moving heavy objects; capstan bars fit holes in the top, for turning it; pawls at the foot of the drum hold it under load when not being turned.

cat—A large timber projecting out over the bows like a crane for drawing up an anchor or other heavy object. Its outboard end was formerly carved to represent the head of a cat.

cavil—One of two crooked pieces of timber, whose lower ends rest in a step or foot fastened to the ship's side. The head branches out like horns and the branches are used to belay to. More commonly Kevel.

ceiling—The inner planking of a vessel or boat.

centerboard—A board that can be lowered to increase the draft of a vessel, providing lateral resistance when the wind is abeam.

chain plates—Thick iron plates bolted to a ship's sides, to which are connected the chains and deadeyes that support the mast by the shrouds.

chainwale—See Channel.

chamfer—To cut away the angle where two planes meet, forming a new surface.

channel—A flat ledge of heavy plank or metal bolted edgewise to the outside of a vessel to increase the spread of the shrouds and carry them clear of the bulwarks. More precisely Chainwale.

Chebacco boat—A type of fishing vessel named for the locality of its origin, Chebacco (now Essex), Massachusetts.

cheek—See Hounds.

cheekblock—A block consisting of a half shell, as one cheek, secured to a mast or other timber, the opposite cheek, the sheave being between the cheeks.

cheek knee—A knee worked horizontally above and below the hawse holes in the angle of the bow and cutwater; it supports the knee of the head.

chess tree—A piece of hardwood fitted and bolted to the outside of a ship abaft the fore channel, with a sheave in the upper end for confining the clew of the mainsail.

chine—The knuckle where the sides of a boat meet the bottom and form a sharp angle. A longitudinal member lying alongside the bilge between the bottom and the topsides.

church ships—Votive models, which see.

cleat—A piece of wood to belay a rope to. It may have two ends projecting beyond the center at which it is fastened to a spar or plank. Cleats are also made of metal.

clevis—A U-shaped shackle with ends pierced to take a pin.

clew—A lower corner of a square sail, or the after lower corner of a fore-and-aft sail. A loop and thimbles at the corner of a sail.

clew garnet—One of the ropes by which the clews of the courses of a square-rigged vessel are hauled up to the lower yards.

clove hitch—A kind of knot.

club—A small spar.

clumsy cleat—A plank fastened across the bow of a whaleboat, just aft the box-warp and on top of the rails, having in its after edge (to port) a notch cut large enough to admit the harpooner's left thigh in order to steady him when using a harpoon.

coaming—The moldings of a hatchway that are raised above the deck.

collar—Any part of a stay or rope formed into a wreath.

combs—Described in the text in the sense used in this book.

companion—A wooden covering for the cabin hatchway.

companionway—A set of steps leading down from the deck to a cabin or saloon below.

cranse iron—An iron band that supports a lower yard and fastens it to the mast; a sort of universal joint. It supplanted chain slings.

cringle—An iron or rope thimble or grommet, or an eyelet.

cross—To send aloft and get in place across the mast.

crossjack yard or *barren yard*—The lower yard of the mizzenmast; a sail was never set on this yard.

crosstrees—Two or more crosspieces of timber or metal supported athwartship by trestle trees at a masthead, which spread the upper shrouds in order to support the mast.

crowsfoot—A number of divergent small cords rove through a long block or euphroe, which see.

cutting-in—The cutting of a whale's

carcass into pieces suitable for the try-pots, etc.

cutwater—The fore part of a ship's stem, which cuts the water.

davit—A crane of metal or wood for raising boats, fishing anchors, etc.

deadeye—A wooden disk scored to take a rope or an iron band around it, and pierced with holes to take a laniard, etc.

dead-flat—The transverse section of a vessel having the largest area. It is the reference station from which other stations are identified aft and forward.

deadlight—A strong shutter made to fit ports or cabin windows and keep out water. A piece of heavy glass in a ship's side to admit light.

deadrise—The rise of the bottom above a horizontal line at the center of a vessel.

dogbody—A Colonial fishing boat type. See the discussion of Plate IV in Chapter Two.

dolphin striker—A vertical spar under the end of the bowsprit, to extend and support the martingale; or a stay supporting the jib boom.

doubling—The parts of a lower mast and topmast where they overlap.

downhaul—A rope to haul down a sail.

draught—The depth in the water to which a ship sinks.

draught—The drawings in the plans for building a ship.

duck tail—Chesapeake Bay term, explained in the text in connection with the bugeye stern. Its function is to steady the rudder.

dumb sheave—A block with a sheaveless hole or a groove in a spar for a rope to be rove through.

earing—A line used to fasten the upper corners of a sail to the yard or gaff. A line for hauling the reef cringle to the yard.

euphroe—A block or long slat of wood, perforated for the passage of a crows-foot, which see.

eye—A loop in a rope, usually at the end.

eyebolt—A bolt with a ring head.

fairlead—A block, ring, or strip of plank with holes, serving as a guide for any rope.

fall—The rope that connects the blocks of a tackle; the hauling part.

fashion piece—One of the timbers at the end of the transom, which define, or fashion, the shape of the stern.

felly—The exterior rim of a wheel, supported by the spokes.

fife rail—A rail about the mast, near the deck, to which running gear is belayed.

fish—To hoist up the flukes of an anchor after it has been catted, in order to stow it.

flare—A spreading outward.

fly block—A block whose position shifts to suit the working of the tackle with which it is connected.

flying (of sails)—Setting without attaching to stays.

frame—Any of the skeleton structures forming the ribs or framework of a vessel.

framed and planked models—Same as built-up models, which see.

frap—To draw tight. To strengthen with bonds, as by passing cables around.

frapping—A lashing binding a thing tightly or binding several things together.

futtock shrouds—Short shrouds leading from the futtock band to the futtock plates; the former is a band near the top of a lower mast; the latter lie across the top of a lower mast, and to them are secured the deadeyes of the topmast rigging.

gallows frame—One of two or more frames amidships on deck for stowing spare spars, boats, etc.

gammoning—The rope or chain which binds the inner quarter of the bowsprit close down to the stem, that it may rest well in its bed.

gangway—The opening through the bulwarks of a vessel by which persons enter or leave it. Either of the sides of the upper deck of a vessel between the deck house and the rail and the quarter deck and forecastle.

garnet—See Clew garnet.

gear—The rigging in general or any specified part of it; specifically, the equipment required for any sail, spar, or function.

gouge—A chisel with a concavo-convex cross section.

gripes—Ropes or canvas straps used to help retain a boat in the boat chocks.

grommet—A ring or wreath of rope used for attaching one thing to another. A metal or metal-lined eyelet.

gudgeon—A metal eye or socket attached to the sternpost to receive the rudder pintle.

gundalow—See Plate II.

gun tackle—A tackle wherein a line leads from the arse of a fixed single block through the sheave of a movable block and then through the sheave of the fixed block; formerly used for moving guns.

gunter yard—A small yard laced vertically to the leech of a fore-and-aft sail. The halliard blocks are bent to the yard and reeve through a block on the masthead. It is used chiefly for club topsails, when the yard is often called a club.

half hitch—A kind of knot.

half-hull model—A ship model made to represent half the hull and mounted on a panel.

halliard or *halyard*—A rope or tackle used to raise or lower spars, sails, or flags to a desired position; a "haul-yard."

hammock netting—A net trough on the bulwarks where the hammocks are stowed during the day.

hanks—Wooden or iron rings on the stays for attaching the sails.

hatch cover—The covering of a hatchway, which see.

hatchway—An opening in a deck.

hawse hole—One of the holes at the bow of a ship through which a cable passes.

hawser-laid rope—Same as cable-laid rope, which see.

head—The fore end of a ship; the bow and adjacent parts. Specifically, that part of a ship within the head rails containing the crew's toilets; hence in modern usage the crew's toilet, even when below decks. The top or upper edge of a sail.

headboard—In a pointed mainsail, a wooden plate at the head over which canvas is sewn.

head knee—See Knee of the head.

heart—A heart-shaped block without sheave through which a laniard is reeved to extend stays.

heel—The after end of a ship's keel. The lower end of a mast, boom, bowsprit, sternpost, etc. To cant or incline.

heeltapper—Precursor of the schooner. See the discussion in connection with Plate IV in Chapter Two.

hog—To curve upward in the middle, like a hog's back.

horse—A footrope. A breastband or similar protection for a sailor in an exposed position. A jackstay. An iron bar on which a traveler (which see) moves.

hounds—Parts of the masthead that project beyond the round to support the trestle trees. Also called cheeks.

hoy—A small vessel used as a tender to larger vessels in port, usually sloop-rigged.

hull—The body of a vessel, exclusive of masts, yards, sails, and rigging.

jack iron—A bar athwartships at a topgallant masthead, to support a royal mast and spread the royal shrouds. An iron performing a similar spreading function elsewhere on a vessel.

jackstay—A rod, wire, or rope stretching along a yard, to which the sails are fastened. A support of wood, wire, or rope, running up and down a mast, on which the parral of a yard travels. A reefing rope stretched along the reefing band of a square sail from hole to hole.

jack yard—A spar to extend a fore-and-aft topsail beyond the gaff.

jeers—Tackles for hoisting or lowering the lower yards of a ship and retaining them in their usual station.

jib—A fore-and-aft sail of a ship forward of the foremast. Hence jib stay, jib boom, etc.

keel—The principal timber of a vessel, extending from stem to stern along the center at the bottom, projecting below the planks. Together with the ribs, it forms the frame. It may be compared to the back bone.

keelson—A structural member parallel with and above the keel, inside the vessel, fastened to the keel by long bolts passing through the floor timbers.

kevel—See Cavil.

knee of the head—The principal member of the head assembly, forward of the stern piece, and supporting the figurehead or billet.

knight—A timber pierced with sheaves through which the halliards run.

knightheads—Heavy timbers each side of a vessel's stem that project above deck. In old vessels they were carved as knights' heads.

knockabout—A vessel with no bowsprit and having the jib stay set up at the stem.

laniard or *lanyard*—A small connecting rope.

lashing rail—A rail fastened about midway above the main deck and below the main rail to the stanchions, the length of the main deck on both sides of the ship. To it are lashed the various parts of the whaling gear used in securing the dead whale to the ship.

lateen rig—See the sail plan of the gundalow, Plate II.

lay—The direction of the twist in a rope. The manner of arranging the strands, etc. See Cable-laid rope, Shroud-laid rope.

lazyjack—A rope or ropes used to confine a sail.

leech—Either side of a square sail. The after edge of a fore-and-aft sail.

leg-o'-mutton—A triangular sail with a pointed head.

lift—A horizontal section of a ship model. A rope leading from a masthead to the arm of a yard below, for raising, supporting, or squaring the yard.

light boards—Boards painted red and green (port and starboard) fastened to the fore shrouds; reflectors for the navigation lights.

lines—The outlines of a vessel from stem to stern and from keel to sheer strake, as exemplified by longitudinal, transverse, and horizontal sections, or as apparent to the eye.

live irons—The harpoons kept in readiness in the crotch of a whaleboat, one of which was made fast to the whale line.

load waterline—The line on the outside of a vessel to which she sinks when properly loaded.

log rail—A rail formed of a single squared timber fastened along the edge of the deck to the tops of the frames,

usually four to six inches high. It has no moldings or finials.

longhead—Chesapeake Bay term for the head of a local-type vessel, characteristically elongated; see the plans for the skipjack and bugeye.

loose-footed—Refers to a sail fastened at the clews only, rather than lashed to a spar along the entire length of the foot or lower edge.

lubber hole—A hole in the floor of the "top" next the mast, through which one may go further aloft without going over the rim by the futtock shrouds. Its chief function is to permit the rigging of the lower mast and yards to come down to the deck of the vessel.

luff—The forward or weather leech of a fore-and-aft sail.

mainsail—The principal sail on the mainmast.

mainsheet—A rope or sheet by which the mainsail is trimmed or secured.

mainsheet band—The iron band around the main boom to which is hooked the upper mainsheet block or blocks.

manger—A mangerlike compartment on the extreme forward part of the deck, having a low bulkhead (the manger board) athwartship to turn back the water which enters the hawse holes and drains off through nearby scuppers.

marline—A small line of two strands, twisted loosely left-handed.

mizzenmast—The aftermost mast in a three-masted vessel. Sometimes, the after mast in a two-masted vessel when that mast is the smaller spar and is secondary in function, as in the bugeye.

monkey rail—A second and lighter rail raised above the main rail of the quarter deck or after part of the main deck of a flush-decked ship.

mouse—A knob made on a stay with spun yarn parceling, or the like, to prevent a running eye from slipping along past it. A turn or lashing across a hook from point to shank, to prevent its unhooking or straightening out. To make a mouse.

nip—To secure or stop a rope with seizing.

outhaul—A rope made fast to a sail for the purpose of hauling it out to the end of a spar.

parral—The loop, or sliding collar, by which a yard or spar is held to the mast in such a way that it may be raised or lowered.

partner—One of the heavy pair of timbers forming a framework about an opening in a deck, to strengthen it for the support of a mast, etc.

pendant—A short rope or chain fixed at one end, having in the other end a block, hook, or thimble that hangs pendant. It serves to connect, or to transmit the effort of, a tackle or other rigging (chiefly braces) to a spar.

perpendicular—In the plans for a ship, the vertical line at either end of and standing perpendicular to the base line. The bow and stern perpendiculars intersect the stem and sternpost at the load waterline.

piggin—A small wooden pail or tub having an extended upright stave for use as a handle.

pinky—A sharp-sterned boat; hence "pink-sterned."

pinrail—A rail or rack which holds belaying pins.

pintle—A pivot pin, part of a hinge, as for a rudder.

poop—A deck raised above the open deck, abaft the mizzen.

port—An opening in a ship's side for any purpose; as entry port, gun port, bridle port. The left-hand side of a ship as a person on board faces the bow, as port light.

preventer—A supplemental auxiliary rope, generally a stay; a feature of the rig of sailing men-of-war. The preventer stay assures support of the various masts should the chief stay be shot away.

profile plan—See Sheer plan.

purchase—A mechanical hold or advantage, e. g., a gun tackle purchase; see Gun tackle.

quarter—The extreme after part of a vessel's side, about ¼ of its length measured forward from the stern. The part of a yardarm outside of the slings.

quarter block—A block fitted under the quarters of a yard, on each side of the slings.

quarter deck—That part of the upper deck abaft the mainmast. In men-of-war, a part of the main deck set aside for the use of officers and the navigation of the ship. Precincts forbidden to the crew.

quarter gallery—A balcony or room projecting from the quarter of a ship. The officers' toilets.

quarter rail—A rail reaching from the gangway to the stern.

rabbet line—The line where the keel meets the hull. A groove to receive the edge of the planking in the stempiece, keel, and sternpost.

rail—The stout, narrow plank or pair of planks that forms the top of the bulwarks. It is usually of two planks with molded edges, the upper being half the thickness of the lower. A light, fencelike structure dividing one part of the deck from another. See also Fife rail, Pinrail, Monkey rail.

rake—To incline from a vertical or horizontal direction. The degree of inclination.

ratline—A transverse rope attached to the shrouds to form a step of a rope ladder. The cordage used for ratlines.

reef—To take up a portion of a sail to reduce its area. The part of a sail so taken up.

reef band—A piece of canvas sewed across a sail to strengthen it at the eyelet holes for reef points.

reef points—Pieces of small rope to pass through the eyelet holes of a reef band for use in reefing a sail.

reeve—To pass a rope through an opening—block, thimble, etc.

rig—The distinctive shape, number, and arrangement of sails and spars.

rigging—The ropes, chains, etc., that support or move the masts, spars, sails, etc., of a vessel.

ringbolt—An eyebolt with a movable ring in the head.

roach—The curved edge of a sail, made by cutting or goring the strips of sailcloth to form a concave surface serving to catch the wind.

room and space—The distance measured between centers of the timbers. The two halves of the timbers occupy the room; the space is the interval between the two surfaces facing each other.

roving—A small piece of rope passing around a yard or jackstay by which a sail is bent to either.

royal—The sail on the royal mast.

royal mast—The mast next above the topgallant mast, usually the highest mast on old-time square-rigged vessels; sometimes integral part of the topgallant mast; it sometimes has shrouds.

royal yard—The yard on the royal mast.

rudder—A flat piece attached to a vessel at the stern in such manner that it can be turned for steering the ship.

rudderhead—The upper end of the rudder stock to which the tiller is attached.

runner—A rope used to increase the power of a tackle.

running rigging—The rigging used in handling sails, movable spars, etc.

saddle—A piece bolted about the mast of a fore-and-aft vessel to support the inboard end of a boom.

sailorman's model—A ship model made by a sailor, usually carved with a knife from a solid block of wood.

samson post—A post (single bitt) stepped on the keelson and extending through the deck of a vessel, just forward of the winch, and chiefly used as the seat of the winch pawl. The heel of the bowsprit was usually let into the samson post, which prevented the spar from coming inboard.

sciatic stay—The stay leading from the mainmast head to the foremast head.

scroll—A curved timber, ornamented with fancy scrolls, bolted to the knee of the head.

scupper—An opening cut through the waterway and bulwarks of a ship, so that water falling on deck may flow overboard.

seize—To bind or fasten together with a lashing of small stuff.

seizing—The cord or lashing used to seize.

set up—To secure, or to be secured. To make taut.

sheave—A pulley, usually in a block but sometimes in a hole cut in a spar, etc. See also Dumb sheave.

sheer—The longitudinal upward curve of the deck, bulwarks, and lines of a vessel when viewed from the side.

sheer plan—A projection of the lines of a vessel on a vertical longitudinal plane passing through its median line.

sheer pole—A pole or rod seized to the shrouds just above the deadeyes and parallel to the sheer of the ship.

sheet—A rope or chain which regulates the angle at which a sail is set in relation to the wind.

shelf—A longitudinal member of a vessel extending its entire length immediately below the deck beams, which rest on and are bolted to it.

shoe—Molding around the centerboard slot on a vessel's bottom.

shroud-laid rope—Four-strand rope in which three strands are laid right-handed around a core.

shrouds—Ropes leading from mastheads to give lateral support to the masts. Lower-mast shrouds lead from the head of the mast to the channels; upper-mast shrouds from the masthead to the top at the outer end of the crosstrees.

sister block—A block having two sheaves, one above the other.

skipjack—See Plate I.

slings—Short ropes or chains used to hang the yards to the mast. Hence, the middle part of the yard, between such gear.

sloop of war—A small armed vessel rigged as a ship, mounting not more than 24 guns on a flush deck. Not to be confused with Sloop, a fore-and-aft rigged vessel with one mast and a single head-sail jib.

snake—To zigzag a light line back and forth between the two parts of a double stay or of two parallel ropes in general. The object was to hold such ropes in position for quick repair if one part was shot away.

space—See Room and space.

spar—Any mast, yard, boom, gaff, or the like.

spencer mast—An auxiliary mast immediately aft another mast, to which the gaff of a fore-and-aft sail is attached to permit of its being raised or lowered on the spar; generally stepped on deck with the upper end bolted between the trestle trees; a feature of the brig rig. The sail is called a spencer.

spreader—A bar holding apart two stays, etc.

springstay—A preventer stay, to assist the regular one.

stanchion—An upright member. It may support a rail or beam, a windlass, a wheel, etc.; the end of the half frame above the main deck to support the bulwarks.

standing part—The part of a tackle that is made fast.

standing rigging—The rigging which sustains the masts and fixed spars, as opposed to the running rigging, which see.

starboard—The right-hand side of a ship as a person on board faces the bow.

station—The location of a frame or rib; see the text for a full discussion.

stem—A piece of timber to which the sides of a ship are united at the fore end.

step—To erect a mast in its place, where it is held by a frame or block intended for the purpose, which is called a mast step.

stern—The after end of a vessel.

stern board—A board athwart the stern of a vessel.

sternpost—The aftermost member of a vessel, extending from keel to deck, and rabbeted to take the ends of the planking.

stirrup—A rope with a thimble in its lower end, or an iron rod with an eye, for supporting a foot rope under a yard or bowsprit, etc.

strake—One breadth of planks on a vessel, either bottom or sides, forming a continuous strip reaching from stem to stern.

strap or *strop*—To fit or furnish with a strap or strop: a piece of rope or metal passing around a block, deadeye, or spar.

studding sail—A light sail set on yards and booms at the side of a square sail.

sweep ports—Ports through which sweeps or oars might be thrust, for moving a vessel when becalmed or for some other reason unable to make headway.

tack—The forward lower corner of a fore-and-aft sail, or the lower forward corner of a square sail when turned. The rope used to haul these corners out or secure them in place.

tackle—An assemblage of ropes and pulleys arranged for hoisting or pulling. Also, the rigging of a ship.

taffrail—The rail around the upper part of a ship's stern.

template—See the text for definition and directions for use.

thimble—A ring of metal formed with a grooved outer edge so as to fit within an eye or loop in a rope. A block may be hooked to a thimble, or a rope rove through one.

tiller—A lever fitted to the rudderhead for turning the rudder from side to side.

top—A platform surrounding the head of a lower mast and resting on the trees, which serves to spread the topmast rigging.

topgallant mast—The mast above the topmast and below the royal mast.

topmast—The mast immediately above the lower mast.

topping lift—A rope to suspend, or top, the outer end of a spar.

topsail—The sail next above the courses on a square-rigged vessel and above the gaff on a fore-and-after.

topsides—The portion of the outer surface of a vessel above the waterline.

trail board—A curved and usually carved board between the cheek knees; generally pierced by the hawse holes.

train tackle—A tackle hooked to a ring-bolt in the deck and to an eyebolt in the train of the gun carriage.

transom—The aftermost of the square frames of a ship, secured to the sternpost and supporting the overhanging stern. Any of several transverse timbers or beams secured to the sternpost.

traveler—An iron ring encircling a rope, bar, etc., and sliding thereon. The bar or rope may be called also a traveler, but is more properly a horse, which see.

traveler iron—See Horse.

treenail—A wooden pin, or peg, used as a nail.

trestle trees—Strong timbers fixed horizontally fore and aft on the masthead; one on either side, to support the cross-trees, the frame of the top, and the topmast.

trice—To haul up or in and secure by a small rope.

truck—A small wooden cap at the head of the topmost mast.

trunk—That part of a cabin projecting above the upper deck of a vessel. A box or funnel around an opening in the bottom of a vessel, rising inside the vessel, sometimes above the deck, to above water level; for example, the centerboard trunk.

trunnion—A pivot or axle projecting from each side of a gun, to support it on the carriage.

truss—A rope employed to confine or slacken a lower yard to or from its mast.

tryworks—The stove used on whalers for rendering blubber.

tub oar crotch—The crotch, or large oarlock for the tub or after oar in a whaleboat. It was high to keep the oar clear of the uncoiling line when the boat was fast to a whale. It was shipped in a wooden socket on the inside of the rail. When the boat was not fast to a whale the oar was used with an ordinary oarlock or thole pins.

tumblehome—The inward inclination of the sides of a ship above the waterline.

tye—A runner or large rope used to convey the effort of the tackle to hoist the upper yards and gaff.

vangs—Braces that steady the peaks of gaffs.

votive models—Ship models placed in churches as votive offerings.

waif—A small pennant or a flag for use in signaling or as a marker.

wale—Certain thick strakes of the outside planking of a vessel. Specifically, the thick and strong planks called the bends.

washboard—A closed part of the rail, or boards arranged to prevent the wash of a sea coming on deck or to carry off surface water.

waterline—Any of several lines on the surface of a vessel, corresponding with the surface of the water when she is on an even keel. Any of certain horizontal lines drawn at fixed distances above the base line in a draught.

waterline model—A model made in lifts so as to exhibit the waterlines.

waterway—A covering board around the deck of a vessel to prevent water entering below decks or between the frames.

welp—A batten on a winch or capstan.

wheelbox—A box or casing over the steering gear of a vessel.

wythe, withe, wye—A metal band, generally with standing eyes, put about a spar for the attachment of rigging.

yard—A long spar used to support and extend a sail. In square-rigged vessels it is tapered to each end; in the lateen rig it is tapered to one end.

yardarm—The outer end of a yard beyond the shoulder, on which are fitted the horses, yard tackle, lift and sheet blocks, and the brace pendant or brace block. About $\frac{1}{20}$ of the yard's length, but this proportion increases as the yards diminish in length.

yard tackle—A tackle used on a lower yard, especially a heavy double or treble purchase for hauling.

INDEX

A

Admiralty models, 18
Agate, whaler, 81-93, V
    dimensions, 85
Albany, U.S.S., 63
American Revolution, 120
Anchor hoy, 63-71, III
Anchors, 147, XIV
    bugeye, 100
    fishing schooner, 79
    skipjack, 55
Apple, 154
Applicators, 152
Ash, 153

B

Backstays, 129
Balsa, 153
Bar, James, 121
Base, in draught, 21
Bateau, oyster boat, 56-8
Belaying-pin layout, 69, 112, 134
Bends, bugeye, 97
Bibliography, 165-6
Bilts, anchor hoy, 65
Black Ball Line, 117
Black Nancy, 57
Blocks, XIII
Boat fall, skipjack, 47-8, 54-5
Boats, 143-4, XIV
Body plan, explained, 20-2
Bone, model material, 17-18
Boom, skipjack, 50-1
Boston Museum, model collection, 17

Bowsprit, anchor hoy, 65
    gammoning, 140-1
    half-hull model, 38, 47
    rigging of, 49
    sloop of war, 43
Boxer, U.S.S., 102-5, VIII
    measurements, 105
Boxwood, 153
Brace blocks, 137-8
Braces, 135, 137-40
Breasthook, half-hull model, 42
Brig, training, 102-5, VIII
Briggs, Enos, 19
Bugeye, 56-8, 95-101, VII
    dimensions, 101
Built-up models, 18
Bulwarks, warship, 107-8
    whaler, 89
Burgess, Edward, 73
Burgess, W. Starling, 73

C

Cabin trunk, half-hull model, 39
Cable-laid rope, 126-7
Cables, 164
Camber, deck, 31
Cant frames, 76
Cardboard, model material, 17
Carrack, 17
Carrie Price, I, 56-9
    measurements, 59
Carving, 35
Cats, XIV
    anchor hoy, 64-5
Celluloid, 121, 152

Center line, in half-hull models, 26, 29
Centerboard, half-hull model, 34, 36
  skipjack model, 45-6
Centerboard trunk, half-hull model, 39-40
Chains, making links, 133
Chapelle, H. I., 73-4, 85, 94, 145-6
Chase Brass Co., 154
Chebacco boat, 72
Cheek knees, half-hull model, 35
Cherry, 153
Chesapeake, U.S.S., 102
Chesapeake Bay, boat types, 56-7, 95-101
Chine, in draught, 21
Chisels, 151
  use of, 28
Church, Albert Cook, 82
Church ships, 18-19
Clay, model material, 17
Clippers, Baltimore, 63
  head, 117
Clothespins, 152
Cole, Benjamin, 121
Collars, XIII
Collins, Joseph, 72
Coppering, 67, 144-5
Cordage, 154
  model, 131
  types, 126-7
Crown, deck, 31
Crowninshield, designer, 73
Crowsfoot, 141
Cumberland, U.S.S., 102
Cutting-in tackle, 91-2

D

Davits, XIII
  half-hull model, 42
  skipjack, 47
Deadeyes, XIII
  stropping, 131-2
Dead-flat, in draught, 21-2
Deck, half-hull model, 31-3
  skipjack model, 46-7
Deck furniture, 143-8

half-hull model, 37-43
  schooner, 75
  skipjack, 47
  whaler, 88
Deck houses, 148
Deck line, in draught, 21
Degama, 154
Dixon & Son, Thomas, 95, 150
Dogbody, fishing boat, 72
Dramatic Line, 117
Draught, explained, 20-3
Drawknife, 149
Drills, 149, 151
Duck tail, 98

E

Eagle head, half-hull model, 35
Edith F. Todd, 95-101, VII
  dimensions, 101
Egypt, ship models, 17-18
England, maritime power, 119
Enterprise, U.S.S., 103
Essex, Mass., shipbuilding, 72, 84
Essex Institute, 116
Euphroe, 141
Eyebolts, 133

F

Fannie M., 60-3, II
  measurements, 61
Fashion pieces, illustrated, 89
Fiber, 154
Filebottoms, fishing boats, 72
Files, 149
Fincham, cited, 68
Findings, 38
Fishing gear, skipjack model, 42
Fittings, 130-1, 152
Flare, 108
Flattie, 57
Foot ropes, 134
Foresheet horse, 53
Fox, Josiah, 105
Frame and batten construction, 19

Framed and planked models, 18
Frames, ship's, 76
Frolic, H.M.S., 105-6
Furniture, 143-8
Futtock shrouds, XIII

G

Gammoning, 140-1
Gear, 143-8
Germanic National Museum, model material, 17
Glass, celluloid for, 39
Glossary, 166-80
Gloucester, fishing fleet, 62
Glue, 154-5
Glueing, technique, 39
Gold, model material, 17
Gondola, 61
Gouges, 151
Grampus, fishing boat, 72
"Great White Fleet," 104
Grice, Francis, 63-4
Grice, Joseph, 63
Grindstone, whaler equipment, 83
Grinell, Russell, 74
Gudgeon, 41
Guerrière, U.S.S., 63
Gun ports, 77, 106-8, 119, 145-6
    dimensions, 159-61
Gundalow, 60-3, II
    measurements, 61
Guns, 143-4, 146
    dimensions, 159-61
    equipment, 162-3
    merchant ships, 119
    Republican, 119
    rigging, 109

H

Hack saw, 151
Hair, rigging material, 18
Hairpins, 38
Half-breadth plan, explained, 20-2
Half-hull model, construction, 17-43

origin, 19
    painted, 37-43
    varnished, 19-37
Hammers, 151
Hammock netting, 108
Hampton flattie, 57-8
Hannah, U.S.S., 74
Hardware, simulation, 20
Hatch coamings, 147
    half-hull model, 40
Hatch covers, 147
    half-hull model, 40
Hawser-laid rope, 126-7
Head, clipper ship, 117
    function, 35
    half-hull model, 35-6
    skipjack, 46-7
    whaler, 89-91
Heeltapper, 72
Helen B. Thomas, schooner, 73
Historical American Merchant Marine Survey, 58, 60, 94-5
Hogging, 47, 59
Holly, 153
Hornet, U.S.S., 105
Horse block, 53
Horses, 134, 137-8
    foresheet, 38
Hoy, function of, 64
Hull, shaping, 45-6
Humphries, Joshua, 118
Humphries, Samuel, 118
Hutton, B., Jr., naval constructor, 105

I

International Yacht Racing Association, 123-5
Ipswich, Mass., 73-4
Iron work, 131
Ivory, model material, 17-18

J

Jack iron, illustrated, 52
Jackstay, 134, 137

Jeers, XIII
Jones, Jacob, 106
Joy C. Parks, 58

K

Keel, half-hull model, 34-5
Keel line, in half-hull model, 26, 29
Knee of the head, 89
Knightheads, half-hull model, 42
Knives, 149
Knots, XIII
Kunhardt, editor, 57

L

Ladder, shroud, 129
Laniards, 129
Lateen rig, 60-3
Lathe, 151-2
Lawlor, D. J., 72, 73
Lay, in cordage, 126-7
Lee board, gundalow, 62
Lexington, U.S.S., 118
Lift construction, 19 *et passim*
  half-hull model, 24-38
  illustrated, 24-38
Lifts, yard, 135-7
Linen cord, 154
Lines, in draught, 21-2
Log-bottom construction, 99
Log canoe, Chesapeake Bay, 96-7
Longhead, 89
  bugeye, 98
  decoration, 99
  half-hull model, 35, 36
  skipjack, 46
Loup Cervier, H.M.S., 105

M

McClain, George, 73
McCutcheon & Co., 154
McManus, Thomas, 73
Mahogany, 23, 153
Manger, 117-19

Manta, Phillip B., schooner, 73
Mare Island, shipyard, 102
Mariner, 145-6
  cited, 94
Maryland, ship types, 56-7
Mast partners, half-hull model, 39
Masts, anchor hoy, 70-1
  dimensions, 163-4
  gundalow, 62
  half-hull model, 39
  skipjack, 49-51, 59
  taper, XIII
  yacht, 124-5
Materials, 38, 152-5
Merchantman, 116-19, X
  general design, 146-7
Merrill, Orlando, 19
Metal, 154
Metropolitan Museum, model collection, 17
Miter boxes, 149-51
Models (*see* Ship models)
Monitor, U.S.S., 93
Mounting, half-hull model, 35-7

N

Navy, U.S., sail in, 102-4
New Bedford, Mass., whaling port, 83, 84-5
Niantic, fisherman, 73

O

Office of Naval Records and Library, 63
Oilstone, 149
"Old Time Ships of Salem," 116-19
Oliver Cromwell, 119-23, XI
  measurements, 123
  spar plan, f. IX
Oriole, Md., boatbuilding, 99
Oyster fishing, 56-8, 95-101

P

Paine, Frank C., 73
Paint, 152

Painting, anchor hoy, 65-7
  Boxer, 104
  bugeye, 99-101
  colonial schooners, 78-9
  merchant ships, 118-19
  Oliver Cromwell, 123
  skipjack, 48
  skipjack half hull, 39-42
  Wasp, 111
  whaler, 93
  yacht, 125
  yards, 135
Panel, half-hull model, 35-7
Panel saw, 150-1
Parceling, 126-7
Parrals, 135
Peabody Museum, 60, 74
Pear wood, 153
Pendants, 137-8
Pennsylvania, U.S.S., 118
Perpendicular, in draught, 21-2
Perry, U.S.S., 63
Pilot boats, Virginia, 63
Pintle, 41
Piscataqua River, ship types, 60-1
Planes, 151
  use of, 27
Pliers, 151
Poictiers, H.M.S., 105-6
Ports, glassed, 39
  (*see also* Gun ports)
Portsmouth, N.H., shipbuilding, 102
Powhatan, U.S.S., 63
Price, Adam P., 58
Price, Carrie, 58
Price, James Henry, shipbuilder, 58
Privateer, 119-23, XI
Profile plan, explained, 20-2
Proportions, 20
Pumps, location, 95
Push boat, 98-9

Q

Quarter galleries, 117
Quincy, Mass., scow building, 94

R

Rabbet line, 21
Rail, anchor hoy, 65-6
  half-hull model, 41-3
  Wasp, 107-8
Ranger, yacht, 123
Rasps, 149
  use of, 26
Ratlines, 129-30
Red Cross Line, 117
Regenia S., 93-5, VI
  dimensions, 95
Relief, U.S.S., 118
Republican, 116-19, X
  spar plan, f. IX
Rigging, 126-42, XIII
  anchor hoy, 67-71
  bugeye, 99-101
  colonial period, 80
  fishing schooner, 80-1
  gun, 109
  gundalow, 62-3
  half-hull model, 42
  material for, 17-20
  running, 135-42
  scale, 20
  size, 157-9
  skipjack, 48-54
  standing, 127-33, 157-9
  Wasp, 110-16
  yacht, 124
Robbins, Joseph E., 98
Roberts, Kenneth L., 120
Rockport, Mass., marine freighting, 94
Romp, schooner, 72
Room and space, 76
Rope, 154
  model, 130-1
  types, 126-7
  wire, 130
Ropework, XIII
Rosewood, 154
Rudder, half-hull model, 34-5, 36, 41

S

Sag Harbor, whaling port, 85
Sailorman's models, 18
Sails, 51-4
    details, XIII
    gundalow, 62
    yacht, 124
St. Ann's Church, model collection, 19
Samson post, half-hull model, 38
San Francisco Bay, water freight trade, 94
Sander, use of, 26
Sandpaper, 152
Saws, 150-1
Scale, 20
    discussed, 23
Scarf-joint, illustrated, 66
Schooner, colonial fishing, 72-81, IV
    development, 72-4
    dimensions, 79
    scow (see Scow schooner), 93-5, VI
    whaling, 81-93, V
Scissors, as tool, 29
Scow schooner, 61, 93-5, VI
    dimensions, 95
Scows, racing, 61
Scrapers, 149
Scuppers, 164
Sectional construction, 19
Seizing, XIII
Serving, 126-7
Severn, U.S.S., 103
Sharpshooters, fishing boats, 72
Sheer line, 21
Sheer plan, explained, 20-2
Sheer pole, 129
Ship, merchant (see Merchantman)
Ship models, collections of, 17-19
    history, 17-19
Ship sloops, 105-16, IX
Shipshape, discussed, 19-20
Shoe, centerboard, 36-7
Shroud-laid rope, 126-7
Shrouds, XIII

cutting and hanging, 127-9
Silk, rigging material, 18
Silver, model material, 17
Size, for models, 23
Skipjack, I
    discussion and history, 56-9
    half-hull models, 19-43
    sails, 51-4
    whole-hull model, 44-5
Slings, 135-6, XIII
Sloop of war, 105-16, IX
Sloops, granite, 94
"Small yachts," Kunhardt, 57
Smithsonian Institution, marine historical collection, 58, 74
Snaking, 110
Spars, dimensions, 163-4
    ivory, 17
    metal bands, 131
    skipjack, 59
    Wasp plan, f. IX
Spencer mast, 70
Splices, XIII
Spritsail yard, 139
Square, tool, 151
Squaring staff, 129
Stanchions, Agate, 86
    anchor hoy, 65-7
    development and function, 76-7
    half-hull model, 41-2
    illustrated, 75
Station lines, 76
    in draught, 21-2
Stays, XIII
Steering gear, 144
    half-hull model, 40-2
    Wasp, 144
    yacht, 124-5
Stem, half-hull model, 34-5
    skipjack, 46
Stern, half-hull model, 41
    privateer, 121-2
Sternpost, half-hull model, 34
    skipjack, 46
Story, Andrew, shipbuilder, 72
Strakes, 108

Sutherland, William, 157
Syren, U.S.S., 105

T

Tackles, XIII
Taylor, D. Foster, 60
Template, use of, 29-30
Terrible Creature, 119-20
Tonnage, to find, 157
Tools, 30, 149-52
Toothpicks, 152
Trail board, 89, 91
Truxton, U.S.S., 63
Tryworks, 88
Tumblehome, 108
Tyes, 135-6

U

United States, privateer navy, 119-20
United States Fish Commission, 72

V

Vangs, 70
Vincennes, U.S.S., 118
Vise, use of, 30
Votive models, 18-19

W

Walen, E. D., 94
Walnut, 153

Warren, U.S.S., 118
Warships, general design, 146-7
Wasp, U.S.S., 105-16, IX
    measurements, 109
Waterlines, in draught, 21
    half-hull model, 35-6
    on lift, 25
Waterline model, 19
Waterways, anchor hoy, 66
    half-hull model, 43
    skipjack, 46
West, Nathaniel, 121
Whaleboat, 82-4, 91, XIV
Whaler, 81-93, V
Wheels, 144
    half-hull model, 40-1
White pine, 23, 153
White wood, 154
Whole-hull model, building, 44-55
Winch, half-hull model, 38
    scow schooner, 95
Windows, 121
Wire, 154
Woods, 152-4
    as model material, 18
Woodwork, technique, 25-6, 28
Worming, 127

Y

Yacht, 123-5, XII
Yardarms, 134
Yards, 134-41
    details, XIII
    dimensions, 162-3